Additional Praise for
Emerging Market Real Estate Investment

"David Lynn and Tim Wang have produced a real winner. Emerging markets real estate is an essential subject for any investor because of its high returns, its contribution to diversification in a global portfolio, and its role as an inflation hedge. This book focuses on the three most important emerging market real estate arenas: Brazil, China, and India. Their long experience in real estate markets and the hundreds of interviews he has conducted gives book unique insights into investing in these markets as well as emerging markets real estate generally. His analysis of property investment approaches and styles is excellent, and his paradigm of location, competition, and growth provides an appropriate framework for the book. The sections on the practical aspects of investing in emerging market real estate provide the reader with a detailed guide through the complex risk, regulatory, legal, and competitive characteristics of each country. This is a notable and unique contribution to emerging markets investing knowledge."

—**Dr. Mark Mobius**
Executive Chairman and Portfolio Manager
Franklin Templeton Investments

"David and Tim have written the 'must read' book for all real estate investors interested in Brazil, China and India. He comprehensively covers the landscape of issues—economic, policy, legal, market, sector, entry, exit, and strategy. Of noted value is their sanguine assessment of the risks and opportunities of alternative strategies in each country. The first outlay for all should be David and Tim's book."

—**Dr. Raymond Torto**
Chief Economist of CB Richard Ellis and the Co-Founder
of Torto-Wheaton Research

"*Emerging Market Real Estate Investment* is a powerful tool for those engaged in foreign investment generally, as well as in China, India and Brazil in particular. It combines a broad general view of competitive strategy with local detail on costs and legal aspects. The book is an intelligent and practical guide to foreign real estate investment."

—**Bowen H. McCoy, CRE**
former Partner and Managing Director, Morgan Stanley

"This book does for international real estate what Paul Samuelson's *Economics* did for economics students—it finally provides a new discipline with its first Bible. Rich in content and filled with practical insights, this book couldn't have come at a better time in the market cycle."

—**Kenneth A. Munkacy**
Senior Managing Director, GID International
Group/GID Investment Advisers, LLC

The Frank J. Fabozzi Series

Fixed Income Securities, Second Edition by Frank J. Fabozzi
Focus on Value: A Corporate and Investor Guide to Wealth Creation by James L. Grant and James A. Abate
Handbook of Global Fixed Income Calculations by Dragomir Krgin
Managing a Corporate Bond Portfolio by Leland E. Crabbe and Frank J. Fabozzi
Real Options and Option-Embedded Securities by William T. Moore
Capital Budgeting: Theory and Practice by Pamela P. Peterson and Frank J. Fabozzi
The Exchange-Traded Funds Manual by Gary L. Gastineau
Professional Perspectives on Fixed Income Portfolio Management, Volume 3 edited by Frank J. Fabozzi
Investing in Emerging Fixed Income Markets edited by Frank J. Fabozzi and Efstathia Pilarinu
Handbook of Alternative Assets by Mark J. P. Anson
The Global Money Markets by Frank J. Fabozzi, Steven V. Mann, and Moorad Choudhry
The Handbook of Financial Instruments edited by Frank J. Fabozzi
Interest Rate, Term Structure, and Valuation Modeling edited by Frank J. Fabozzi
Investment Performance Measurement by Bruce J. Feibel
The Handbook of Equity Style Management edited by T. Daniel Coggin and Frank J. Fabozzi
The Theory and Practice of Investment Management edited by Frank J. Fabozzi and Harry M. Markowitz
Foundations of Economic Value Added, Second Edition by James L. Grant
Financial Management and Analysis, Second Edition by Frank J. Fabozzi and Pamela P. Peterson
Measuring and Controlling Interest Rate and Credit Risk, Second Edition by Frank J. Fabozzi, Steven V. Mann, and Moorad Choudhry
Professional Perspectives on Fixed Income Portfolio Management, Volume 4 edited by Frank J. Fabozzi
The Handbook of European Fixed Income Securities edited by Frank J. Fabozzi and Moorad Choudhry
The Handbook of European Structured Financial Products edited by Frank J. Fabozzi and Moorad Choudhry
The Mathematics of Financial Modeling and Investment Management by Sergio M. Focardi and Frank J. Fabozzi
Short Selling: Strategies, Risks, and Rewards edited by Frank J. Fabozzi
The Real Estate Investment Handbook by G. Timothy Haight and Daniel Singer
Market Neutral Strategies edited by Bruce I. Jacobs and Kenneth N. Levy
Securities Finance: Securities Lending and Repurchase Agreements edited by Frank J. Fabozzi and Steven V. Mann
Fat-Tailed and Skewed Asset Return Distributions by Svetlozar T. Rachev, Christian Menn, and Frank J. Fabozzi
Financial Modeling of the Equity Market: From CAPM to Cointegration by Frank J. Fabozzi, Sergio M. Focardi, and Petter N. Kolm
Advanced Bond Portfolio Management: Best Practices in Modeling and Strategies edited by Frank J. Fabozzi, Lionel Martellini, and Philippe Priaulet
Analysis of Financial Statements, Second Edition by Pamela P. Peterson and Frank J. Fabozzi
Collateralized Debt Obligations: Structures and Analysis, Second Edition by Douglas J. Lucas, Laurie S. Goodman, and Frank J. Fabozzi
Handbook of Alternative Assets, Second Edition by Mark J. P. Anson
Introduction to Structured Finance by Frank J. Fabozzi, Henry A. Davis, and Moorad Choudhry
Financial Econometrics by Svetlozar T. Rachev, Stefan Mittnik, Frank J. Fabozzi, Sergio M. Focardi, and Teo Jasic
Developments in Collateralized Debt Obligations: New Products and Insights by Douglas J. Lucas, Laurie S. Goodman, Frank J. Fabozzi, and Rebecca J. Manning
Robust Portfolio Optimization and Management by Frank J. Fabozzi, Peter N. Kolm, Dessislava A. Pachamanova, and Sergio M. Focardi
Advanced Stochastic Models, Risk Assessment, and Portfolio Optimizations by Svetlozar T. Rachev, Stogan V. Stoyanov, and Frank J. Fabozzi
How to Select Investment Managers and Evaluate Performance by G. Timothy Haight, Stephen O. Morrell, and Glenn E. Ross
Bayesian Methods in Finance by Svetlozar T. Rachev, John S. J. Hsu, Biliana S. Bagasheva, and Frank J. Fabozzi
The Handbook of Municipal Bonds edited by Sylvan G. Feldstein and Frank J. Fabozzi
Subprime Mortgage Credit Derivatives by Laurie S. Goodman, Shumin Li, Douglas J. Lucas, Thomas A. Zimmerman, and Frank J. Fabozzi
Introduction to Securitization by Frank J. Fabozzi and Vinod Kothari
Structured Products and Related Credit Derivatives edited by Brian P. Lancaster, Glenn M. Schultz, and Frank J. Fabozzi
Handbook of Finance: Volume I: Financial Markets and Instruments edited by Frank J. Fabozzi
Handbook of Finance: Volume II: Financial Management and Asset Management edited by Frank J. Fabozzi
Handbook of Finance: Volume III: Valuation, Financial Modeling, and Quantitative Tools edited by Frank J. Fabozzi
Finance: Capital Markets, Financial Management, and Investment Management by Frank J. Fabozzi and Pamela Peterson-Drake
Basics of Finance: An Introduction to Financial Markets, Business Finance, and Portfolio Management by Frank J. Fabozzi and Pamela Peterson-Drake
Simulation and Optimization in Finance: Modeling with MATLAB, Risk, or VBA by Dessislava Pachamanova and Frank J. Fabozzi
Probability and Statistics for Finance Svetlozar T. Rachev, Markus Hoechstoetter, Frank J. Fabozzi, Sergio M. Focardi Active Private Equity Real Estate Strategy* by David Lynn

Emerging Market Real Estate Investment

*Investing in China,
India, and Brazil*

DAVID J. LYNN, PH.D.
with TIM WANG, PH.D.

WILEY

John Wiley & Sons, Inc.

Published by John Wiley & Sons, Inc., Hoboken, New Jersey.
Published simultaneously in Canada.

For general information on our other products and services or for technical support, please contact our Customer Care Department within the United States at (800) 762-2974, outside the United States at (317) 572-3993 or fax (317) 572-4002.

Wiley also publishes its books in a variety of electronic formats. Some content that appears in print may not be available in electronic formats. For more information about Wiley products, visit our Web site at www.wiley.com.

Library of Congress Cataloging-in-Publication Data:

Lynn, David J.
  Emerging market real estate investment : investing in China, India, and
Brazil / David J. Lynn.
      p. cm. – (Frank J. Fabozzi series ; 196)
    Includes index.
    ISBN 978-0-470-90109-0 (cloth); 978-0-470-91256-0 (ebk); 978-0-470-91257-7 (ebk);
978-0-470-91258-4 (ebk)
    1. Real estate investment–China.   2. Real estate investment–India.   3. Real estate
investment–Brazil.   I. Title.
    HD926.L96 2010
    332.63'24–dc22   2010026720

10 9 8 7 6 5 4 3 2 1

Contents

Preface

This book focuses primarily on private equity real estate investment in China, India, and Brazil. Much attention has been devoted in recent years to the "BRIC" countries—that is, these three countries plus Russia. Several analysts have argued that China, India, and Brazil will be among the world's largest economies by the year 2050.[1] These countries encompass a significant percentage of the world's land coverage, 30% of the world's population and amount to a combined GDP (PPP) of US$12.4 trillion. They are among the biggest and fastest-growing emerging markets.

We decided to exclude Russia in this analysis as China, India, and Brazil feature more of the characteristics of typical emerging markets—that is, young, large populations with significant long-term growth and arguably deeper and more diversified economies. Russia's demographic profile (older, shrinking population), its less diversified economy, and issues with endemic corruption led us to omit it from this book.

An objective of this book is to develop a general approach to commercial real estate investment in emerging markets. We believe that a discussion of the three largest emerging markets illustrates some common approaches, strategies, and analytical methods that can be used in emerging market real estate.

This book is a departure from other studies of international real estate investment in that it focuses on broad investment themes and strategies as well as economic and legal/institutional factors, rather than the minute details of local market analyses. An inherent thesis is that real estate is a derivative of the overall economy and institutional framework and one can only understand real estate drivers of demand in this context. The analysis and recommendations are designed to be pragmatic, pithy, and actionable.

We specifically do not delve into extensive detail about items such as current capital values and rental rates except for illustrative purposes in certain areas of the text. Pricing of this nature is subject to changes in the short term. Instead, we focus on the forces that determine pricing and values.

The primary audience for this book is the foreign commercial real estate investor. Nevertheless, domestic investors should find the book of interest as well, as it covers many of the same issues, opportunities, and impediments foreign investors face.

The research for this book was based on a combination of direct data sources, third-party reports, and on-the-ground research. The on-the-ground research was essential in developing our pragmatic and strategic approach. On-the-ground research consisted of collecting and organizing data and information available only in the local market. We also conducted hundreds of in-person and telephone interviews with local, regional, and national real estate investors, developers, brokers, consultants, government officials, architects/planners, economists, and other agents involved in the commercial real estate value creation process.

We relied upon both top-down and bottom-up research in developing the book. We believe this approach is intrinsic and essential in all rigorous real estate analysis (Exhibit P.1). The economic, political, demographic, and institutional macroeconomic forces are of essential importance in commercial real estate, particularly in emerging markets. A part of this top-down analysis involves legal, institutional, and regulatory factors that are fundamental in investment structuring and economic returns expectations. For example, legal restrictions on commercial real estate investment can render some sectors and strategies virtually off limits to foreign real estate investment. The bottom-up analysis includes submarket economics and real estate fundamentals as well as property-specific factors such as capital values, operating income, and other local or property level data.

Our approach is highly strategic and pragmatic in nature, outlining opportunities for investing in these markets. Our analysis is based upon what

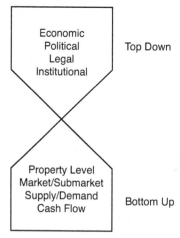

EXHIBIT P.1   Top Down and Bottom Up Approaches

we call our **LCG Framework**. This framework states that the attractiveness of real estate foreign direct investment (REFDI) in emerging markets is a function of three main variables: **Locational** factors, the **Competitive** environment factors, and **Growth** factors.

That is, $(REFDI) = f(L, C, G)$

It follows that the firm must obtain some kind of advantage over the costs of investing and operating domestically in order to take on the added risks of international activities.

Thus, Profit = Total Revenues − Total Costs (Cost of Investing/Operating Internationally) and $P_i > P_d$ based upon a given amount of marginal capital, where P_i is international profit and P_d is domestic profit.

We apply this framework implicitly throughout the market and strategy sections of the book. We supplement this strategic analysis with a pragmatic review of markets and investment options.

Locational factors include geographic location, natural features, and institutional/legal factors such as natural endowments (i.e., in labor, raw materials). It can also mean, particularly in the case of real estate, controlling or owning specific locations within an urban market that confer special advantages (i.e., local monopolies of a sort). The value of real estate has often been largely ascribed to location. There is an old saying that the only three things an investor need know about real estate are "location, location, and location." While this is a gross oversimplification, there is a kernel of truth in this notion. Real estate is a highly idiosyncratic asset and very site- and market-specific.

Competitive factors can consist of advantages firms possess (core competencies of firm-specific advantages) in the competitive environment. Real estate investment must be competitive vis-à-vis other types of investment. The firm with advantages abroad, relative to domestic competitors, may achieve higher returns or lower costs, thus leading to more total profit. These advantages may include greater access to investment capital, better practices and processes, better management, superior technology, and so on. Branding and brand-equity are a part of this factor. Firms with more recognizable and trusted brands may receive better terms on financing, stronger relationships with suppliers, and higher customer demand.

Growth factors are related to locational factors, but are considered separately because they are such a critical driver of real estate demand. Without growth, both current and long-term, most real estate investment would not be economically feasible. All things being equal, local, regional, and national markets that are characterized by sustainable growth are usually preferred to those with minimal or diminishing growth. In many mature countries of Europe and in Japan, long-term growth prospects in terms of the economy and real estate markets appear limited.

The LCG Framework includes several of Michael Porter's considerations (as described in *The Competitive Advantage of Nations*), including:

- **Factor conditions**, such as human resources, physical resources, knowledge resources, capital resources, and infrastructure. Specialized resources are often specific for an industry and important for its competitiveness. Specific resources can be created to compensate for factor disadvantages.
- **Demand conditions** in the home market can help companies create competitive advantage, when sophisticated home market buyers pressure firms to innovate faster and to create better products that those of competitors.
- **Related and supporting industries** can produce inputs that are important for innovation and internationalization. These industries provide cost-effective inputs, but they also participate in the upgrading process, thus stimulating other companies in the supply chain to innovate.
- **Firm strategy, structure, and rivalry** constitute the fourth determinant of competitiveness. The way in which companies are created, set goals, and are managed is important for success. But the presence of intense rivalry in the home base is also important; it creates pressure to innovate in order to upgrade competitiveness.
- **Government and the legal and institutional framework** can influence each of the above four determinants of competitiveness. Clearly, government can influence the supply conditions of key production factors, demand conditions in the home market, and competition between firms. Government interventions can occur at local, regional, national, or supranational levels.

CHARACTERIZING EMERGING MARKET REAL ESTATE

Emerging markets can be characterized as "embryonic and growth oriented." The shaded regions of the market matrix (Exhibit P.2) describe the current state of the real estate markets in China, India, and Brazil. These are young and growing markets. Prior to the recent global recession, there had been significant property appreciation, which we expect will resume in the near term. All three markets benefit from large national economies and demand based on solid growth fundamentals.

CHINA, INDIA, AND BRAZIL

China, India, and Brazil have gradually evolved their economic and political systems to embrace and flourish in global capitalism, reducing barriers and

EXHIBIT P.2 Market Typology Matrix

Descriptors	Embryonic	Growth	Mature	Aging
Market Growth Rate	Accelerating; accurate rate cannot be calculated because the base is too small.	Faster than GCP, but constant or decelerating.	Equal to or slower than GDP; cyclical.	Industry volume cycles but declines over long term.
Industry Potential	Difficult to determine.	Substantially exceeds the industry volume, but is subject to unforeseen developments.	Well known; primary markets approach saturation industry volume.	Saturation is reached; no potential remains.
Breadth of Product Lines	Basic product line established.	Rapid proliferation as product lines are extended.	Product turnover, but little or no change in breadth.	Shrinking and increasingly specialized.
Number and Quality of Competitors	Increasingly rapid number of relatively unsophisticated players.	Increasing to peak; followed by shake-out, differentiation, and consolidation.	Stable with increasing capability and segmentation.	Declines, but business may break into many small regional suppliers.
Market Share Stability	Volatile.	A few firms have major shares: rankings can change, but those with minor shares are unlikely to gain major shares.	Firms with major shares are entrenched.	Concentration increased as marginal firms drop out; or shares are dispersed among small local firms.

(Continued)

EXHIBIT P.2 (*Continued*)

Descriptors	Embryonic	Growth	Mature	Aging
Purchasing Patterns	Little or none.	Some: buyers are aggressive.	Suppliers are well known; buying patterns are established.	Strong; number of alternatives decreases.
Ease of Entry	Usually easy, but opportunity may not be apparent.	Usually easy; the presence of competitors is offset by vigorous growth.	Difficult; competitors are entrenched, and growth is slowing.	Difficult; little incentive to enter.
Ease of Exit	Legal preclusions, absence of market, high transactions costs.	Developing market; increasing number of buyers.	Strong secondary market; securitization occurring; many buyers and liquidity.	Highly liquid market but weak demand and unattractive market.
Technology and Productivity	Concept development and early product design.	Product line refinement and extension.	Processes and methods refinement; new product line development to spur growth.	Role is minimal as underlying market fundamentals render both technology and productivity less vital.

Source: ING Clarion Research & Investment Strategy, based on a diagram in A. C. Hax and N. Majluf, *Strategy Concept and Process: Pragmatic approach.* Upper Saddle River, NJ: Prentice-Hall (1995), 307.

EXHIBIT P.3 Country Summary of Salient Economic Rankings

	Brazil	India	China
Countries by total area	5th	7th	3rd
Countries by population	5th	2nd	1st
Countries by GDP (nominal)	10th	12th	3rd
Countries by GDP (PPP)	9th	4th	2nd
Countries by exports	21st	11th	2nd
Countries by imports	27th	17th	3rd
Countries by current account balance	47th	5th	1st
Countries by received FDI	16th	29th	5th
Countries by foreign exchange reserves	7th	4th	1st
Countries by number of mobile phones	5th	2nd	1st
Countries by number of Internet users	5th	4th	1st

Source: M. Kobayashi-Hillary, *Building a Future with BRICs: The Next Decade for Offshoring.* Berlin: Springer (2008).

impediments around the flow of trade goods and capital. China and India are expected to become the dominant global suppliers of manufactured goods and services, while Brazil is becoming a similarly dominant supplier of raw materials.

Combined, these countries have an expanding middle class, which will double in number within three years and reach 800 million people within a decade! This massive rise in the size of the middle class in these nations will create demand for a wide range of economic goods including real estate. This suggests that a huge increase in demand will not be restricted to basic goods but result in greater demand for all consumer segments. High economic growth combined with enormous populations of these nations will translate into a large aggregation of wealth, creating ever more attractive world markets. Multinational corporations will no doubt view these countries as major expansion markets.

Exhibit P.3 illustrates the three countries according to a variety of rankings.

Exhibit P.4 shows the changing GDP positions of the BICs vis-à-vis the current GDP leaders.

China

China's growth has been breathtaking, with an average annual real GDP growth rate of 9.1% from 1978 to 2008, faster than that achieved by any East Asian economy during their fastest-growing periods. While China has

EXHIBIT P.4 Forecast GDP Comparison

	2008			2050	
Rank	Country	GDP (millions of USD)	Rank	Country	GDP (millions of USD)
1	United States	14,204,322	1	China	70,710,000
2	Japan	4,909,272	2	United States	38,514,000
3	China (PRC)	4,326,187	3	India	37,668,000
4	Germany	3,652,824	4	Brazil	11,366,000
5	France	2,853,062	5	Mexico	9,340,000
6	United Kingdom	2,645,593	6	Russia	8,580,000
7	Italy	2,293,008	7	Indonesia	7,010,000
8	Brazil	1,612,539	8	Japan	6,677,000
9	Russia	1,607,816	9	United Kingdom	5,133,000
10	Spain	1,604,174	10	Germany	5,024,000

Source: World Development Indicators database, World Bank, 2009; "The N-11: More Than an Acronym," Goldman Sachs study of N11 nations, Global Economics Paper No: 153, March 28, 2007.

a huge population, it is also one of the fastest-aging populations due to the one-child policy and increasing longevity of the elderly. Despite the slowing labor force growth, there will be an ongoing increase in human capital accumulation. Advances in human capital investment and educational attainment of the general population have boomed.

We believe that one of the keys to sustaining long-term growth will be the gradual shift of the Chinese economy away from exports and towards more domestic, demand-driven growth. To facilitate this, China will gradually let its currency appreciate, thereby making imports more affordable for Chinese consumers. It will also likely develop its consumer market as well as its consumer financial services sector to facilitate a wider range of consumer credit products available to the average Chinese household. The expanded use of credit cards would likely spur retail demand and imports, while long-term affordable mortgages will boost housing demand and the concomitant accoutrements associated with home ownership.

India

Since 2003 India has been one of the fastest-growing major economies in the world, leading to rapid increases in per capita income, increasing demand and integration with the world economy. India has made structural reforms that have led to its growing prowess in certain sectors of the service economy as well. Should the government maintain a growth orientation with respect to economic policy, trade, and globalization, India's GDP in dollar terms could rival that of the United States by 2050.

The increase in service and manufacturing productivity has been a large component of India's surging GDP. The gradual opening up of the economy introduced competition that forced the private sector to restructure, emerging leaner and more competitive. Leading this change have been international trade, financial sector growth, and the spread and adoption of information technology.

The twenty-first century will likely see a majority of India's population living in urban areas for first time in history. India has 10 of the 30 fastest-growing cities in the world and is witnessing rapid urbanization. This is happening not only in the larger cities, but in small and mid-size cities as well. We believe India's rapid urbanization has implications for demand in housing, urban infrastructure, and location of offices, retail, and hotels. The increasing expenditures in infrastructure will likely drive growth in the transportation sector, spur demand for vehicles, contribute to increasing real estate values along road corridors, boost suburban growth and accelerate the next phase of urbanization.

Brazil

Brazil is forecast to be among the world's fastest-growing economies for the next several decades. By 2050, Brazil is predicted to be the world's fourth-largest economy. The country possesses vast natural resources, sizable pools of labor, growing productivity, and high investment rates. Unlike most other Latin American economies, its debt position has improved, having moved from the world's largest emerging market debtor to a net foreign creditor by 2008. Since the early 2000s, Brazil has made great progress towards putting into place the foundations for growth, with particular emphasis on achieving macroeconomic stability. Brazil's growth rate has lagged behind China and India in part because of the stabilization measures, which have acted as a drag on the economy, but nevertheless should serve as a strong foundation for future growth.

The economy still remains relatively less open to trade compared with other fast-growing emerging market countries. Brazil has gradually been opening up its markets and lifted barriers to trade. While still primarily a domestically focused economy, a boom in the global demand for raw materials and increased openness pushed the share of imports and exports to a quarter of GDP in 2007. Going forward, a combination of capital accumulation, population growth, and total factor productivity should continue to boost growth. In terms of productivity, increased human capital associated with a growing middle class should be a significant driver of economic expansion. We believe this should help move Brazil rapidly up the value chain in terms of its commodity and raw materials sector and further expand its manufacturing base.

OUTLINE OF THE BOOK

Following this preface, the first two chapters of the book provide a general overview of the fundamentals of commercial real estate and of international real estate investment. The basic structure for each country-specific chapter then follows this general framework:

- A brief overview and analysis of the economic, institutional, and political environment
- A discussion of the main features of the real estate market, including real estate foreign direct investment (FDI)
- A review of the major real estate markets and submarkets in the country
- An analysis of the four or five primary real estate sectors in the country: office, retail, residential, industrial, and hotel where applicable
- A discussion of investment options and strategies
- The appendix of the book includes statistical summaries of information on property market business practices and the bibliography.

Units of measurement follow prevailing property market practice in each country. Thus, metric measurements are used in China and Brazil, while the English system is used in India (though the metric system is more prevalent outside their real estate industry).

NOTE

1. Goldman Sachs, *Dreaming with the BRICs: The Path to 2050*. Global Economic Paper No. 99. 2003.

Disclaimer

This publication is not investment advice or an offer or solicitation for the purchase or sale of any financial instrument. While reasonable care has been taken to ensure that the information contained herein is not untrue or misleading at the time of publication, the authors makes no representation that it is accurate or complete. The assumptions used in making forecasts rely on a number of economic and financial variables. These variables are subject to change and may affect the likely outcome of the forecasts. The information contained herein is subject to change without notice. The authors are not responsible for any liability for any direct or consequential loss arising from any use of this publication or its contents. Copyright and database rights protection exists in this publication and it may not be reproduced, distributed, or published by any person for any purpose without the prior express consent of the authors (and further, John Wiley & Sons). All rights are reserved. Any investments referred to herein may involve significant risk, are not necessarily available in all jurisdictions, may be illiquid, and may not be suitable for all investors. The value of, or income from, any investments referred to herein may fluctuate and/or be affected by changes in exchange rates. Past performance is not indicative of future results. Investors should make their own investment decisions without relying on this publication. Only investors with sufficient knowledge and experience in financial matters to evaluate the merits and risks should consider an investment in any issuer or market discussed herein and other persons should not take any action on the basis of this publication. Additional information is available on request. At the date hereof, the authors may be buying, selling, or holding significant long or short positions; be represented on the board of the issuer; and/or engaging in market making in securities mentioned herein.

Acknowledgments

This book benefited greatly from the perspectives contributions, suggestions, and insights of Jeff Barclay, Bohdy Hedgcock, Shane Taylor, Maria-Luisa Paradinas, Richard van den Berg, Tim Bellman, Jingning (Jessie) Yang, Yanni Jin, Angela Du, Richard Price, Jeff Organisciak, Matson Holbrook, Karen Schumacher, Yu Pei Chang, Cassie Mehlum, Nicholas Brown, Yi Jin, Max Michaels, Jingjing Zhou, and Suzanne Franks. The work of Shane Taylor was extensive and invaluable in the chapter on Brazil. We are grateful to the administrative assistance provided by Sanela Osmanovic and the graphics of Jeremy Sumpter. Many business leaders, academics, and government officials gave freely of their time. They consented to interviews and provided useful comments on investment strategies and the nuances of the business environments of cities and countries. This project could not have been carried out without their help and cooperation. It is unfortunate that space precludes acknowledging each one individually. We are most appreciative of all of their help. We would like to thank Jennifer MacDonald, Evan Burton, and Kevin Holm at John Wiley & Sons for their expert guidance and multi-faceted assistance in this work. Any inadvertent errors or omissions contained in this book are entirely the responsibility of the authors.

Fundamentals of Real Estate Investment

Commercial real estate has been increasingly recognized as an asset class by institutional investors over the past 15 years because of its high current cash flow, diversification benefits, and as a hedge against inflation. Broadly speaking, the universe of commercial real estate investment opportunities can be divided into four categories based on whether the properties are held in public or private market vehicles, and whether the investment structures are equity or debt. This Four Quadrant Model, shown in Exhibit 1.1, illustrates the range of real estate investment opportunities available to investors today.

In each strategy, the fundamental revenue source is derived from leases paid by tenants who occupy commercial real estate properties. This income revenue is potentially augmented by capital appreciation of the asset realized at the time of sale. Private equity investment involves the purchase and management of commercial buildings, including office buildings, industrial warehouses, multifamily apartment complexes, hotels, and retail shopping centers. This investment may be made through direct property, closed-ended, or open-ended commingled funds, and separate accounts. Most real estate investment in emerging markets falls within the private equity quadrant. Public equity investment involves the purchase of shares in real estate investment trusts (REITs) and real estate operating companies (REOCs), providing investors with exposure to real estate via publicly traded securities. Private debt investment includes the origination and acquisition of senior debt (whole mortgages) on commercial properties. The public debt market includes the origination and trading of commercial mortgage-backed securities (CMBS).

The four sectors can be differentiated by their relative risk and liquidity profiles. Debt assets provide a senior claim on future rents at a specified rate and over a specified period. These investments sacrifice some potential return

	Equity	Debt
Private	Direct Investment in Real Estate	Direct Investment in Real Estate Mortgages
Public	Real Estate Investment Trusts (REITs) Real Estate Operating Companies (REOCs)	Commercial Mortgage Backed Securities (CMBS)

EXHIBIT 1.1   Four Quadrants of Real Estate Investment

in favor of predictability. Equity investments, on the other hand, are higher risk because the claim on future rents is subordinate to the debt position. The benefit of the equity position lies in an enhanced ability to control the property through active management and to benefit from the growth of future rents and property appreciation. Private equity real estate investors generally anticipate relatively higher returns than public equity, reflecting the lower liquidity and higher risk of the private market, compared to the public equity markets. While REIT shares can be actively traded through an organized, efficient, and transparent market where abundant information exists, private equity transactions are conducted between individual buyers and sellers with less information.

The debt markets have evolved to provide an increasing number of sophisticated financial products to investors. Public debt investing, predominantly in the form of CMBS, emerged as a strong global trend beginning in the early 1990s. The liquidity provided by trading CMBS in a public market, as well as the ability to securitize large income streams and tranche loans into various risk profiles, helped to make CMBS an increasingly attractive investment opportunity. While the current upheaval in the capital markets has severely impacted the origination and values of CMBS tranches, we nonetheless expect an eventual return to long-term origination and trading volumes. Private debt, which for many years was the primary vehicle for commercial debt investment, has taken on an increasingly prominent role recently as the CMBS market has "seized" in the current crisis. Exhibit 1.2 illustrates the various risk and liquidity characteristics of some of the major commercial real estate investment vehicles. Investors are able to craft portfolios based upon their needs for liquidity and risk, while balancing the risk and return profiles.

This chapter focuses mainly on investment strategies for private equity real estate investment, as this is still the main way of investing in emerging markets. Private equity has historically also been a cornerstone of most

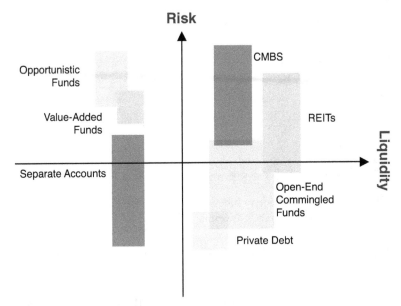

EXHIBIT 1.2   Real Estate Investment Vehicles Risk and Liquidity Spectrum
Source: ING Clarion Research & Investment Strategy.

institutional portfolios, and we believe it provides a good foundation for understanding the additional strategies.

INVESTING BY PROPERTY SECTOR

Private equity real estate investments are generally focused on the five main property sectors: office, industrial, multifamily, retail, and hotel. Investment preferences may vary depending on current and forecast economic conditions, lease types, professional management requirements, and other characteristics unique to each sector. For example, the benefits of a generally low vacancy rate in the multifamily sector are balanced against the requirement for intensive, active management. We believe, therefore, that local market knowledge and management experience are particularly important in the multifamily sector to maximize returns and mitigate risks. Similarly, while the hotel sector has historically been the most volatile in terms of returns, it is also typically the first sector to recover after an economic downturn, presenting the potential for high returns with careful market timing.[1]

In the United States, institutional-quality real estate investments are tracked by the National Council of Real Estate Investment Fiduciaries

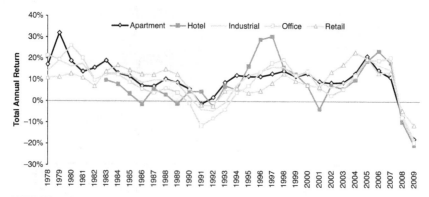

EXHIBIT 1.3 NCREIF Property Index Annual Total Return by Property Sector
Source: ING Clarion Research & Investment Strategy, NCREIF, as of 2009Q4.

(NCREIF). The NCREIF Property Index (NPI) is a good representation
of investment performance for the five core property sectors over several
market cycles (see Exhibit 1.3).

Globally, International Property Databank (IPD) tracks real estate returns for dozens of countries and has recently begun publishing a global
index. While the global returns data series is not as lengthy or robust as the
U.S. series, it does suggest that the property sectors appear to follow similar
patterns globally as what we see in the U.S. NCREIF data (see Exhibit 1.4).

Office

Office sector properties are generally categorized based upon location and
quality. Buildings may be located in Central Business Districts (CBDs) or
suburbs. Buildings are also classified by general quality and size, ranging

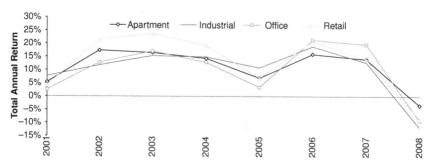

EXHIBIT 1.4 IPD Global Property Index Annual Total Returns by Property Sector
Source: ING Clarion Research & Investment Strategy, IPD, as of 2009Q4.

from highest-quality and generally large-scale Class A buildings to below investment grade Class C buildings; institutional investors tend to focus on only Class A or B buildings. So-called trophy office buildings are generally found in supply-constrained markets such as Manhattan, London, Shanghai, and Mumbai; typically, they are of the highest quality with notable architecture and outstanding locations.

The longer duration of office leases, which typically run 5 to 10 years, helps to mitigate the office sector's historic volatility.[2] It is generally understood that the complexity and size of many office projects contribute to long construction timelines. This limits the developer's ability to pull back on projects when the economy deteriorates, sometimes leading to the delivery of new space in a time of weak fundamentals. In addition to long construction timelines, CBD office properties are capital-intensive, requiring a high capital outlay to purchase the property as well as significant levels of expenditure for renovations and tenant improvement when leases roll over.

Industrial

Industrial properties are generally categorized as warehouses, research and development (R&D) facilities/flex space, and manufacturing.[3] NCREIF returns for the industrial sector illustrate generally less volatility than in the other property sectors, suggesting investment in this sector as a relatively more defensive strategy.[4] The shorter construction timeline—typically six to nine months for warehouse properties—allows the sector to be much more responsive to changes in demand, helping to avoid significant overbuilding. Industrial properties typically require relatively modest capital expenditures for maintenance and tenant turnover. The triple-net lease structure, common to the sector, helps the owner to mitigate many of the risks associated with rising expenses. However, industrial properties tend to have lower total values than the other sectors, and constructing a sizable and diversified industrial portfolio one property at a time may be difficult. As such, portfolio acquisitions have been relatively more common in the industrial sector than other sectors.

Apartment or Multifamily

Multifamily properties are generally defined as having five or more dwelling units. There are three main types of multifamily product—garden (mostly one-story apartments), low-rise, and high-rise. Typically, institutional-grade apartments consist of at least 20 or more units. The apartment sector is similar to the industrial sector in that both feature relatively short construction periods and may be developed in phases, making them more responsive to changes in demand. Apartments typically have the lowest vacancy rates of any sector—rarely above 10% even in economic recessions.[5]

Retail

The retail sector is comprised of five main formats: neighborhood retail, community centers, regional centers, super-regional centers, and single-tenant stores. Like the hotel and apartment sectors, retail properties also require a high degree of active management. Location, convenience, accessibility, and tenant mix are generally considered to be among the key criteria for successful retail investments. Retail leases tend to range from 3 to 5 years for smaller tenants and 10 to 15 years for large anchor tenants. Leases, particularly for anchor tenants, may include a base payment plus a percentage of sales. The cost of upgrading and renovating retail properties can be significantly higher than for the other sectors, and upgrades may be required on a more regular basis to maintain functional utility. Overall, returns on retail investments tend to closely track the economy—both local and national. Income and population density are generally considered to be key drivers of local retail demands.

Hotel

We believe that hotel investment is best understood as both a real estate sector and an operating business. Generally characterized as a noncore asset class, the hotel sector exhibits the highest volatility of the five main property types according to NCREIF returns. This is primarily due to the extremely short effective lease terms, as hotel rooms are essentially leased on a daily basis. As such, hotel owners/operators are able to adjust their rates quickly in response to economic activity. As a result, hotel revenue has been largely correlated with gross domestic product (GDP) activity. Hotel demand is derived from business travelers, meetings/conventions, and leisure travelers. Although hotels are the most volatile of the five sectors, they can offer the highest return potential during an economic recovery.

Mixed-Use

Mixed-use, as the name implies, is a combination of uses (sectors) within one property. Mixed-use properties may include multiple uses in a single structure (vertical mixed use) or multiple uses within close proximity of one another in an integrated development (horizontal mixed use). This development style has become much more popular in recent years due to the renewed popularity of urban living, urban redevelopment, and brownfields renewal efforts, which all aim to maximize development potential and density on increasingly expensive land. Mixed-use is also much more prevalent in emerging markets due to greater urban densities and the need to optimize land uses. This product type often combines high-density residential, office, and retail in one site. Integrating the various components of a mixed-use project demands a higher attention to design than the other property sectors, generally increasing costs. These types of projects have historically been large in scale and located in high-profile urban areas, but the increasing popularity of these projects has resulted in a growing number of smaller projects in suburban locations as well.

INVESTING BY STYLE

A range of investment styles allows real estate investors to pick a preferred level of risk. There are three main investment styles: core, value-added, and opportunistic. These strategies offer a continuum of options along the risk-return spectrum, as indicated in Exhibit 1.5.

Core Strategy

Core real estate has historically accounted for more than half of all real estate commitments.[6] It is generally understood to represent a long-term, low risk/low return strategy. Investors are typically attracted to core real

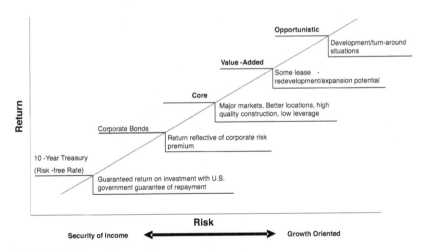

EXHIBIT 1.5   Real Estate Investment Strategies
Source: ING Clarion Research & Investment Strategy.

estate because of its high yield, stable bond-like characteristics, diversification, and inflation hedging benefits. Investment in core real estate focuses on the acquisition of existing, well-leased and high quality properties in established markets. Investments are focused in the four primary property sectors: office, industrial, retail, and multifamily. The hotel sector is often not considered to be a core sector, given its high volatility and the fact that it is extremely management-intensive. Core properties typically demonstrate stable and predictable income flows from strong credit tenants. A high proportion of the anticipated total return in this strategy is generated from current income and cash flow. Property appreciation plays a lesser role, but the stability of the properties helps to provide more predictability of future property values and potential purchasers. Low-to-moderate leverage is used for asset acquisition, further minimizing risk. The target total returns are in the 7–10% range.

Value-Added Strategy

The value-added strategy spans the spectrum from less risky core-plus style to higher risk and more opportunistic plays. In its most fundamental form, value-added real estate investment involves buying a property, improving it in some way, and selling it at an opportune time for a capital gain. Capital appreciation normally comprises a significant portion of the investment's total return. Properties with management problems, operational issues, or ones that require physical improvements are prime candidates for this strategy. Significant expertise and experience in re-tenanting and rehabilitating the properties are required for successful execution. The value-added strategy normally uses 40–70% leverage and the target total returns are in the 13–17% range.

Opportunistic Strategy

Opportunistic investing represents the highest risk/highest return strategy available in private equity real estate. In the past, most institutional investors had minimal exposure to opportunistic investments in their portfolios. However, the search for higher returns in recent years spurred growing interest in this strategy. Opportunistic investments are made based on their return potential with little or no consideration given to diversification, either by property type or by geographic region. Opportunity funds target distressed assets (property or debt), development projects, and emerging markets. In general, these investments are more complicated and risky and could involve nontraditional/specialized property types, complex financial restructuring, highly leveraged transactions, ground-up development, and international markets. Opportunistic investing often uses high leverage (>70%) and target total returns start at 20% and above, with a limited income component.

INVESTING BY PHASE

Investors can also choose to invest in a specific stage of the property life cycle. The three basic stages are (1) development, (2) stabilization, and (3) repositioning/redevelopment. This approach allows the investor an additional opportunity to balance the level of risk and reward.

Development

Development is typically part of an opportunistic strategy. In a market with significant barriers to entry, development can be justified if existing properties regularly sell at a premium to their development cost. High barrier-to-entry markets are often characterized by strong demand fundamentals (high occupancies and rents) and low capitalization rates (cap rates).[7] In markets characterized by low barriers to entry, new properties run the risk of being priced close to or at their development cost, which generally does not justify the risk premium for development.

Stabilization

Stabilization occurs when the construction phase is finished and leases are in place to reach a target occupancy level. These types of properties are the focus of a majority of investment activity, partly because the risks of owning stabilized buildings are partly mitigated by the clear record of historic operating income and expenses. This stable income allows for a more accurate projection of future income. Stabilized properties generally demand a higher price (a lower cap rate) than development or redevelopment properties, given the lower relative risk. As such, stabilized properties also generally have lower total returns. Stabilized investments are typically preferred by large institutional investors. A typical strategy for stabilized assets is to hold for income returns and sell when the spread between return on investment and the cap rate is the greatest.

Repositioning/Redevelopment

This is also known as the value-added phase. When stabilized properties command large price premiums in high barrier-to-entry markets, repositioning/redevelopment is a logical investment strategy. Poorly managed or

EXHIBIT 1.6 NCREIF Historic Return Correlations

NCREIF Historic Return Correlation	10-Year	30-Year
S&P 500	0.21	0.11
Barclays Capital Aggregate Bond Index	−0.17	−0.07

Source: ING Clarion Research & Investment Strategy, S&P, Barclays Capital, as of March 31, 2010.

cash-strapped properties with high potential are typical targets in repositioning/redevelopment investments.

ASSET ALLOCATION

According to Modern Portfolio Theory, the inclusion of low or negatively correlated assets in a diversified portfolio can minimize overall portfolio risk. Real estate as an asset class exhibits low to negative correlations with equities and bonds (see Exhibit 1.6). We believe that an allocation between 10% and 20% of real estate assets into a mixed asset portfolio can potentially enhance investment returns and reduce portfolio risks over a long-term investment horizon.[8]

Real estate has typically been underweighted in mixed-asset portfolios.[9] We believe that there are a few reasons for this. First, real estate is perceived to be risky. Second, many investors feel that real estate is relatively illiquid and inaccessible to small investors. As we have seen above, this has been changing with the proliferation of real estate investment options.

NOTES

1. General conclusions based upon a review of historic returns data in the U.S. from the National Council of Real Estate Investment Fiduciaries (NCREIF), historic returns data, 1978–2008.
2. W. Wheaton, "The Cyclic Behavior of the National Office Market," *American Real Estate and Urban Economics Association Journal* (1987). Volume 15, Number 4, December 1987, pp. 281–299.
3. Manufacturing space tends to be a small focus for investors, as it typically is owned directly by end-users, not investors.
4. National Council of Real Estate Investment Fiduciaries (NCREIF), historic returns data, as of Q4 2008.

5. For example, according to Torto Wheaton Research, the national vacancy rate has not topped 8.2% since 1994. Torto Wheaton Research, Outlook XL Online, Apartment Sum of Markets, as of Q1 2010.
6. Real Capital Analytics, Q1 2010.
7. A capitalization rate is calculated as the expected net operating income divided by the current property market value, either for the previous year or for the first year of ownership.
8. T. Bellman, M. Paradinas, and S. Taylor, "The Case for Real Estate: Asset Class Performance at the Cusp of Recession," ING Real Estate Internal Publication (2008).
9. P. Sivitanides, "Why Invest in Real Estate: An Asset Allocation Perspective," *Real Estate Issues* (1997). Volume 22, April 1997, 30–37.

2

Investing in International Real Estate

Increasing global economic integration makes the opportunities in international real estate investment, including emerging market real estate, more compelling than ever before—especially given the weakness and slow growth in the domestic real estate markets of most developed economies. While traditional international capital flows were largely directed toward U.S. and Western European opportunities, in the last several years, substantial interest has developed for markets in Asia. More recently, investment has been growing in Latin America, Eastern Europe, and Russia.

Although most capital currently going into international real estate has an "opportunistic" risk/reward structure, we expect that, over the next few years, "value-added" and "core" strategies will follow as comfort with international real estate grows and reduction in portfolio risk becomes more attainable. This chapter provides information on the rationale for making an investment in international real estate, as well as identifying the risks that such an investment entails.

WHY INVEST IN INTERNATIONAL REAL ESTATE?

The same logic drives investment in international real estate as in domestic real estate: higher returns, portfolio diversification, and the ability to hedge inflation. The international dimension also provides two additional factors: potential to invest in an expanded universe of real estate investments and the need to match international asset holdings to the increased international liability exposure of multinational corporate pension funds.

To summarize, we believe that investing in international real estate facilitates the potential for:

- Higher returns
- Increased diversification
- Inflation hedging
- Expanded real estate universe

The Potential to Earn Higher Returns

Countries that offer investment-grade opportunities are subject to more diverse supply and demand conditions than those countries without investment-grade opportunities, leading to different returns by country. As shown in Exhibit 2.1, which displays total returns for five countries, several economies produced greater total returns than the United States in certain years. These were earned on unleveraged, investment-grade real estate by institutional and private investors and therefore warrant further consideration as an investment opportunity.

Among the major markets, annual returns in the UK, the United States, France, Spain, and Japan fell into negative territory, while Australia, Canada, Germany, and South Korea recorded positive figures but below 5% (IPD as

EXHIBIT 2.1 Long-Term (1990–2008)* Total Returns YoY by Asset Type and Major Market

	AU	CA	NL	UK	US	Global
Bonds	10%	9%	7%	9%	7%	8%
Private Real Estate	8%	8%	10%	8%	8%	8%**
Equity/Stocks	10%	9%	10%	8%	10%	6%
Public Real Estate	12%	2%	7%	7%	14%	9%
Commodities	N/A	N/A	N/A	N/A	N/A	14%***

Sources: IPD/NCREIF. Thomson Financial Datastream (TFD)/FTSE (EPRA); TFD/Citigroup (CGBI); TFD/Morgan Stanley (MSCI). TFD/ML (MLCX), ING Real Estate Research & Strategy, as of 4 June 2009.

*Unless otherwise stated, mention of years refers to the calendar year, thus 1990 refers to 1 January 1990 to 31 December 1990.

**The global IPD index has an eight-year history.

***Commodities data are for 1991–2008. Private real estate figures for the Netherlands include the ROZ and IPD figures without adjustments. Figures provided by ROZ up to 1994 are more transaction based and may contain some regression noise, unlike IPD figures.

EXHIBIT 2.2 2008 Total Returns YoY by Asset Type and Major Market

	AU	CA	NL	UK	US	Global
Bonds	12%	11%	7%	9%	12%	14%
Private Real Estate	2%	4%	3%	−22%	−7%	−5%
Equity/Stocks	−37%	−31%	−45%	−29%	−37%	−38%
Public Real Estate	−54%	−40%	−34%	−45%	−41%	−49%*
Commodities	N/A	N/A	N/A	N/A	N/A	−43%

Sources: IPD/NCREIF. Thomson Financial Datastream (TFD)/FTSE (EPRA); TFD/Citigroup (CGBI); TFD/Morgan Stanley (MSCI); TFD/ML (MLCX), ING Real Estate Research & Strategy, as of 4 June 2009.
*FTSE/EPRA Developed Index. Note the private real estate return is based on the IPD Global Index 2008, and the value is based on the "local currency" figure.

of June 2009). However, the downturn has been general and widespread across all asset classes. Total returns in 2008 behaved mostly as they "were expected to," in terms of volatility and return levels. As shown in Exhibit 2.2, private real estate was the second-best performing asset in 2008, only outperformed by bonds, which was the best asset class globally. General equities and listed real estate recorded the deepest falls, in a range between −29% (UK equity) and −54% (Australian listed real estate), of those five countries in our study.

Despite the widespread downturn in 2008 and 2009, we believe that long-term private real estate returns remain attractive. The asset class that outperforms and underperforms over the long term varies by country, and there is no common pattern, but private real estate returns in each country range between 7.5% and 10.2% per year, which we believe remains at the upper-end of the range of returns usually required by investors for private real estate as an investment asset.[1] The hybrid nature of real estate offers a stable income return similar to bonds; however, capital appreciation may occur as the economy grows, and this feature is similar to equities. It is for this reason that over the long term, real estate is expected to provide a return somewhere between equities and bonds in general terms. Available data show that private real estate has been the best-performing asset in the Netherlands in the long term, while public real estate has been the best-performing asset in Australia and the United States, providing investors with double-digit returns (Exhibit 2.3).

Over the long term, private real estate has offered attractive returns compared to bonds and relatively lower volatility compared to equities and public real estate, which makes it a potentially attractive asset for risk-averse investors. Investors who are less risk-averse and are looking for higher

EXHIBIT 2.3   Annual Total Returns for Mixed Assets: 1983–2007

Asset	Index	Total Return	Std Dev	Return/ Risk
U.S. Intermediate Bonds	Barclays/Lehman	8.30%	5.10%	1.63
U.S. Private Real Estate	NCREIF	9.38%	6.16%	1.52
Ireland Private Real Estate*	IPD-Ireland	14.65%	11.80%	1.24
UK Private Real Estate	IPD-UK	10.90%	8.96%	1.22
U.S. Large-Cap Stocks	S&P 500	13.78%	15.55%	0.89
U.S. Public Real Estate (REITs)	NAREIT	14.37%	16.40%	0.88

Sources: ING Clarion Research & Investment Strategy; NAREIT; NCREIF; IPD; Standard & Poor's; and Lehman Brothers.
*IPD-Ireland data are from 1984 through 2007.

returns might turn to equities and public real estate to complement their portfolio.

The relationship between returns and volatility has resulted in a favorable risk-adjusted return, which ranks private real estate between bonds and equities for every country we have considered, for the period 1990–2008, with the exception of the Netherlands, where private real estate shows the best ratio.

As a means of illustrating the diversification benefits of real estate in a mixed asset portfolio, we use a hypothetical portfolio of U.S. stocks, bonds, private and public real estate, and then examine the impact of adding international private real estate investment in the UK and Ireland. These countries were selected because of data availability and because they exhibit different risk/return behavior from one another.

In Exhibit 2.3, the calculated values for the mean return, the standard deviation of the returns, and the return-to-risk ratio of six asset classes are reported. Three of the asset classes are positioned at the lower end of the risk spectrum: U.S. intermediate bonds; U.S. private real estate; and Ireland private real estate. The other three are located at a higher risk level: U.S. public real estate; U.S. large-capitalization stocks; and UK private real estate.

The expected return and volatility of these returns are estimated for each of the portfolios and are expressed in efficient frontiers (Exhibit 2.4).[2] In the portfolio demonstrating the highest return and lowest risk, the inclusion of international real estate resulted in a better alternative than a purely domestic one.

While this is a naturally selective example, it clearly demonstrates the point that portfolio performance can be enhanced through widening the assets under consideration to include international real estate. In addition to the risk-adjusted returns, there are other compelling return-related

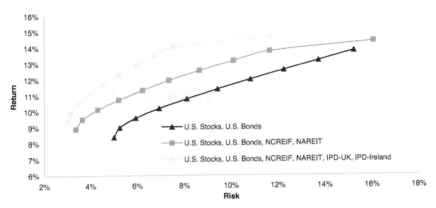

EXHIBIT 2.4   Efficient Frontier with and without International Real Estate
Sources: ING Clarion Research & Investment Strategy; NAREIT; NCREIF; IPD; Standard & Poor's; and Lehman Brothers.

arguments that encourage cross-border investing, particularly in emerging or developing countries. *Most importantly, we believe this is where the higher growth markets will be.* Higher economic growth rates have been found in developing rather than in developed economies for the past several decades, and we believe that this trend will continue for the foreseeable future. In faster-growing economies, the demand for new buildings and facilities should expand proportionately. In some cases, such as China, India, and Brazil, there is significant pent-up demand in several sectors. As a result, investors should expect more development opportunities coupled with the need for additional inbound foreign capital in these countries. Each country is likely to develop its own stock of investment-grade real estate to meet the needs of its expanding economy. This is the Growth Factor of the LCG Framework.

We believe that cross-border investing creates an opportunity to transfer the knowledge of real estate management and investment acquired by individuals and firms in developed markets to emerging markets, that is, the Competitive Factor of the LCG Framework. The widespread trend by a number of countries to create structures similar to the real estate investment trust (REIT) structure in the United States is an example of knowledge transfer of an investment vehicle in the real estate industry. Over the last several years a number of countries around the world including Japan, the UK, Germany, Singapore, and Malaysia have pushed legislation enabling REITs, and expectations are that the international market capitalization will rapidly approach that of the United States' REIT sector.[3] We believe that knowledge transfer, and the attendant competitive advantage conferred to the foreign investment firm, is a powerful return enhancement technique.

In emerging countries, the capital markets are typically underdeveloped. A cross-border investor with access to capital markets can make the investment that a domestic investor with no, or limited, access to capital markets would be unable to undertake. Cross-border direct investment into emerging countries has experienced a tremendous increase over the last decade as astute investors pursued the opportunities for higher returns and discovered that the increase in risk can be well rewarded. Investors pumped a record US$782 billion into emerging markets in 2007, encouraged by favorable economic conditions and a search for high returns.[4]

Increased Diversification

A common measure of risk for an individual asset, such as real estate, is the standard deviation of returns for that asset. This risk measure can be partitioned into two parts, systematic or market risk, and unsystematic or property-specific risk (also called idiosyncratic risk). By investing in multiple properties, rather than just one, the standard deviation of the portfolio of properties declines from that of the individual asset, meaning that the multiproperty investment is less risky. This is the Locational Factor of the LCG Framework.

The same benefits of diversification apply when a new asset class is added to a portfolio. Adding real estate to a stock portfolio will reduce portfolio risk. The greater benefit is obtained from lower correlation between the two assets.

Using the same data series that produced Exhibit 2.3, the correlation coefficients between the asset pairs considered in the portfolio example were calculated and are shown in Exhibit 2.5. In the search for a diversification

EXHIBIT 2.5 Correlation of Annual Total Returns for Mixed Assets: 1983–2007

	NCREIF	NAREIT	IPD-UK	IPD-Ireland*	U.S. Stocks	U.S. Bonds
NCREIF	1					
NAREIT	−0.05	1				
IPD-UK	0.41	0.15	1			
IPD-Ireland*	0.54	−0.19	0.37	1		
US Stocks	0.05	0.27	0.07	0.25	1	
US Bonds	−0.23	0.14	−0.36	−0.35	0.28	1

Sources: ING Clarion Research & Investment Strategy; NAREIT; NCREIF; IPD; Standard & Poor's; and Lehman Brothers.
*IPD-Ireland data are from 1984 through 2007.

benefit, the desire is for assets that are not highly, positively correlated (values near +1.00 are undesirable).

However, another element to be observed is that private real estate was the asset type with a lower correlation level both in the earlier and the more recent periods. Despite the increased integration of capital, private real estate investments rely heavily on variables with a high local component, which suggests that a global portfolio of private real estate investments might be better diversified than a global portfolio of other asset types.

Based on the results reported in the figure above, two observations are made:

1. Private real estate provides diversification benefits to a portfolio of stocks and bonds that otherwise would include no or limited private real estate investments; the observed correlation coefficients between stocks or bonds and any of the real estate assets are consistently low.
2. Public real estate and private real estate behave quite differently in a portfolio; they represent two different asset classes for investment purposes.

When the portfolio perspective is that of a global investor, then all real estate, in all forms in all markets, could potentially be placed in the portfolio. It is highly unlikely that the optimum portfolio for this investor would actually comprise only real estate from one country as this scenario would not capture diversification benefits. While any attempt to obtain an optimum mix of assets from a modern portfolio theory perspective might result in a preference for a concentration of assets in some subset of countries, the likelihood of a single country as the only source of real estate assets for inclusion in the portfolio is nearly zero.

Inflation Hedging

An inflation hedge is a protection against the loss of purchasing power as inflation occurs. To be effective, the real return to the asset must be independent of the rate of inflation. An asset is viewed as a complete hedge against inflation if the nominal return of the asset varies directly with both expected and unexpected inflation. The empirical results to date support the view that private real estate is effective as a hedge against expected inflation and in special cases for unexpected inflation.[5]

The inflation-hedging capability of real estate tends to work best during extended periods of low inflation. During periods of rapid inflation, real

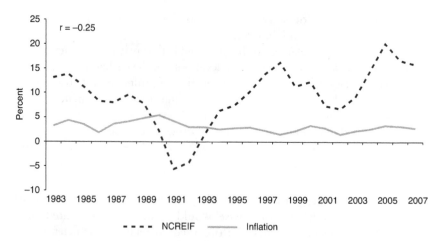

EXHIBIT 2.6   Inflation and Private Real Estate in the United States
Sources: ING Clarion Research & Investment Strategy; Bureau of Labor Statistics;
NCREIF.

estate markets are unable to match inflation with rent increases, and the
hedging capability diminishes. Also, the hedge is most effective when the
real estate markets are in equilibrium. There is very limited pricing power
when markets are overbuilt; in other words, rent increases are difficult when
vacancies are high. The effect of overbuilding in the United States can be seen
during the years 1991–1992 when real estate returns diverged significantly
from the trend of inflation (see Exhibit 2.6).

   The ability of real estate to hedge inflation is determined by the structure
of the typical lease in the market. When the normal lease is for a long term
at a fixed rate with little or no provision for review, then the underlying
property will not serve as an effective hedge against inflation since rental
rates would not increase over its lease term.

   On the other hand, if the lease has frequent reviews or contains pro-
visions where the rents adjust with inflation, then the hedging capability
is increased. Typical lease terms differ substantially from one country to
another as well as from one product type to another. While it is conceiv-
able that an international investment in private real estate might be made to
hedge domestic inflation, it appears very unlikely, since the logical choice for
hedging domestic inflation would be domestic real estate. However, when
the decision to diversify internationally has been made and the choice of asset type is the issue, then international private real estate would appear to be
superior as an inflation hedge to the other usual asset choices of international
stocks and bonds.

Expanded Real Estate Universe

Most real estate investors seek high returns over the long term. Sometimes, the investor will exhaust domestic markets and thus be constrained in reaching the investment objective. Consideration of international real estate greatly increases the opportunities to achieve alpha. For example, the investor may desire to invest in central business district (CBD) office buildings in supply-constrained markets. In developed economies, supply-constrained markets do exist but they are finite, and other investors pursue the same strategy pushing up prices and lowering returns. By increasing the universe to international real estate and finding supply-constrained CBD office buildings in other countries, the investor can continue to pursue the desired strategy. This is, again, an example of the Locational Factor.

The ability to engage in international real estate investment is made easier by the continually expanding universe of investment-grade real estate throughout the world. The estimate of the global stock of investment-grade real estate in 2008 was US$17.8 trillion, with US$4.6 trillion, or 23.3%, in the United States (Exhibit 2.7).[6] In other words, most real estate suitable for the portfolio of an institutional investor is now in countries other than the United States.

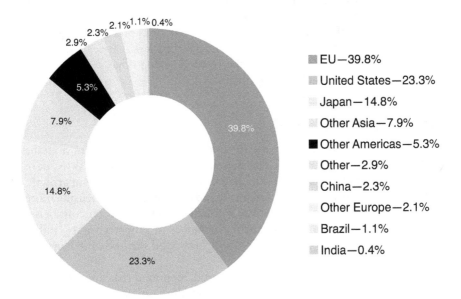

EXHIBIT 2.7 The Investment-Grade Real Estate Universe: 2008
Source: Urban Land Institute; PricewaterhouseCoopers; and ING Real Estate Research & Strategy.

The globalization of economic activity has accelerated the development of commercial real estate over an ever-widening array of countries. The process should continue as more countries are added to the list in the future. The market share for smaller countries on the current list will likely expand at the expense of developed economies, with China, India, and Brazil all expected to see significant increases.

RISKS IN INTERNATIONAL REAL ESTATE

Country risk is the risk that cross-border cash flows will not be realized because of disequilibrium between the domestic platform and that of another country.[7] Given this potential concern, one may require higher returns from an investment as an offsetting factor. Factors that influence country risk can be partitioned a number of ways. For our purposes, we will use a simple two-factor approach.

Political Risk

Political risk is concerned with government structure, policy, leadership and stability, conflicts, tensions and war, political parties, and bureaucracy. A measurement of political risk would attempt to capture the degree of movement along the continuum of political freedoms that lead to stable environments over time. Much of the research to date has tended to use qualitative factors in such measurement.

Economic Risk

Economic risk is concerned with the stability of exchange rates and the performance of the economy. The measurement of economic risk is more quantitative, and insight can be obtained from factors such as output growth, inflation, debt, current account balances, and exchange rates. Focusing more directly on business and real estate transactions, factors to be considered include contract law and enforcement, the nature of property rights, ability to meet financial obligations, bankruptcy laws, and methods for handling defaults.

The various dimensions of political and economic risk are interactive and interconnected. Consequently, we will explore only a few of the many factors that influence country risk and try to gain some insight as to the level of risk currently present in the global arena. The factors considered are presented in Appendix A. The division of the countries by income status is based on the World Bank classification of economies.

We believe that the probable single best indicator of the level of country risk is the level of income received by each citizen. As per capita income levels increase, the pressures for political change are likely to be reduced, and economies flourish, producing a decline in country risk for the cross-border investor. The per capita income measurement presented in the Appendix is adjusted for purchasing power parity (PPP), providing a more realistic measure of differences in the standard of living by country.[8]

The absolute level of gross domestic product (GDP) is also an indicator of reduced country risk, even after adjusting for the factor of high per capita income. In general, larger economies are less risky economies. As economies expand, the level of country risk usually declines. Sound monetary policy, resulting in low levels of inflation, is also a feature of countries with a lower level of country risk. By contrast, rapidly expanding money supplies and persistent high levels of inflation result in heightened pressures for currency devaluation.

One strategy that reduces country risk is to monitor the movement of the markets and economic structures toward free and competitive markets. The Fraser Institute annually rates the economic freedom of countries, taking into consideration five major areas: size of government expenditures, taxes, and enterprises; legal structure and security of property rights; access to sound money; freedom to trade internationally; and regulation of credit, labor, and business.[9] As a final outcome of their assessment process, the Economic Freedom of the World (EFW) rating is produced, measured on a scale from 1 to 10 with the higher value indicating the greater freedom. In their recent Annual Report, they provided current ratings (reported here) and historical values of the index. Comparing ratings from 1995 to those of 2005, significant improvement was found.[10] Collectively, the world continues on a path to free and competitive markets according to the annual report.

One of the most visible risks to an international investor is currency risk. The potential movement of exchange rates during the holding period of an investment definitely adds risk to the investment in another country should the currency of the country where the asset is located devalue.

MITIGATING COUNTRY RISKS

When the various dimensions of country risk are identified, then strategies can be employed to mitigate that risk. Some will be partial solutions, while others might render the particular risk neutral.

Currency Risk

In an ideal risk-neutral situation, the exchange rates between two countries would remain unchanged during the life of an international investment. While such a perfect relationship is difficult to find over extended periods of time, there are ways to deal with the problem.

Hedge the Currency Examples of hedging devices include both forward contracts in the currency and currency swaps. Unfortunately, these methods to hedge risks are available on a limited basis, usually for the major currencies of the world, and have a cost associated with their use. The dollar, yen, and euro are easily hedged for extended holding periods, as these are the most actively traded currencies. However, the same cannot be said for currencies of developing and transitional economies where the risk of currency movement is the greatest.

Use Local Currency-Denominated Leverage Borrow funds in the target country to purchase the real estate asset in that country. The debt will be denominated in the same currency as the held asset, and the risk of differential currencies on that portion of the investment is neutralized. In order to utilize this strategy, there must be capital available in the target country. While the capital markets of emerging economies are improving, there remain many countries with limited ability to support this strategy.

Invest in Markets Where Real Estate Leases Are Dollar- or Euro-Denominated With the growth of multi-country trading zones and the increased activity of multinational firms, this strategy is becoming more widely available. The currency risk is transferred from the owner of property to the tenant.

Build a Portfolio of Currencies An international investment in real estate is *actually two investments, one in real estate and one in a currency.* By investing in multiple countries, the portfolio of currencies is diversified and currency risk is reduced.

Political/Economic Risks

Beyond the issue of currency risk mitigation, there are ways to mitigate some of the other political and economic risks that may be encountered when making an international investment.

- When country risks are perceived to be high, a strategy of making only short-term investments can mitigate some of the risk. In the short term, the direction of the economy is much easier to forecast. In a like manner, the effects of political change are more visible over a shorter time horizon. As a result, short-term currency movements are more predictable since they are often tied to short-term economic and political health.
- Given the wide variety of local practices and procedures for engaging in business and real estate transactions, the selection of a local partner for *participation in a joint venture* can serve to mitigate much of that risk.
- Staying with the theme of "using local knowledge," many financial services companies have global operations. Since the mid 1980s, the global financial services sector has been merging and consolidating. In the process, local operations for banking and insurance have been acquired and incorporated into the firms. These units are, in turn, a source of local knowledge for the institutional investment arms of the consolidated company.

Beyond active strategies for risk mitigation, there is an underlying trend toward economic integration sweeping across the globe. Regional trading zones have been and are being created.[11] The income levels of developing nations are growing at rates above those of developed nations leading to a convergence of real income levels and standards of living.[12]

International real estate investment increases risk-adjusted returns and the diversification of a portfolio. Investment-grade real estate is dispersed around the globe and should become more so. Economic convergence is likely to increase information about and the demand for international real estate.

International real estate investment involves increased risks. Country risks can be identified and substantially mitigated. Political and economic risks have been declining globally for some time and should continue to do so as the global economy integrates further.

Despite the increasing synchronization of the global capital markets, the diversification benefits of private real estate support a case for real estate and, more than ever, a case for international real estate. Private real estate presents the lowest cross-border correlation levels of all major asset classes, even in recent years. When several international markets are considered, investors can access a higher level of returns at the same level of risk. Local market characteristics continue to create differences in performance of local real estate markets, especially due to divergent economic performance. This suggests that a deep knowledge of the local markets would help to build a more efficient diversified portfolio. Private real estate may have become more global from a capital markets perspective, but in terms of market fundamentals it retains its local roots in a local economy.

NOTES

1. Average annual return for 1990–2008 in Australia, Canada, the Netherlands, the UK and the United States, according to IPD and NCREIF total returns.
2. The real estate return series from NCREIF was adjusted for smoothing using the technique presented in David Geltner, "Estimating Market Values from Appraised Values without Assuming an Efficient Market," *The Journal of Real Estate Research* 8, no. 3 (Summer 1993): 325–345. The IPD series were examined for temporal lags and judged not to require such a significant modification.
3. Ernst & Young, "2008 Real Estate Market Outlook," 9.
4. "Capital Flows to Emerging Market Economies." Institute of International Finance, March 6, 2008: 1.
5. Haibo Huang and Susan Hudson-Wilson. "Private Commercial Real Estate Equity Returns and Inflation." *Journal of Portfolio Management* (September 2007).
6. The Urban Land Institute and PricewaterhouseCoopers LLP; "Emerging Trends in Real Estate, 2008"; and ING Real Estate Research & Strategy.
7. It should be noted that there are several countries with less country risk than the United States.
8. Purchasing power parity is the rate of currency conversion that eliminates the differences in price levels between two countries. Thus, per capita output measures based on PPP-converted data reflect only differences in the volume of goods and services produced.
9. The Fraser Institute, Chapter 1, "Economic Freedom of the World, 2005," in *Economic Freedom of the World: 2007 Annual Report*: 9.
10. Ibid., 19.
11. Roberto V. Fiorentino, Luis Verdeja, and Christelle Toqueboeuf, "The Changing Landscape of Regional Trade Agreements: 2006 Update," Regional Trade Agreements Section of the Trade Policies Review Division of the WTO Secretariat (2007): 3–4.
12. The International Bank for Reconstruction and Development/The World Bank, "Global Economic Prospects 2007: Managing the Next Wave of Globalization" (2007): 41–42.

CHAPTER 3

China

INTRODUCTION

China represents a significant opportunity for real estate investment. All of the main drivers of real estate demand are strong—economic growth, demographics, urbanization, rising per capita and household incomes, domestic investment, as well as foreign direct investment (FDI). China is moving along a path of (albeit sometimes uneven) economic development, liberalization, and privatization. Opportunities abound in both the primary markets and increasingly the secondary markets.

China reported a total population of 1.3 billion and GDP of US$4.9 trillion in 2009. The country's per capita GDP reached US$3,315 that year (nominal term). Per capita GDP is as high as US$9,000 in first-tier cities: that is, Beijing, Shanghai, and Guangzhou. China started the transition from a centrally planned to a market economy in 1978 and made tremendous economic progress over the next 30 years, registering an average annual GDP growth of above 9.8%. However, Chinese economic development has been uneven among regions. The western regions of the country remain relatively undeveloped while the eastern regions tend to be much more industrialized.

There are dangers of speculative excess. Corruption is still a major issue in China, particularly in the real estate sector. In some locales, government officials expect and receive bribes for approving entitlements and real estate transactions. In other cases, some developers operate largely on a cash basis, declaring little profit to the tax authorities. Another risk is that the legal and institutional framework is vague and seemingly arbitrary in terms of real estate rights, title, and investment regulations. Perhaps the biggest risk currently is the capricious nature of the government (mainly national level) with respect to laws governing real estate, particularly real estate FDI. The changes to real estate FDI in July 2006 radically altered the rules of the game for investment by foreigners. This was done with virtually no warning. This kind of unforeseen, rapid-fire changing of the rules of the game has the potential to wreak havoc on investment. Working with established in-country partners and trusted consultants is fundamental to helping to mitigate these risks.

China is a market brimming with opportunity, but risks are higher due to issues with insecure property tenure, unpredictable government actions, a weak and ever-changing legal/regulatory framework, and low transparency and high corruption. However, the market is also one of the most promising in the world. A recently passed law now allows diverse pension funds to invest in real estate. This could potentially mean billions of dollars of new investment to the Chinese real estate sector. The fact that China is higher risk should not dissuade investors from pursuing investments in the country. Foreign investors need to consider carefully the level of risk for potential reward. While China is ostensibly a "communist" country, it is the capitalist workshop of the world with unprecedented growth. The devil is in the details. Real estate horror stories abound about how deals have gone sour or how gross yields were hit by a number of unforeseen taxes and hidden costs to render a very low effective yield. Gross yields mean far less in China than in many other markets. Each investment must undergo, at least initially, an extraordinary degree of due diligence.

China offers a large variety of investment opportunities. Typically, real estate markets are roughly correlated with size. The same is true with China where, more or less, the potential investment locations are located in the country's largest cities (see Exhibit 3.1). The estimated population as of 2010 according to the United Nations of the 10 largest cities by population are shown below.

Shanghai	15,789,000
Beijing	11,741,000
Guangzhou	9,447,000
Shenzhen	8,114,000
Wuhan	7,542,000
Tianjin	7,468,000
Chongqing	6,690,000
Shenyang	4,952,000
Dongguan	4,850,000
Chengdu	4,266,000

Source: United Nations, World
Urbanization Prospects, as of 2008.

This chapter focuses on the three *primary* markets: (1) Beijing, (2) Shanghai, and (3) Guangzhou/Shenzhen as well touching on several important *secondary* markets including Chengdu, Wuhan, and Dalian. China possesses many more promising secondary markets, which could not be covered in the scope of this book. Some additional high potential secondary markets include Hangzhou (near Shanghai), Qingdao, Tianjin (near Beijing), Nanjing, and Chongqing to name a few. It is important to note that China is so large and possesses so many high-growth cities with populations exceeding one million, the list of potential secondary markets could be very long (in fact over 100 cities). Moreover, nearly all major cities in China are growing rapidly with attendant demand for real estate of all types surging.

OVERVIEW OF THE MARKET ENVIRONMENT

General Overview

A new powerhouse of capitalism that will eventually be (if trends continue) the world's largest economy has seen strong growth despite the recent global recession. As China has become the manufacturer for the world, its growth and development have significantly transformed the country's built environment. In "purchasing power parity" (PPP) terms, China is already the world's second-largest economy, and in PPP terms will likely eclipse the United States as the world's largest economy by 2020. The resurgence of China after three centuries of stagnation has been a miracle of free market capitalism and Keynesian economics. No nation of this magnitude has ever grown so quickly. In the past 20 years, the quadrupling of China's per capita income has helped more than 250 million people move out of poverty, a phenomenon the World Bank calls "unprecedented in human history." Demand for Chinese manufactured goods continues to increase at record levels. Will the growth continue? It is anyone's guess, and many critics have proclaimed that China's growth will slow or stop, but it has continued to be an ongoing economic juggernaut.

China is called the "world's workshop" for good reason. China completely dominates the world's low-cost manufacturing. It manufactures two-thirds of the world's copiers, microwaves, DVD players, and shoes. Walmart, the world's largest corporation, uses 6,000 suppliers of which 5,000 are from China. China has pursued a modernization and economic growth path that is astonishing. China's economy has grown by about 8% annually for more than 25 years—the fastest growth rate for a major economy in recorded history. It has also become the world's largest consumer of basic food and industrial goods. China now consumes more meat, grain,

EXHIBIT 3.1   Map of China
Source: © Map Resources, www.mapresources.com.

steel, coal, cell phones, televisions, and refrigerators than any other country in the world. The country's total demand has been largely responsible for driving up commodity prices around the world.

There are three main growth zones, corresponding to the three primary real estate markets: Bohai (Beijing), Yangtze (Shanghai), and the Pearl River Delta (Guangzhou/Shenzhen). These three growth zones have been registering local GDP growth above the already high national average in recent years. The Bohai has distinct growth drivers in services, high-tech, and government. Yangtze is a major industrial and financial services zone. The Pearl River area specializes in a range of manufacturing, export zones, and tourism, particularly from Hong Kong.

China's consumer class is growing prodigiously. There are currently more than 64 million households earning more than the equivalent of

US$5,000 per year. This is the level at which discretionary consumption begins to grow. Underlying this growth is an increase in real income driven by new financial products and a change in consumer behavior. The growth of the consumer class boosts demand not only for retail properties, but also for residential and leisure property sectors as well.

The ownership structure of China's secondary industry has also undergone great transformation since 1978. In the prereform era, output was dominated by state-owned enterprises (SOEs). In the 1980s, collective enterprises under the local governments, particularly the township and village enterprises in the eastern regions, had been the driving forces behind the growth of industrial output. Since the mid-1990s, local private entrepreneurs, together with foreign investors (either in wholly owned enterprises or in joint ventures with Chinese interests) have played an increasingly important role in manufacturing production. By 2007, the private sector accounted for 44% of the total manufacturing output. However, large state-owned enterprises or state-holding companies (where the state holds more than 50% of the firm) remain the backbone of the country's key industries.

The Economic and Institutional Environment

GDP China has maintained the momentum of rapid economic growth in recent years, despite the global economic slowdown. After growing by 13% in 2007, national GDP slowed to a still-healthy 9.6% in 2008 and 8.6% in 2009.

The EIU has raised its forecast for real GDP growth to 9.9% in 2010 amid clear signs that the Chinese economy has started to recover (Exhibit 3.2).[1] Trade restrictions on Chinese exports as well as growing imports, particularly energy, will lead to slower growth in the external account.

Real GDP growth has been driven by fixed investment and net exports. Total investment in fixed assets grew 25.5% in 2008, and the trade surplus reached US$295.5 billion, US$263.5 billion higher than that in 2004. Fixed investment has grown rapidly in some sectors such as financial services, leasing and commercial services, and electrical equipment manufacturing. Urban investment in financial services and leasing and commercial services increased year on year by 62.6% and 50.6% respectively in 2008. The government is trying to cool down investment in some areas, as it might lead to overheating and raise risks for the future.

Inflation Inflation remained low until 2006 in China, but has risen rapidly since 2007 (Exhibit 3.3). According to the National Bureau of Statistics (NBS), consumer prices rose by 6.6% in 2007, a sharp increase from the

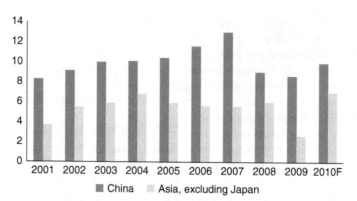

EXHIBIT 3.2 China and Asia (Except Japan) Gross Domestic
Product (GDP) History/Forecast (% change, year on year)
Source: Economist Intelligence Unit (2010).

prior year. The inflation rate slowed over the past two years, but is expected
to rise again in 2010, to an annual rate of 3.4%.

Monetary Policy   Monetary policy is an important aspect of China's economic policy and continuing growth, particularly growth derived from exports. China has carefully managed its currency for well over a decade,

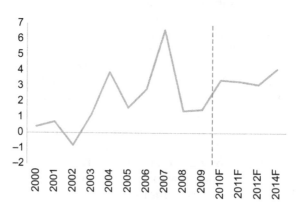

EXHIBIT 3.3 Consumer Price Inflation History/
Forecast (%)
Source: National Bureau of Statistics of China,
China Statistical Yearbook, 2000–2008; Economist
Intelligence Unit, 2010.

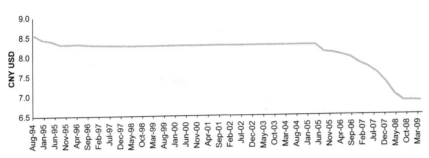

EXHIBIT 3.4 Chinese Renminbi Exchange Rate History
Source: Bank of China, Renminbi Exchange Rate Quotations, 1994–2009.

artificially keeping the value of the RMB low, hovering around RMB 6.8 to the USD (see Exhibit 3.4). The United States has been exerting pressure for China to reevaluate its currency, particularly in light of the enormous and growing current account surplus with the United States. Since the exchange rate reform in 2005, through July 2009, the renminbi appreciated by 15.8% (Exhibit 3.4). In the future, the government will continue to intervene in foreign exchange market to limit the rise of renminbi, but the appreciation process is expected to continue in 2010 and beyond as China's economy continues to strengthen. As the government permits the currency to become more widely used internationally, it will also pursue gradual liberalization of the capital account.

In addition to currency revaluations, monetary policy influences these short-term capital flows. In particular the interest rate differential with the United States is highly correlated with short-term capital flows into and out of China. The central bank has not raised interest rates over the past year in an effort to increase the interest rate differential with the United States and reverse some of the short-term speculation against the local currency. The government raised interest rates on mortgages in March 2005, in a successful effort to cool rising real estate prices, but has not followed the U.S. lead in raising interest rates more broadly, partly in order to reduce speculative pressure on the currency. In 2009, the central bank of China loosened monetary policy by eliminating loan quotas, slashing official interest rates, and cutting the bank reserve ratio in order to stimulate economic growth.

The Chinese central bank adopted a new exchange-rate regime for the renminbi in July 2005, scrapping the currency's peg to the U.S. dollar and replacing it with a managed float against a weighted basket of currencies. The initial central point against the U.S. dollar was set at RMB/US$8.11, representing a 2.1% appreciation compared with the previous pegged rate. The Chinese currency is expected to continue to appreciate, but at a gradual pace, given the government's caution about the issue. The RMB averaged RMB/US$6.81 in 2009 and is likely to appreciate to RMB/US$6.59 in 2010.[2] The Chinese currency is supported by large financial and foreign direct investment flows into China, and the external trade surplus. In the past, a considerable amount of capital denominated in U.S. dollars has flown into China in anticipation of this lift.

Liquidity   At more than 800%, China has the highest liquidity ratio of any sovereign rated by Fitch, well above the 138% median for "A"-rated countries. Reserves were US$2.0 trillion (equivalent to 18.4 months of import cover) at the end of 2008 and have exceeded US$2.4 trillion through June 2010. Gross foreign debt is estimated by Fitch at US$43.4 billion at the end of 2008 (10% of GDP and an extremely low 21.7% of reserves) and is projected to remain low in both relative and absolute terms. Debt service was only 4.1% of current account receipts in 2008, much lower than the 12.3% median for "A"-rated countries. Short-term debt is also very low in absolute terms, US$18 billion in 2008, but somewhat high relative to total foreign debt, 42% of the total, an indication that much of the debt is trade finance. China is a net foreign creditor with US$207 billion (48.8% of GDP) more in foreign asset holdings than foreign claims on Chinese assets, one of the strongest external ratios for an "A"-rated sovereign, according to Fitch Ratings, and significantly above the median of a net debtor position equivalent to 11.3% of GDP.

Finance Sector   China has suffered from a relatively weak banking sector and a significant numbers of nonperforming loans (NPLs). Official statistics claim that the level of nonperforming loans (NPLs) was only 2.45% by the end 2008, down sharply from 6.16% at the end of 2007. However, almost all international institutions estimated that the actual number was much higher than that. Regardless of the actual size, they agreed the number was dropping, and the improvement was the result of increased lending (which could turn out to be a fresh batch of bad loans given recent history), past government purchases of bad loans, and a recent round of recapitalization of three of the largest state-owned banks.

    The real estate sector has been a large component of the NPL problem. Until reforms in recent years, real estate lending was a case of classic crony capitalism. Relationships were key, and investment performance was secondary. The cleanup of the industry is creating a need for international capital as well as partnerships to improve the public image of real estate firms.

The banks followed the government's advice in moving into mortgages, auto loans, and credit cards over the past two years, and the rating agencies expect high NPLs to emerge from this latest round of lending, given the lack of consumer credit skills in Chinese banks or even a national credit agency. The banking sector was opened up to foreign competition at the end of 2006, but foreign ownership of the banking system remains low at 2.4% of total assets by the end of first quarter of 2008. The stock market (Shanghai Composite Index) meanwhile started to decline after reaching an all-time high of 6,124 points in October 2007, ending 2008 down at a record of 65%, partly due to the impact of the global economic crisis. However, at the end of 2009, the stock market index has increased by 73%.

Credit Rating   Due to its strong current account, low domestic and foreign debt levels, and generally conservative fiscal management, China has maintained high, positive credit ratings:

- Moody's Investors Service: A1; Stable
- Fitch: A+; Stable
- Standard & Poor's: A+; Stable

FDI   Foreign investment in China, especially in real estate, has remained strong in recent years. Huge foreign capital inflow continued to dominate the country's capital flows. According to official figures, FDI inflows totaled around US$40 billion a year in the late 1990s, and rose to an all-time high of US$92.4 billion in 2008.

Despite a contraction in Chinese exports, EIU forecasts that disputes with trade partners will continue and some restrictions on capital flows will be eased in the future. Capital account liberalization will continue at a slow pace as well. Capital inflows are forecasted to decrease to US$71.4 billion in 2009, but rise again in 2010.

Manufacturing   China has become a key player in the global manufacturing industry. With export growth usually topping 20% a year, China's rise as an exporter of manufactured goods has taken all recipient economies by surprise. The country's evolving role in the manufacturing industry and its climb up the value-added ladder has been staggering.

China has emerged as the last stage in a pan-Asian production system that has become one of the most important features of global manufacturing.

Regional economies including Taiwan, Singapore, and Korea are rapidly offshoring their manufacturing operations to China.

However, China is not the always ultracompetitive manufacturer it is assumed to be. Its competitiveness is both sector- and region-specific. China's exports are primarily in labor-intensive sectors that include apparel, footwear, and electrical equipment. Guangdong province accounts for almost 60% of China's total exports. Other regions of the country, notably the west and northeast, are far less productive.

Even though products may be "Made in China," roughly 60% of China's exports are produced by foreign-invested enterprises. As the economy continues to restructure, its input costs will escalate, and its price competitiveness is expected to begin to erode. This is already seen in the low end of some (owner-value-asset) goods being produced in countries such as Vietnam and Cambodia.

Tourism   Tourism in China is surging and promises to become a leading growth sector of China's economy. In Beijing, a broad mix of business is driving current increases in demand. In Shanghai, the MICE (Meetings, Incentives, Conventions, and Exhibitions) sector is expected to drive demand growth. The Shanghai Municipal Government is projecting a total of 1,500 international conferences and exhibitions in the city by 2010. China dominates Asia as the biggest tourist destination (Exhibit 3.5).

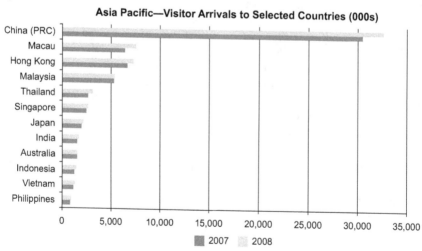

EXHIBIT 3.5   Asia Pacific Visitor Arrivals
Source: World Tourism Organization, World Tourism Barometer (2009).

Rural Unrest   The rural areas are the location of China's greatest poverty. The majority of the population, 62%, resides in the countryside. Increasing income inequality is especially poignant when comparing the incomes of middle-class urban dwellers in the coastal cities to peasant incomes inland. The coastal provinces have a GDP *three times higher than the rural interior*. Some demonstrations and protests have occurred around the country regarding the government's policies and economic maldistribution. This will be an ongoing issue in China and will be a continuing source of friction as China's massive wealth accumulation continues.

Urbanization   Unlike many emerging market countries, which possess only a few major cities, China possesses over 100 cities with a population exceeding one million inhabitants; this staggering level of urbanization will no doubt be a major driver of real estate demand. Urban areas run the length of the east coast of the country as well as many cities inland. Many of its provinces would qualify as countries in any other part of the world. Exhibit 3.6 portrays the regional breakdown of provinces within China. While the bulk of the population is concentrated on the eastern coast, it is important to note that a significant portion of the population is inland (Exhibit 3.6).

Corruption   One of China's biggest problems for the foreign investor is corruption. Corruption is especially acute in the real estate sector where financing for investments was often done, until recently, with a handshake. Bribes to local and national governmental officials for entitlements and various approvals are commonplace. Developers frequently under-report their revenues, frequently selling only for all cash, then not reporting or under-reporting the sales revenue. Transparency International rates China 72nd (a score of 3.6, where 10 represents absolutely free of corruption and zero equals totally corrupt) on its 2008 Corruption Perception Index, which represents an improvement from the 3.4 score recorded in the 2004 survey. China is below some of its regional peers, such as South Korea (5.6), but slightly above Thailand (3.5).[3]

Work Force   The official unemployment rate of urban residents remained low at 4.2% in 2008. Employment growth continues to slow. New job creation in the cities is estimated at only 8 million annually, while 24 million new workers join the workforce each year, leaving a 16 million gap. More problematic, there are an estimated 150 million unemployed rural workers, 20% of the 800 million rural population. A study by the government's Chinese Academy of Social Sciences (CASS) estimated that the Gini

EXHIBIT 3.6 Regional Demographic Trends

	Population (m)	% of Total	GDP (RMB bn)	% of Total	Foreign Direct Investment (US$ m)	Foreign Trade (US$ m)
North	156.9	11.9%	4,773	12.2%	22,291	414,132
Beijing	17.0	1.3%	1,049	3.5%	6,080	271,850
Tianjin	11.8	0.9%	635	2.1%	7,420	80,539
Hebei	69.9	5.3%	1,619	5.4%	3,420	38,420
Shanxi	34.1	2.6%	694	2.3%	2,720	14,390
Inner Mongolia	24.1	1.8%	776	2.6%	2,651	8,933
Northeast	108.7	8.3%	2,819	7.2%	15,563	108,681
Liaoning	43.2	3.2%	1,346	4.5%	12,020	72,440
Jilin	27.3	2.1%	642	2.1%	993	13,341
Heilongjiang	38.3	2.9%	831	2.8%	2,550	22,900
East	382.4	29.1%	12,243	31.3%	70,594	1,202,719
Shanghai	18.9	1.4%	1,370	4.6%	10,084	322,138
Jiangsu	76.8	5.8%	3,000	10.0%	25,120	392,270
Zhejiang	51.2	3.9%	2,149	7.1%	10,070	211,150
Anhui	61.4	4.6%	887	3.0%	3,490	20,440
Fujian	36.0	2.7%	1,082	3.6%	10,026	84,832
Jiangxi	44.0	3.3%	648	2.2%	3,604	13,749
Shandong	94.2	7.1%	3,107	10.3%	8,200	158,140
Southeast	374.3	28.5%	14,978	38.3%	32,704	757,730
Henan	94.3	7.1%	1,841	6.1%	4,033	17,528
Hubei	57.1	4.3%	1,133	3.8%	3,245	20,567
Hunan	68.5	5.2%	1,116	3.7%	4,005	12,566
Guangdong	95.4	7.2%	3,570	11.9%	19,167	683,261
Guangxi	50.5	3.8%	7,172	23.9%	971	13,284
Hainan	8.5	0.6%	146	0.5%	1,283	10,524
Southwest	196.0	14.9%	2,704	6.9%	7,018	45,296
Chongqing	28.4	2.1%	510	1.7%	2,729	9,521
Sichuan	81.4	6.1%	1,251	4.2%	3,340	22,040
Guizhou	37.9	2.9%	333	1.1%	149	3,371
Yunnan	45.4	3.4%	570	1.9%	777	9,599
Tibet	2.9	0.2%	40	0.1%	23	765
Northwest	96.9	7.4%	1,629	4.2%	1,970	39,235
Shaanxi	37.6	2.8%	685	2.3%	1,370	8,368
Gansu	26.3	2.0%	318	1.1%	128	6,080
Qinghai	5.5	0.4%	96	0.3%	220	688
Ningxia	6.2	0.5%	110	0.4%	62	1,882
Xinjiang	21.3	1.6%	420	1.4%	190	22,217
National Total	1,315.3	100.0%	39,146	100.0%	150,140	2,567,793

Note: Totals reported by provinces may not match national totals.
Source: National Bureau of Statistics of China, Statistical Communiqué on the 2008 National Economic and Social Development of Municipalities and Provinces (2008).

coefficient, a measure of income inequality, has more than doubled in the past 20 years and now stands at around 0.50, higher than the regional average. Urban residents now earn more than four times the income level of rural residents.[4]

Agriculture is an important sector of the Chinese economy. Although agricultural production accounted for only 11.3% of GDP in 2008, around 307 million people—comprising 40% of total nationwide employment—still made a living from farming, forestry, animal husbandry, and fisheries. The labor force is huge at about 775 million workers.

As a developing country in transition, the Chinese economy has undergone considerable structural changes in the past quarter century. The share of agricultural output in GDP declined from 28% in 1978 to 11% in 2008. The output share of secondary industry, mainly manufacturing and construction, rose from 48.2% of GDP in 1978 to 48.6% in 2008. The output share of tertiary or services industry rose from 23.7% of GDP in 1978 to 40.1% in 2008.

Infrastructure   The Chinese government has put great emphasis on the development of the country's infrastructure, in order to meet the demands of its booming economy. China's infrastructure is one of the best of all major emerging market economies. India is often compared to China, but India is far behind in terms of this critical dimension. A recent national effort stresses the central government's fiscal spending will be concentrated on improving transport and infrastructure, especially in poorer provinces in central and west China.

Infrastructure in some ways is the backbone of real estate and the economy in general. Without adequate roads, rail, and communications, the utility and therefore value of real estate is greatly diminished. Because of the classic problem of market externalities, it rarely makes economic sense for the private real estate developer to provide much in the way of public infrastructure. Having the infrastructure already in place solves this problem. To its credit, China plans and builds not just for the present, but also for future expansion. Many real estate fortunes have been made by piggybacking on the public investments in infrastructure.

For the longer term, the government has proposed a RMB2 trillion (US$293 billion) railway development program that would take place over 15 years, comprising a series of measures to expand the railway network including double-tracking and line upgrades. The plan will be implemented in stages, beginning with the corporatization of railway operations, so that property rights can be clarified in preparation for sales. Funding options under consideration include issuing bonds and opening the market to domestic and foreign equity investors.

There has been huge investment in shipping and port construction as well, which has greatly eased congestion in the sector. In 2008, port transportation in China was 5.9 billion tons of cargo and 128.4 million twenty-foot equivalent units (TEUs) for container shipping. This figure will be considerably raised, with the on going construction at the new deepwater port at Yangshan near Shanghai and other port expansion projects. The country's total port capacity is projected to reach 8 billion tons of cargo and 136 million TEUs by 2010. This growth in container traffic capacity will boost supply greatly and may bring down freight rates.

China just started to build its interprovince highway network a few years ago. In 2007 the total length of expressways in China reached 53,913 km, and the total length of roads was 3.6 million km in 2007. By the end of 2008, the government had connected 89% of villages across the country. However, despite these improvements, the road network is likely to remain inadequate in relation to the demands for transport in China.

The country's port facilities have improved rapidly in recent years. China has over 200 seaports, and their handling capacity increased to 5.9 billion tons in 2008 from just 483 million tons in 1990. Shanghai is the largest seaport, but, access to the port is restricted by its limited depth. Currently, Shanghai is developing a new US$16 billion offshore deepwater port at Yangshan, the first phase of which was inaugurated in 2005 with a capacity of around 3 million TEUs a year. The full project will be completed by 2020. China's best existing deepwater port is at Ningbo, near Shanghai, in Zhejiang province. Other major ports include those at Dalian in the northeast, Tianjin, Qinhuangdao in Hebei province, Qingdao in Shandong province, Xiamen in the southeastern province of Fujian, and Guangzhou and Shenzhen, near Hong Kong.

China has also made good progress in developing aviation infrastructure over the past 10 years. Dozens of new airports and airport renovations have been completed, including large projects in cities like Beijing and Shanghai. These projects have helped to support explosive growth in civil aviation. Passenger numbers soared from 16.6 million in 1990 to 190 million in 2008, and freight traffic in the same period climbed from 369,722 tons to 4 million tons. Domestic flights account for over 90% of air passenger numbers and over 70% of freight in 2007. But international routes are now available to most of China's large cities. The number of domestic routes has climbed from 385 in 1990 to 1,216 in 2007, and the number of international routes has risen from 44 to 290.

Transportation and Communications China's transportation system is inadequate, especially in rural and western areas of the country, but large sums of money are being spent on upgrading it. The backbone of the system remains the railways, which carry about one-third of all cargo and passengers. The movement of commodities such as coal still clogs up the railway system, and the network is congested and overloaded for both cargo and passengers, especially during China's annual public holidays. Recent infrastructure investments are aimed at improving the current problems.

A high-speed rail link between Beijing and Tianjin was completed and put into operation in 2008, which reduced the travel time between Beijing and Tianjin to half an hour. It is part of a program to build a wider high-speed network. The total length of railways in operation in China reached 78,000 km in 2007, up from 53,400 km in 1990. Nearly 40% of this was double-track railway.

Port facilities have improved rapidly in recent years. China's 14,500 km coastline hosts over 200 seaports, which handled 3 billion tons of goods in 2008, up from just 483 million tons in 1990. Most ports—including some of the largest, such as Shanghai—are relatively shallow, and this prevents modern container ships from using many of them. However, this is changing.

China's telecommunications sector is booming—from fixed-line to internet services. China now boasts more cable television subscribers (around 163 million at the end of 2008) and mobile phones customers (641 million in 2008) than the United States, as well as 341 million fixed-line users in 2008. In addition, the internet is gaining in popularity, with 300 million users in 2008. Penetration rates increased greatly, from around 26 subscribers per 100 people in 2004 for mobiles to 48 subscribers per 100 people in 2008. Internet protocol (IP) telephony is displacing conventional international and long-distance trunk traffic, and third-generation (3G) mobile systems have been rolled out. Optical fiber cable links in the home may allow every urban household to have broadband multimedia access as early as 2010.

Porter Critique of China's Competitive Positioning

Given China's singular role in the world's economy, it is useful to examine the dynamics of China's economy, using Michael Porter's analytical framework for analyzing national competitive factors. In his book *The Competitive Advantage of Nations,* Porter introduced a model that examines why some nations and industries within nations are more competitive than others. This model of determining factors of national advantage has become known as "Porter's Diamond" (Exhibit 3.7). It suggests that the national home base of an organization plays an important role in shaping the extent to which it is likely to achieve advantage on a global scale. This home base provides basic factors, which support or hinder organizations

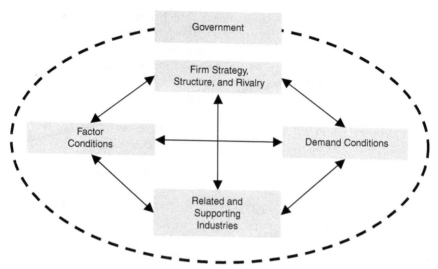

EXHIBIT 3.7   Porter Diamond Model for the Competitive Advantage of Nations
Source: Based upon Michael E. Porter, *The Competitive Advantage of Nations* (1988).

from building advantages in global competition. Porter distinguishes four determinants.

Factor Conditions   The situation in a country regarding production factors, like skilled labor, infrastructure, and so on, are relevant for competition in particular industries. These factors can be grouped into human resources (qualification level, cost of labor, commitment, etc.), material resources (natural resources, vegetation, space, etc.), knowledge resources, capital resources, and infrastructure. They also include factors like quality of research in universities, deregulation of labor markets, or liquidity of national stock markets.

These national factors often provide initial advantages, which are subsequently built upon. Each country has its own particular set of factor conditions; hence, each country will develop those industries for which the particular set of factor conditions is optimal. This explains the existence of so-called low-cost countries (low costs of labor) and materials, agricultural countries (large countries with fertile soil), or the start-up culture in the United States (well developed venture capital market). Porter points out that these factors are not necessarily nature-made or inherited. They may develop and change. Political initiatives, technological progress, or sociocultural changes, for instance, may shape national factor conditions.

Home Demand Conditions This factor describes the state of home demand for products and services produced in a country. Home demand conditions influence the shaping of particular factor conditions. They have impact on the pace and direction of innovation and product development. According to Porter, home demand is determined by three major characteristics: their mixture (the mix of customers needs and wants), their scope and growth rate, and the mechanisms that transmit domestic preferences to foreign markets.

Porter states that a country can achieve national advantages in an industry or market segment, if home demand provides clearer and earlier signals of demand trends to domestic suppliers than to foreign competitors. Normally, home markets have a much higher influence on an organization's ability to recognize customers' needs than foreign markets do.

Related and Supporting Industries This factor relates to the existence or nonexistence of internationally competitive supplying industries and supporting industries. One internationally successful industry may lead to advantages in other related or supporting industries. Competitive supplying industries will reinforce innovation and internationalization in industries at later stages in the value system. Besides suppliers, related industries are of importance. These are industries that can use and coordinate particular activities in the value chain together, or that are concerned with complementary products (e.g., hardware and software).

Firm Strategy, Structure, and Rivalry These are the conditions in a country that determine how companies are established, are organized and managed, and that determine the characteristics of domestic competition. Here, cultural aspects play an important role. In different nations, factors like management structures, work place morale, or interactions between companies are shaped differently. This will provide advantages and disadvantages for particular industries. Family-business–based industries that are dominated by owner-managers will behave differently from publicly quoted companies. Porter argues that domestic rivalry and the search for competitive advantage within a nation can help provide organizations with bases for achieving such advantage on a global scale.

We review China's economy through this framework below. Since a full Porter analysis would not be appropriate for this book, we use the framework as an outline to briefly highlight some of the strengths and weaknesses of China's economy vis-à-vis the competitive market environment.

Factor Conditions of China

China is well endowed with a full range of natural, economic, and human capital resources. China enjoys an enormous supply of low-cost and motivated labor. Given the vast and ongoing rural-to-urban migration, there is little pressure on labor cost increases. China also has an abundance of educated human capital as it possesses a large and geographically dispersed number of colleges, universities, and technical training schools. China is rich in raw materials of nearly every type. While China is technically a communist country, it behaves in many ways like a capitalist country, promoting business and investment in a wide range of sectors. The government encourages foreign direct investment in part to build capability in its industrial base. Intellectual property theft seems to be a de facto policy of the government. This has enabled the country to rapidly advance up the value chain in many industries, including high technology. It also has a variety of different climate conditions, making it suitable for a wide range of different agricultural products. China has an extensive coastline with a large number of natural seaports and harbors. Most of China is still rural, but it is urbanizing quickly. The government has been a partner in the country's growth, encouraging investment in high–value-added sectors and industries, while liberalizing and reforming restrictive regulations, and encouraging foreign direct investment. China is also the geographic center of Asia facilitating supply chain and investment decisions. Countries such as Japan, Korea, Taiwan, Vietnam, Malaysia, and Singapore will increasingly be viewed as the spokes around the hub of China.

Factor-Creating Mechanisms   The government, at the national, regional and local levels, has been effective in maintaining a high rate of infrastructure investment to facilitate growth. Both government and traditional Chinese culture have placed a premium on education. Thus China has an abundant supply of highly educated and motivated labor. China's labor is a bargain by world standards, and with its managed currency it continues to be a key competitive factor allowing the country to produce low-cost goods. The government continues to guide and encourage the private sector to move up the value chain in a variety of sectors and industries including high-tech, bio-tech, and a range of heavy industries. China has aggressively obtained the best and latest technology from throughout the world, allowing the private sector to freely copy, reverse engineer, and otherwise purloin the intellectual property of the world at an extremely rapid pace—perhaps faster than any other Asian country before it. The government's encouragement of FDI, particularly of R&D has been a part of this strategy which has been paying off spectacularly. There has been a sea-change in the perception of China over the last few years. In the 1990s, China was seen as a highly risky, "wild west" market. It was a location unsuitable for regional head-quarters, R&D, and most high-skilled, high-technology investment. This has all changed. Multinational corporations (MNCs) who formerly invested in fringe countries of Southeast Asia such as Taiwan, Thailand, Malaysia, and Singapore, are now investing directly into China. China is being perceived by the international business community as a lower-risk, almost business-friendly country. Importantly, with the exception of the Bird Flu scare, the country has been out of the high risk factor news since Tiananmen Square in 1989. Its managed currency has kept the cost of its exports very low and has spurred growth of key industries.

Selective Factor Disadvantages The extreme growth has led to labor shortages of highly skilled labor in some parts of the country. The educational system in the rural areas is still mostly poor and ill-suited for a modernizing, increasingly industrial economy. The masses of poor unemployed in the countryside and a growing number in some cities could turn into a huge political risk if these people fail to integrate into the economy and mobilize. The increasing income disparity has also been the cause of growing unrest. The world business language is English, which is still not widely spoken or understood in the country. This makes doing business in China harder than say Hong Kong, Singapore, or India. The infrastructure in parts of the country, particularly the rural, noncoastal regions, is under-developed, hindering economic progress. China for all its progress is still very much of an emerging market economy with a whole host of challenges to doing business in the country. Corruption is still a problem, particularly in the real estate industry.

Demand Conditions of China China has a huge advantage in the fact that its domestic market is already the largest in the world. This means that Chinese companies can first develop, sell, and create great and large companies, brands, and products in their home market and then venture forth internationally in a strong position. The acquisition of IBM's PC division by Lenovo and several white goods companies by Heier are two of many examples. The Chinese consumer has been overly characterized as commodity-oriented and price-sensitive. The growing middle class is creating a demand for all sorts of product segments beyond the low end. The domestic consumers are increasingly quality- and brand-conscious. Chinese also seem to crave the quality and perceived prestige of top Western brands and companies. The much-touted high savings rate of the Chinese is somewhat distorted by the fact that that the consumer finance sector is nascent. With the spread of easy consumer credit, it is expected to see a surge in consumer demand of all types. As for housing, more variety in home mortgages (i.e., longer terms, adjustable rates, interest-only) will increase demand, particularly for middle-class housing.

Related and Supporting Industries in China   China has a large backbone of heavy industry in every major sector. This has supported its large and still growing manufacturing sector. Nearly all major inputs, except certain raw materials can be sourced domestically. China's main weakness is its relatively weak service sector, which has not kept pace with its industrial growth. There is a widely cited problem of the country having great "hardware" (the industrial base and infrastructure) but a poorly developed "software" (the services sector) side to the economy. This is limiting China's growth into certain higher value-added sectors, such as software exports. Consumer service industries are particularly underdeveloped. China has also not been on the cutting, innovative edge of many industries, leading to an ongoing need for foreign technology. For China to be a leader in business segments, it needs to develop the capacity to innovate.

Firm Strategy, Structure, and Rivalry in China   There is still a large state-owned enterprise (SOE) sector. These SOEs are largely inefficient, taxing public resources and crowding out private sector investment. The private sector has spawned a large number of entrepreneurial firms across all industries. The family firm is thriving and possesses clear advantages in the terms of the ability to move quickly into markets and motivating its managers. However, family firms face limitations in their scalability. SOEs exist primarily to produce low-cost undifferentiated goods for the mass market. Private sector firms, however, are extremely competitive in price and quality. Firms whose products are destined for the export market are nearly on par with Western firms in terms of quality, yet are still cost competitive. Professional business managers with international experience are in short supply. The entrepreneurial nature of the Chinese culture ensures a steady supply of new competitors in most high-growth sectors.

The Role of Government   The government plays an active role in economic development, targeting industries and setting goals for economic composition and growth. The government has been effective in channeling investment in key areas of infrastructure such as highways, rail, mass transit, airports, and telecommunications. The government is continuing to make progress in reforms and economic liberalization. The government can also be a negative in that it is prone to making sudden, unexpected blackbox decisions that can have widespread, sometimes negative implications. While the government deserves rightful credit for much of the economic progress and reforms, it is seen as a risk factor by most foreign companies. The fact that the government is communist makes many international investors nervous. Unilateral, top-down decisions are made daily. Private property rights are still a far cry from what they are in the West.

The Role of Chance China has a long coastline, with many deepwater ports, making export from the coastal cities particularly efficient and cost effective. China lies in the center of the region with the greatest economic growth potential in the next 50 years. China is also fortunate to have a culture that encourages hard work, entrepreneurial activity, wealth creation, and education. China's government is also singularly committed to economic development and is not only bogged down by the special interest politics of other emerging market countries. The leadership of the country at the current time seems unusually capable of efficient, "technocratic" governance. China's enormous population (1.3 billion), once considered a major disadvantage, is now looked upon as a key advantage, giving it the ability to be a leading economic, political, and cultural force in the world.

Future Competitive Advantage China is winning not only at the low cost end, but also increasingly at the quality and product segmentation end of the market in a variety of goods and sectors. With the country's abundant supply of cheap labor continuing to stream into the cities, pressure on wage increases will be minimal. Chinese industry as well as government seems committed to constantly moving up the value chain in all industries, whether building design, construction, or automobiles. They will likely continue to borrow, adopt, or purloin the best and most innovative practices, processes, and technology from around the world. China keeps increasing the list of industries and products in which it has a strong or dominant market share. MNC FDI is growing at a staggering pace, bringing with it all of the capital and capability to fuel China's torrid growth. Social unrest, which could destabilize the economy and leaders, is a risk to future competitive advantage. Factors behind this could be income disparities, unemployment, and the coastal-hinterland dichotomy. War with Taiwan is unlikely but could prove disruptive if it were to break out.

THE REAL ESTATE MARKET

It is generally accepted that the current rate of growth of the real estate sector will continue at least for the next five years. In the coming years, growth is expected to be driven less by fixed-asset investment and more through consumer spending. Real estate investment is expected to become more dispersed around the country. Urbanization will be a key driver of real estate. Estimates on urban population growth reach 200 million new urban residents by 2015, when 60% of the population would reside in urban areas.[5] This growth will fuel demand for housing, consumer goods, and infrastructure. The consumer class is expected to grow prodigiously with higher wages and a declining savings rate.

The lack of sufficient investment-grade properties is one of the main barriers to investing in China. There is the greatest potential in the second-tier cities, but much of this will have to be through development as there are few investment-grade properties to be purchased. The tax regime, including lack of predictability, differing tax structures (local, regional, provincial, national), and high capital gains often forces investors to buy out the shares of an existing property holder so as not to effect the transfer of the property itself. This practice exposes the buyer to additional risk and due diligence requirements. Finding a suitable domestic Chinese real estate partner is a key challenge, given potential nonalignment of competencies, interests, and reputation. However, Chinese development partners are continually improving in skills and sophistication. This means that much investment will be value-added or new development—moving investment up the risk curve from simply core investment. Repatriation of profits has become easier and less risky over the past several years with the implementation of State Administration of Foreign Exchange (SAFE) regulations; however, SAFE registration has slowed the acquisition process, which has made pursuit of prime properties (given shorter acquisition periods) more difficult. More is mentioned of these regulations in the appendix.

China's real estate sector is highly fragmented—even the largest developer does not command a market share of more than 10% in any given city. Most local developers come from non–real estate backgrounds such as manufacturing or heavy industry. This is a result of those companies' accessibility to land and financing. Due to the rapid rate of urbanization, many highly labor-intensive factories and plants are located in prime locations. The closure, relocation, and redevelopment of these locations have been one of the major themes in Chinese real estate over the last 10 years. Developers with an inside track on these deals, often lacking in capability, experience, and professionalism, rushed in to capitalize on these opportunities.

Foreign real estate companies began to enter the market in the late 1990s. They are predominately from Hong Kong, Singapore, Japan, and South Asian countries, and account for 9% of total real estate companies in China. American companies are relatively recent arrivals, though their involvement has increased exponentially over the past several years. Explosive growth of major international retailers (e.g., Walmart, Carrefour, and Metro) is indicative of a trend that will continue. Most foreign investors are still not comfortable investing in major deals outside of the first-tier cities.

There has been a great dichotomy between the rate of economic development between the coast and the inland areas. The government has been making strenuous efforts recently to focus more investment and development in the noncoastal cities. As was the case in America during the nineteenth century, the government is emphasizing a policy of "go west." In China, this means inland, to provincial centers that have yet to experience the development common in many parts of the country.

It is likely that investment capital will continue to flow into the real estate sector unless performance of the equities market dramatically improves. Over the past decade, about 80% of all real estate investment in China has been directed into the residential sector. Since 2001, however, commercial and other types of real estate have gained investment share—a trend that is expected to continue. Policies encouraging home ownership and liberal lending allowed investment in the residential sector to increase over six times from 2000 to 2008, while over that same period investment in commercial real estate increased about four times.

Investors are drawn to China because its properties remain relatively cheap despite a strong run in the past five years, the government is spending massively on infrastructure, and the renminbi has been appreciating, making renminbi-dominated assets more valuable. The attraction of Chinese real estate has led to a boom in property shares. It also has spurred Hong Kong developers and foreign banks to set up property ventures on the mainland.

Concerns about overheated real estate markets and speculative bubbles have prompted the Chinese government to take measures to cool down the real estate markets.

According to DTZ Debenham Tie Leung, after a robust growth of 19% in 2007, the invested stock in the Asia Pacific Region declined by 8% in local currency terms and 1% in U.S. dollar terms in 2008, for the first time since 2001, because of the effects of global downtown.[6] However, China is forecasted to recover to positive territory in 2010, ahead of other key markets such as Japan, Hong Kong, and Singapore.

In longer terms, China's real estate sector, despite the current slowdown caused by the global economic downturn, is expected to expand rapidly, especially in the large cities. In particular, regions around Beijing received a boost from the 2008 Olympics Games that were hosted by the capital city. The Shanghai area should receive a similar stimulus from the 2010 World's Fair to be held there. China's entry into the WTO has also supported the upward trends of its real estate market, with stronger demand for commercial properties.

Real Estate FDI

One of the fastest-growing areas of capital spending in recent years has been real-estate investment. Investment in property development has increased by about *20% annually in every year since 2000,* with growth topping 30% in 2003 and 2007.[7] Booms in real estate investment are not unknown in post-reform China, with government funds intended for "productive" investment, especially in much-needed infrastructure projects, frequently being diverted by lower-level officials to spending on hotels, town halls, and pure property speculation.

China's real estate sector, including the development of both residential and nonresidential buildings, has been one of the country's "hottest" and fastest-growing industries. The expansion of the real estate sector has been driven by strong economic growth and rapid urbanization of the Chinese population.

For the country's urban areas as a whole, total stock of building space reached nearly 17 billion sqm by the end of 2008, more than quadruple the number in 1990. Of the total, floor space of nonresidential buildings increased by 2.6 times from 1.98 billion sqm in 1990 to 5.12 billion sqm in 2008, while residential floor space increased by more than six fold during the period (Exhibit 3.8).

However, since 2000, much of the heightened activity has instead been driven by real demand, as in the late 1990s when people gained the right

EXHIBIT 3.8 Floor Space of Buildings in Chinese Urban Areas (billion sqm)

	1990	1995	2000	2005	2008
Total floor space of buildings	3.98	5.73	7.66	15.44	17.19
Floor space of residential buildings	2	3.1	4.4	10.3	12.1
Floor space of nonresidential buildings	1.98	2.63	3.25	5.16	5.12

Source: National Bureau of Statistics of China, China Statistical Yearbook, 1990–2008.

to buy their own homes (previously, most urban housing was provided either free or at low rents by government institutions or SOEs). Even so, the government intervened in 2004 and 2005 to try to prevent overinvestment in real estate, and prices in the frothiest markets, such as Shanghai and the capital, Beijing, eased in 2005. Several policies to cool down overheated real estate had been introduced since 2006 until the recent global economic crisis, when the government reversed its policy again.

Characterizing the Real Estate Market The overall real estate market in China is dynamic and is growing fast in terms of capital flow and investment volume. There are over 5,600 *foreign funded real estate* companies, including China-foreign joint ventures (JVs) or cooperative enterprises, and over 1,000 wholly foreign-owned companies currently operating in China. Hong Kong is the top investor, accounting for over 75% of total foreign investment, followed by the United States and Taiwan.

China can be characterized as an embryonic and growth-oriented market. There is ample opportunity to innovate and to build market share. The inherent returns in many strategies can be very high.

Market Growth Rate (and Size) The market growth rate is astounding. China is potentially the largest in the world with very large primary markets and over 100 secondary markets. The massive growth is underpinned by surging demand—GDP growth, incomes, population, urbanization, demand for higher quality product, and other factors are strong and will continue to fuel real estate.

Industry Potential The industry holds enormous potential. Primary and secondary markets are expanding at a considerable rate. China is the workshop of the world. Its industrial sector and soon its service sector are creating a gigantic demand for all sorts of real estate—residential (for-sale, service apartment, and rental), office (CBD and R&D), retail (malls, power centers, shops), hotel (luxury and business class), and industrial (warehouse and logistics, particularly at the ports).

Breadth of Product Lines Product lines are still emerging, and some do not exist at all. There is significant pent-up demand for many different types of real estate products. There exists a large potential for significant product segmentation in both the luxury segment as well as for the middle tier to respond to the growing wealth and quality-seeking middle-class population.

China has seen one of the fastest growth rates in the world for the number of High Net Worth Individuals (HNWIs), defined as those with at least US$1 million in financial assets, excluding the value of home real estate.

Number and Quality of Competitors There are about 62,500 real estate developers in China and significantly more businesses involved in some way or another in real estate investment. The quality of the competition ranges considerably. Most are new companies or offshoots from industrial companies lured to the high returns and the perceived glamour of real estate development. Most of these companies are inefficient, have little knowledge of best practices, and produce dubious quality product. Property management is still nascent and is often seen as a scam to skim fees for long-term revenue. There are few regional players and national firms. Many firms are unsophisticated, with most personnel having relatively little real estate experience. Financial analysis, design, construction management techniques, project management, marketing, and asset management are all generally amateurish.

Ease of Entry and Exit Entry and exit are rather difficult, requiring considerable time, planning, legal groundwork, and careful execution. China is not a market one simply jumps into without careful planning, research, and necessary ground work. China is not very transparent. It is relationships-driven. Relationships must be developed with business partners as well as with local, regional, and national government officials before you kick off serious business in the country. A wrong early misstep could cost a city or region. How one establishes the legal entity and investment vehicles is very important and must be planned early.

Technology and Productivity China is eager to catch up and surpass the world in everything, including the real estate and construction industries. There are many examples where world-class designers and construction techniques have been imported. However, by and large, the real estate and construction industries are characterized by inefficient techniques and technology resulting in sub–Class A product, but this is changing rapidly. In general, the southern regions bordering Hong Kong (Shenzhen and Guangzhou), Shanghai, and Beijing display a higher level of technology and productivity. These urban areas also benefit from foreign investors and developers.

Legal and Regulatory Considerations

Perhaps more than both India and Brazil, one of the leading considerations for doing business in China is the business, legal, and regulatory environment. The purpose of this chapter is not to render detailed legal advice but merely to sensitize the investor at a high level of a few primary considerations. China's real estate market has only been available to private investors for less than 20 years. The legal framework is one of the key risk factors of doing real estate business in China. Primarily it is in a constant state of flux. Problematically, these changes are often major, done unilaterally, and are sudden with little or no warning. This kind of behavior is not conducive to large fixed capital investment to say the least. Before doing any business at all, the legal structure should be considered first. Without the proper underlying legal foundation, one may face significant difficulties in funding investments and repatriating profits. More detailed information on the legal and procedural aspects of conducting business can be found in Appendix B: Property Market Practice in China.

Foreign investment in Chinese real estate typically takes the form of a Foreign Investment Enterprise (FIE) structured as a foreign equity joint venture (an "**EJV**"), a Foreign Cooperative Joint Venture (a "**CJV**") or a wholly foreign-owned enterprise (a "**WFOE**").

A WFOE is a Chinese entity owned entirely by foreign investors, and is generally established as a company with limited duration and with the liability of the shareholders limited to the amount of subscribed capital. According to the Ministry of Commerce, WFOEs now account for the majority of foreign direct investment in China in terms of both number of entities and invested capital. Owners may transfer equity in a WFOE subject to prior approval from the Ministry of Commerce or its local branch, as appropriate.

A CJV may be established by one or more foreign investors and one or more Chinese investors as a limited liability company with limited duration with a legal personality or as a contractual joint venture between foreign and Chinese coventures (similar to a common law partnership) without separate legal status. A CJV's structure is relatively flexible. For example, the shareholders of a CJV may agree to share profits and losses that do not correspond to the ratio of the parties' respective ownership interests. Owners may transfer equity in a CJV subject to prior approval from the Ministry of Commerce or its local branch, as appropriate.

An EJV is a limited liability Chinese entity with limited duration established by one or more Chinese investors and one or more foreign investors. Investors in an EJV share profits and losses strictly in proportion to their respective equity interests. EJVs resemble Western-style corporations in many respects. Owners may transfer equity in an EJV subject to prior approval from the other parties to the EJV, and the Ministry of Commerce or its local branch, as appropriate.

The formation documents of a FIE must indicate the total amount that will be invested in the FIE. A portion of this amount must be contributed as registered capital (i.e., minimum equity), depending on the size of the total

EXHIBIT 3.9 FIE Schedule

Total Amount of the Deal	< US $100 million	Time	> US $100 million	Time
Asset Deal	Shanghai Foreign Investment Committee	1–2 months	Ministry of Commerce	3–4 months
	State Administration of Foreign Exchange, Shanghai Branch	1–2 weeks	Shanghai Foreign Investment Committee	1–2 months
	Shanghai Municipal Housing, Land and Resource Administration Bureau	1–2 months	State Administration of Foreign Exchange, Shanghai Branch	1–2 weeks
			Shanghai Municipal Housing, Land and Resource Administration Bureau	1–2 months
Equity Deal	Shanghai Foreign Investment Committee	1–2 months	Ministry of Commerce	3–4 months
	State Administration of Foreign Exchange, Shanghai Branch	1–2 weeks	Shanghai Foreign Investment Committee	1–2 months
			State Administration of Foreign Exchange, Shanghai Branch	1–2 weeks

Source: Shanghai Municipal Commission of Commerce (2008).

investment, in accordance with the example from an investment in the city of Shanghai in Exhibit 3.9.

In July of 2006, new regulations were issued that prohibit foreign investors from directly investing in Chinese real estate from offshore, thereby effectively forcing foreign investment into the more traditional onshore corporate structure.[8] As part of this regulatory tightening, establishment of onshore companies to invest in Chinese real estate will also be subject to a higher level of administrative scrutiny and will require a higher level of equity contribution as a percentage of the total investment.

The regulations mandate:

1. *Offshore investment prohibited.* In order to purchase Chinese real estate, foreign institutions and individuals are (subject to the self-use exception discussed below) now required to use an onshore ownership structure. This means that foreign investors will need to obtain approval to establish foreign investment enterprise(s) (FIEs) in order to invest in all forms of Chinese real estate.
2. *Self-use exception.* Foreign institutions with China branch(es) or representative office(s), and foreign individuals working or studying in China, are allowed to purchase real estate for self use.
3. *Onshore investment restrictions.*
   (i) A higher equity ratio is required for setting up larger real estate FIEs. The previous general foreign investment requirement that 33% of the total investment be contributed to the FIE as registered capital for larger transactions (previously defined as total investment of US$30M or above) is now increased to 50% (and the total investment threshold is lowered to US$10M or above) for investments in real estate.
   (ii) In the case of acquisitions, the foreign purchaser must meet all of its acquisition payment obligations in one up-front payment.
   (iii) Equity transactions involving real estate FIEs, as well as foreign acquisitions of domestic real estate companies, are now subject to strict scrutiny, and Ministry of Commerce (MOFCOM) approval (as well as other required approvals) is likely to become more difficult.
   (iv) State Administration of Foreign Exchange (SAFE) will deny conversion of foreign currency purchase money if the real estate FIE (a) has not fully paid its registered capital and (b) has not properly obtained the land use certificate.
   (v) No fixed-return provision is allowed among foreign and domestic investors in a real estate FIE.

In July 2008, the China National Development and Reform Commission issued a guideline entitled "Circular of the National Development and Reform Commission on the Further Enhancement and Regulation of the Administration of Foreign Investment Projects." The guideline provided that those real estate projects with foreign investment of US$50 million and above shall be approved by the National Development and Reform Commission, and those real estate projects with foreign investment less than US$50 million shall be approved by provincial development and reform commissions. It reduced the required application time for foreign investment in real estate to some extent.

PROPERTY SECTORS

This section provides a general overview of the property market and goes into a detailed analysis of each sector. The China property market is, in some ways, one of the most promising real estate markets in the world. It is enjoying strong demand across all sectors with only localized oversupply concerns in a few markets. There are unique and serious risk factors associated with the market, however. These include, among others, the variability in government policies, limitations on foreign investment, an overly frothy market in some cities, and restrictive real estate regulations.

It is generally accepted that the current rate of growth of the real estate sector will continue at least for the next five years. In the coming years, growth is expected to be driven less by fixed asset investment, and more through consumer spending. Commercial real estate investment is expected to become more dispersed around the country. Urbanization will be a key driver of real estate. Estimates on urban population growth reach 200 million new urban residents by 2015.[9] This growth will fuel demand for housing, consumer goods, and infrastructure. The consumer class is expected to grow prodigiously with higher wages and a declining savings rate.

There is perhaps the greatest potential in the second-tier cities, but much of this will have to be realized through development as there are few investment-grade properties to be purchased. REITs are expected to become a popular exit strategy in the future. Securitization is on the horizon and should play an important role in China. Local banks are in the process of establishing residential mortgage-backed securities (RMBS); however, the current financial malfunction has delayed the process. Due diligence and lack of transparency are major issues in Chinese real estate investment. The tax regime including lack of predictability, differing tax structures (local, regional, provincial, national) and high capital gains often forces investors to buy out the shares of an existing property holder so as not to effect the transfer of the property itself. This practice exposes the buyer to additional risk and due diligence requirements.

Finding a suitable domestic Chinese real estate partner is a key challenge given potential nonalignment of competencies, interests, and reputation. The lack of sufficient investment-grade properties is one of the main barriers to investing in China. This means that much investment will be value-add or new development—moving up the risk curve. Repatriation of profits has become easier and less risky over the last two years with the implementation of State Administration of Foreign Exchange (SAFE) regulations; however, SAFE registration has slowed the acquisition process, which has made pursuit of prime properties (given shorter acquisition periods) more difficult.

Before the 1980s, most real property was owned by the state. There was no consumer housing sector. After the economic reforms starting in 1978, China's government began separating ownership and land use rights, and legal private ownership of real estate emerged. A major milestone was the elimination of restrictions on foreign ownership of real estate in China. This was changed in 2001 when the entire domestic market was opened to both domestic and foreign players. Under the present system, the government retains the title of ownership, but sells the marketable and renewable land use rights to developers under a long lease, which lasts between 40 to 70 years. In the past, most land was acquired through private negotiation. Consequently, sponsors with strong relationships with local developers could secure prime sites at very low prices. However, many large city governments have adopted the practice of selling state-owned land in a single open market through auction or tender.

The retail mortgage market was also liberalized. Housing loans can be obtained from the Housing Provident Fund or through numerous commercial banks. For mortgage loans provided by commercial banks, the maximum mortgage term has been increased to 30 years from 10 years, and the loan-to-value (LTV) has been increased to 80% of the property value. This has in turn stimulated housing demand, particularly for newer, more expensive housing that cannot be easily purchased with cash only.

China's real estate sector has approximately 62,500 real estate developers. The industry is highly fragmented—even the largest developer does not command a market share of more than 10% in any given city. Most local developers come from non-real estate backgrounds such as manufacturing or heavy industry. This is a result of those companies' accessibility to land and financing. Due to the rapid rate of urbanization, many highly labor-intensive factories and plants are located in prime locations. The closure, relocation, and redevelopment of these locations have been one of the major themes in Chinese real estate over the past 10 years. Developers with an inside track on these deals, often lacking in capability, experience, and professionalism, rushed in to capitalize on these opportunities. Foreign real estate companies began to enter the market in the late 1990s. They are predominantly from Hong Kong, Singapore, Japan, and South Asian countries and account for

9% of total real estate companies in China. American companies are recent arrivals. Hines Interests, for example, completed its first project in China in 2002, but now it has developed or invested in six projects in Beijing and Shanghai, including office, apartment, condominium, and mixed-use properties.

The three primary real estate markets are (1) Shanghai, (2) Beijing, and (3) Guangzhou/Shenzhen. The second-tier cities are defined as cities with populations exceeding one million. Most investors concur that the greatest potential growth will be in the secondary cities. However it is generally more difficult to find investment-grade projects in these cities. Thus investment in the secondary cities will probably be more development-oriented and value-added in nature. Some players have capitalized on second-tier city growth by focusing on retail and logistics properties in those areas. Explosive growth of major international retailers (e.g., Walmart, Carrefour, and Metro) is indicative of a trend that will continue. Many investors are still not comfortable with doing major deals outside of the first-tier cities.

The Office Sector

The demand for Class A office buildings remains strong across major cities such as Shanghai, Beijing, Guangzhou, and Shenzhen. The strong demand in these cities continued to put upward pressure on prices and rents, as company tenants competed for office space (Exhibit 3.10).

There have been improvements in building quality in the past few years, as foreign investors are beginning to team up with local developers. As a result, tenants for office buildings now have more and better-planned space options. Tenant profiles have gradually shifted in recent years from primarily manufacturers and consumer goods producers to service providers such as consultants, accountants, and lawyers.

The majority of office buildings in China are still far from international standard, but building design and specifications are improving across major and secondary cities.

There is pent-up demand as the supply of true international Class A buildings around the country is quite low. As the service sector continues to grow, so will office demand. Moreover, as Chinese companies become leading world players on the corporate stage, they will need high profile corporate and regional offices.

China's opening up of its financial sector in 2006 has led to stronger demand for Class A office premises as foreign financial institutions increase their presence in a bid to secure a larger market share. As the domestic market continues to see substantial growth in foreign investment, especially

EXHIBIT 3.10 Office Market Overview

Market Factor	Market Characteristics	Drivers	Future Trends	Business Opportunity
Demand for New Development	Strong demand for office space concentrated in major cities.	Rapid growth in financial and service sector.	Demand is likely to grow even stronger, with increasing needs expanding industry.	Growing demand for Class A, state of the art office buildings in first-tier markets.
Supply of New Development	Concentration in primary markets, improving design and quality.	Appreciation of RMB, capital support and demand for new spaces.	Scalable development concepts to continue; speculative developments could depress rent growth.	Look for more supply constrained locations such as infill CBD locations.
Investment Market Support	Insufficient transactions to derive meaningful return data.	Most capital grows from traditional fixed income investments.	Gradual movement towards entity level investments, vis-à-vis asset level investments.	Channel U.S. fixed income investment for higher core returns in China.
Debt Market	Long project cycle; abundant liquidity in 2009.	Government encouraged lending to boost the economy.	Interest rates could firm up by about 50–100 bps as regulators crack down on excess lending.	Leverage lower cost U.S. and international debt.

in the finance, insurance, retail, and telecommunication sectors, MNCs will continue to demand more premium office space.

The Residential Sector

Residential property development activity slowed down in some Chinese cities in 2008 and early 2009, on the back of the government's tightening measures and the global economic crisis, but signs of recovery have been strengthening since mid 2009. The boom in residential property markets was mainly driven by "fundamental needs," with Chinese residents gaining the right to buy their own homes in the late 1990s. However, in recent years, an increasing volume of transactions in Beijing and Shanghai have been speculative in nature. On concerns of a property bubble the government intervened in the markets in 2004–2005 and moved to cool off the property markets and only eased the policies in late 2008 when there were worries about slowed economic growth.

The government adopted a series of measures to tame speculation, including removing tax deductions for homebuyers, tightening controls on bank loans for land purchases, and raising mortgage rates, minimum down-payment requirements, as well as capital gain taxes in resales of newly purchased houses (Exhibit 3.11).

China is expected to increase 5.5 to 6 billion sqm of housing floor space, or 70 million housing units in the coming 10 years, according to Yang Shen, President of China Real Estates Association. Statistics from Ministry of Construction show that from 1980 to 2000, China's real estate industry had kept a rapid growth momentum with newly built houses in rural and urban areas to have reached 20.3 billion sqm, an increase of twofold compared with the past 30 years.[10] As the quality of life improves, housing consumption will become an important motivation for economic growth. Owning a spacious and comfortable house will be a major goal for the majority of Chinese people.

According to statistics from the Ministry of Construction at the end of 2007, about 83% of the urban residents in China owned their own homes. The average residential space per capita was about 28 sqm (about 300 square feet). Among those who do not own residential properties, 51% plan to purchase their homes within 10 years, and 12% plan to buy after 10 years. Only 18% plan to rent rather than buy their homes.

The Retail Sector

Despite the size of China's overall population, the real trend to watch is the growth of the consumer class. At present, there are approximately

EXHIBIT 3.11 Residential Market Overview

Market Factor	Market Characteristics	Drivers	Future Trends	Business Opportunity
Demand for New Housing Stock	Relatively high portion of home ownership; high speculative transaction in primary markets.	Increasing urban population; government stimulus through interest rate.	Demand for higher quality of housing will increase as the middle class in the country increases.	Development of international standard housing in major markets meeting with exceptionally strong demand. Demand for Class A apartments could be addressed.
Supply of New Housing Stock	Highly concentrated in primary and secondary cities, expanding to surrounding markets.	Increased home ownership, accessibility to financing, government investment.	Cautions on speculative transaction and housing market bubble.	Demand of lower-to-middle income families can be fixed which is increasing along with the rapid urbanization.
Investment/ Developer Market	Short project cycle and abundant capital support first mover advantage to existing players.	Increasing urban population; increasing living standards.	Should be increased domestic and international competition in residential development. Competition for the best deals and development partners to heighten. Look for increased regulation because of unscrupulous developers.	Provide capital (preferred equity) to local developers; leverage local expertise.
Debt Market	For homeowners: 6% interest rates for a 15 year mortgage.	Opportunities exist if Chinese government and domestic banks discourage lending.	Interest rates likely to increase as the government moves to stabilize the housing market.	First mortgage is possible, but investment returns may be inferior to preferred equity.

31 million households earning more than the equivalent of US$5,000 per year—the level at which economists generally believe discretionary consumption spending becomes possible. It is clear that this number is poised to grow and to grow quickly. Underlying this growth will be an increase in real income driven by higher wages and increased productivity, and a decrease in the savings rate driven by new financial products and a change in consumer behavior. The growth of the consumer class will create numerous retail opportunities.

The prime retail property market witnessed buoyant demand in major Chinese cities. Overseas retailers continued their expansion and even entered some secondary markets in China. Case in point: in January 2009, Walmart opened 17 stores in China in a single month. Its expansion plan is still aggressive amid the current global economic downturn (Exhibit 3.12).

The Industrial Sector

The industrial sector is booming on the back of China's ongoing industrial expansion. The scale and speed of China's industrialization is perhaps unmatched. With industrial manufacturing and exports surging to new records year after year and the globalization of China's industrial base and economy, the demand for new, institutional-grade warehouse and logistics facilities is strong, particularly in port cities with an industrial economic base. In the last few years, MNCs have been moving production lines to China. This has not only increased the demand for manufacturing buildings, but also for warehouse and logistics centers. Foreign companies have become active in the sector as Chinese law has been changed as a result of China entering the WTO, allowing them to distribute their own products. An additional driver for foreign companies opening up a China manufacturing facility is the ability to tap into the local Chinese consumer market.

The expansion of the industrial sector has also been correlated with the growth of "industrial zones." China's industrial zones are graded by level of government sponsorship, including central, provincial, municipal, or district governments. The higher the level of government, the easier to get financial support, infrastructure investment, and land supply. The development of industrial zones is also facilitated by strong inflow of foreign direct investment, including those from Hong Kong and Taiwan.

Previously, foreign companies were mainly interested in manufacturing facilities for production of exports. More recently, foreign firms have been opening manufacturing facilities to tap into the Chinese local consumer markets. In addition, MNCs are increasingly locating their R&D centers in China in order to benefit from the abundant supply and low cost of

EXHIBIT 3.12 Retail Market Overview

Market Factor	Market Characteristics	Drivers	Future Trends	Business Opportunity
Demand of New Retail	Rapid growth of retail malls across metros in China. Most of these are vertical, "infill malls."	Real income driven by higher wages and increased productivity; surging middle class.	Growth of consumer class with discretionary consumption.	Larger, international-class malls and lifestyle centers are expanding. Opportunity to segment the market, to improve the quality of the shopping experience and design of centers.
Supply of New Malls	Mainly in primary cities and expanding in secondary markets.	Surging Chinese middle class and rising household income.	Consolidation likely for mall spaces. Supply could be retarded to address the glut in the market.	Supply does not appear to be constrained in most urban areas.
Investment/ Developer Market	Short project cycle and abundant capital support first mover advantage to existing players.	Supply of malls has spurred interest. Strata title sales on the rise.	Investment will continue to flow to the sector as new markets open up, particularly in secondary and tertiary cities.	Investment in mall development companies and be cautious in asset level investment because of potential oversupply.
Debt Market	Plenty of commercial lending from domestic banks in 2009.	Opportunities exist if Chinese government and domestic banks discourage lending.	Primary markets may be oversupplied with shopping centers.	Better opportunities may exist in secondary markets.

qualified professionals in the fields of engineering, IT, science, and other research areas (Exhibit 3.13).

In terms of location, manufacturing plants have been mainly concentrated in major urban areas such as Beijing, Shanghai, and Guangzhou. However, as a recent trend some companies are relocating out of these first-tier cities into secondary or emerging cities in the western and inland areas, such as Xi'an and Chengdu. Increased pressure for land in the major cities is likely to result in further increase in land values and shortage of industrial sites in metropolises. Thus, more companies are expected to consider second- and third-tier cities for their industrial facilities in the future.

In late 2004, the General Office of the State Council issued a notice demanding stricter measures of control over the national land market, as part of the central government's efforts of cooling down fixed investment and property markets. More restrictions were imposed and fewer approvals granted for industrial usage of land. As a result, industrial land supply became tighter in major cities. Currently, vacant sites are scarce in the major industrial zones.

- More manufacturing plants, which used to be concentrated in cities like Beijing, Shanghai, and Guangzhou, are relocating out of these cities into secondary or emerging cities in the western and inland areas of China, like Xi'an and Chengdu. The overall infrastructure in these cities is improving rapidly, and these cities can still offer cost savings in terms of competitive land prices and cheaper labor.
- Other cities in China are becoming more popular as options, not just for manufacturing facilities but also for R&D centers.

Investment in the industrial sector is now growing, not just for export-oriented activity, but domestic industrial and logistics growth.

The Hotel and Hospitality Sector

The Beijing and Shanghai markets have seen strengthening hospitality demand since 2000. In Beijing, five-star hotels witnessed the highest average daily rate (ADR) of 1,236 yuan (US$181) during 2008, although the occupancy rate fell to 52%. Shanghai is also a preferred investment location, given its position as China's financial center. In 2008, ADR for Shanghai's five-star hotels was 1,233 Yuan (US$180), with an occupancy rate of 60%. Due to the global economic crisis and a large hotel supply in Beijing before the 2008 Olympic Games, ADR and occupancy rate in both Beijing

EXHIBIT 3.13 Industrial Market Overview

Market Factor	Market Characteristics	Drivers	Future Trends	Business Opportunity
Demand for New Development	Demand is high as the country continues its expansion in industrial manufacturing and export.	Globalization, growth of industrial manufacturing and export as China's industrial base.	Demand for new, institutional-grade warehouse and logistics facilities is strong, particularly in port cities.	Scarcity of land would make the second- and third-tier cities favorable options for industrial development.
Supply of New Development	Supplies largely concentrated in primary markets; secondary markets are gaining attention from both manufacturing and R&D.	Increasing land price; strict regulation and entitlement on industrial land.	More domestic industries and logistics are creating increasing demand for industrial property.	Markets in primary cities are well developed and tight, while the second-tier markets are offering new opportunities.
Investment Market Support	Increasing concentration on second-tier markets and domestic facilities.	China continues to dominate world's manufacturing exports; imports also on the rise.	This should be an important investment sector with China's ongoing economic development.	There could be significant financial interest in the sector if there were more investable assets and companies.
Debt Market	Plenty of commercial lending from domestic banks for now.	Opportunities for international industrial players to bring in foreign capital.	Primary coastal markets may be oversupplied with warehouse distribution centers.	Better opportunities may exist in secondary markets.

and Shanghai have been negatively impacted, and they still face pressure over the next two years. However, in the long term sustained growth is still forecasted.

In China, the cost of land is rising rapidly, and investment remains challenging. Nevertheless, opportunistic investors have profited from small and speculative initial investments, such as a low-end hotel conversion. The majority of hotels are still owned by the government. The hype about growth comes from operators, rather than investors, who are keen to capitalize on the extraordinary levels of growth forecast over the next decade. China is expected to become the world's largest tourism destination. In preparation for this, the country is improving its infrastructure with approximately 80 airports being constructed and about 30,000 kilometers of highways planned over the next 20 years. International hotel chains are keen to capture some of this growth and are seeking further management opportunities as a more expeditious way to enter the market.

According to the World Tourism Organization, China is expected to have 100 million foreign tourists in 2015 and become the world's top destination country before 2020.[11] The country received 130 million overseas travelers in 2008, including visitors from Hong Kong, Macau, and Taiwan. Asia in general has seen a boom in tourism travel over the last few years (Exhibit 3.14).

PRIMARY MARKETS

Most real estate investment is directed towards the three primary markets—Beijing, Shanghai, and Guangzhou/Shenzhen. These markets offer some supply of investment-grade properties as well as sufficient infrastructure. These markets also have the best coverage from the leading property and consultancy firms. These would be the logical starting point for an investment program. Office investment over the last year has mainly been focused on Beijing and Shanghai, buoyed by the expansion of the banking and insurance sectors as well as other professional service providers, including accounting and consulting companies. The steady growth in middle-class disposable incomes in China's urban areas is underpinning rapid expansion in organized retail and is stimulating interest on the part of overseas retailers.

Beijing

Beijing is the capital city of China, and it is also the largest city in the country. It has an urban area population of approximately 16.95 million and a GDP

EXHIBIT 3.14 Hotel Market Overview

Market Factor	Market Characteristics	Drivers	Future Trends	Business Opportunity
Demand for Hotel Rooms	High demand, increased business travel and tourism.	Great demand from foreign and domestic tourists.	Demand likely to increase for the next decade.	Development of Class A hotels in primary and secondary cities as well as business class hotels is dictated by strong and increasing demand.
Supply of Rooms	Occupancy was negatively impacted in 2008; large amount of supply in a short-term yet sustained market growth from a long-term perspective.	Number of foreign travelers to be increased by 100 million in 2015; increasing domestic tourism to major cities.	Supply is expected to pick up due to completion around the Olympics and Shanghai Expo.	Supply is increasing as the country is becoming one of major global destinations and government investment on infrastructure increases. Opportunities are found in these growth trends and hospitality management as well.
Investment/ Developer Market	Investments are small and speculative; dominated by domestic investors.	Extraordinary growth forecast in next decade.	Increasing demand for high-end hotels. Expanding international hotel chains in China.	New development as well as purchasing and adding value to existing assets. International chains and operating hotel companies are viable strategies to investigate.
Debt Support	Domestic lending relatively robust.	Expanding international hotel chains may bring in additional capital.	Increasing standardization of hotel services across the country.	Opportunities may exist when partnering with expanding international hotel chains in the Chinese market.

of US$153 billion in 2008.[12] It also registered a GDP growth rate of 9% YoY in 2008. Property investment accounted for 49.6% of Beijing's total fixed asset investment in 2008, slightly down from 50.3% in 2007.

Office The Beijing office market has been cooling off since 2008 due to the global economic crisis and an increasing level of supply before the Olympics. Much of this supply has to do with the requirement that there should be no major construction during the time of the Olympics in 2008. This meant that developers and investors scrambled to get projects started and completed regardless of the market take-up scenario, temporarily oversupplying the market.

The total market size for Class A office stands at about 5,400,000 sqm. Oversupply is a problem that the Beijing office property sector has faced only in recent years. Supply forecasts suggest that a total of 1.3 million square meters of new supply will enter Beijing's office property sector in 2009, with a majority of this supply to be located in the Central Business District (CBD).

Good quality office buildings in the eastern part of Beijing continued to draw the attention of foreign and high profile domestic companies. For example, media companies such as CCTV and BTV have shifted to the CBD area which will strengthen the media functions in that area. CTV purchased some 3,000 square meters in Winterless Centre. Furthermore, Class A office developments such as Beijing Fortune Center and Gateway Plaza have been well accepted by the market and consequently achieved satisfactory leasing results.

In early 2009, overall office rents accelerated their downward trend reflecting gloomy economic expectations of both tenants and landlords. Compared with Q4 2008, net effective rents of Class A office in Q1 2009 saw a decrease of 9% to RMB207 (US$30) per square meter per month. Class A office rents across all the submarkets declined in 2009.

Beijing's office market is comprised of six major office submarkets, (Exhibit 3.15) four of which are located in western Beijing and the remaining two on the eastern side.

Whether or not a strong rebound in the leasing market can be anticipated in 2010 will depend heavily upon global and domestic demand expectations for production output over the next two years. In terms of the investment market, a return in the confidence of the global financial market's ability to function properly is required before international investment activity will experience a noticeable pick-up; a revival in the level of domestic investment activity could be seen as early as the end of 2009, as favorable domestic

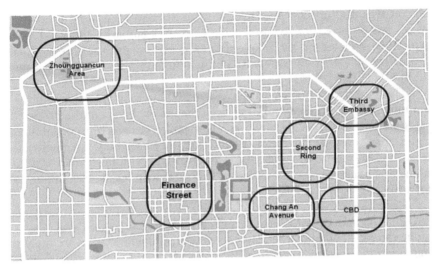

EXHIBIT 3.15   Six Key Office Submarkets in Beijing
Source: Clarion Partners, Canstockphoto.com.

lending conditions and the indirect effects of fiscal stimulus attract domestic investors back to the market.

Residential   In the first half of 2009, sales volume in Beijing's residential market was encouraging, after a dismal year in which transaction volume declined by about 40%. The average daily transaction number was reminiscent of peak levels in 2007, with 500 to 600 transactions recorded per day.

In spite of the strong growth in the mass residential market, most high-end residential projects saw very few transactions during the period.

Multinational companies in response to bleak growth expectations for the year ahead have begun to reduce housing allowances as well as business trip accommodation allowances of their employees. These cutbacks have had a noticeable influence on the serviced apartment property sector: The average vacancy rate for serviced apartments increased by 2.7 percentage points quarter-over-quarter (Q-o-Q) to 29.2%; rents dropped by 7.2% Q-o-Q to RMB171.3/sq m/month as of the first quarter of 2009.

In the luxury leased apartment sector average vacancies continued to increase to 21.2% as of Q1 2009. Rents, following the same trend as the serviced apartment segment, dropped to RMB105.3/sq m/month. Weakening rental growth and increased vacancies in this property segment can be attributed to overseas employees' budget cutbacks. The luxury villa leasing market was also affected by the fall off in demand for leasing property, which has occurred following housing allowance cutbacks and what was typically a slow season for villa leasing. The average price for luxury villa properties in Q1 2009 was RMB112/sq m/month with market vacancy of 20.4%.

The incentives introduced at the end of 2008 were successful in improving purchasing sentiment and have been the major drivers in the property sales boom in the market. However, these policy changes aim to stabilize, rather than revitalize the sector. In addition, they have only marginally affected Beijing's top-end residential market so far. With more than 10,000 units supplying the market in 2009, pressure on prices will continue to intensify.

Retail   The majority of Chinese retail consists of unorganized small shops along the road and in marketplaces. However, Chinese retailers are rapidly migrating to organized retail formats, particularly of an international standard. With their growing wealth, there is a heightening concern for quality, fashion, and brands, particularly Western brands. Department stores and shopping centers predominate. Hypermarkets and category killers hold tremendous promise. Shopping centers can be further broken down into ultraluxury and high-end. The ultraluxury centers are still too far ahead of the incomes of all but the very rich. The high-end shopping center on the other hand is experiencing overwhelming success. Many goods sold here are within the purchasing power of the middle class. The food concessions (food court) within shopping centers attract all family members, which in turn leads to longer shopping times and greater expenditures on standard household items.

Uncertainty in regards to the short-term direction of the domestic economy, brought forth by the global financial crisis, has noticeably constrained the current level of personal consumption in Beijing's retail markets. Retailers have felt the full brunt of dampened levels of consumption as sales revenues have begun to decline and sales competition has increased. Following lower levels of business activity, a number of retailers have postponed previous expansion plans, focusing more attention on the management and operation of their currently occupied outlets.

Under the backdrop of the current economic environment, investment interest in retail properties, relative to that of office and residential properties, has increased. The transportation access, construction quality, structural design, fixtures, facilities, and, most important, the stability of rental income for retail properties in the Beijing market have undergone noticeable improvements from previous years; as a result, foreign and domestic investors have begun to regard retail properties as more favorable investment options.

There is limited land supply for true Class A shopping centers in the city. There is a general trend of movement out of the downtown area to along the peripheral areas of the city including third, fourth, and fifth ring roads. The retail market is expanding both through the growth of domestic retailers as well as international retailers with the later increasingly more willing to move into the middle-class segment of the market. Department stores will see a smaller market share due to the increasing number of shopping centers and hypermarkets in Beijing. Demand in the retail sector is expected to remain strong in the long term.

Industrial An open competition mechanism has been introduced to assign industrial land, and the "bid-auction-listing" system has been implemented. Most industrial premises in the Beijing market are built-to-suit, with a limited number of properties procured for institutional investment purposes. However, with relatively low entry barriers to foreign investment and room for added value, the industrial property sector holds vast investment potential. Following a rise in demand for logistics warehousing and increased interest towards research centers and office park properties brought forth by the state-planned focus to increase the production value of domestic-made goods, investment opportunities in the industrial property sector should begin to broaden.

One of the recent trends that have negatively affected the industrial/warehouse sector is stricter environmental control by the government. In order to protect air and water quality, the government has forced many polluting manufacturing plants to relocate far from the Beijing metro. Consequently, demand for industrial warehouse space is shifting from the manufacturing storage type to the consumer distribution purpose type.

Hotel/Hospitality The five-star hotel market has been a picture of dramatically increasing fundamentals since 2003, but with a fall off in demand in 2008 and 2009. The 2008 Summer Olympic Games in Beijing significantly boosted hotel investment and construction in the city. However, as the games ended, so did the occupancy. As of the end of 2008, the average room rate for five-star hotels in Beijing was US$88 per night with average occupancy at 52%, the lowest level since 1999. According to Beijing Tourism Bureau, there were 132,733 rooms in these hotels as of December 2008. It is evident that the Beijing hotel market is oversupplied in the near term, and investment performance could suffer as a result.

Shanghai

Shanghai is a coastal city directly administered by the central government and has been a major recipient of foreign investment. The city is China's largest commercial center and has many trading links with neighboring provinces, municipalities, and administrative districts. Shanghai has developed a number of satellite towns in the suburbs to reduce the congestion in the city. Shanghai is a leading city in the Yangtze River Delta, an important economic center and one that has recorded China's highest regional GDP growth. Over the last decade, Shanghai has developed a reputation as an investor-friendly city with less red tape and procedural delays than other provinces.

Shanghai recorded double-digit economic growth from 2000 to 2007, and in 2008 its GDP growth rate still reached 9.7% amid the gloomy global economy (Exhibit 3.16). Foreign trade volume reached a record US$322 billion in 2008, increasing by 13.8% compared to 2007. With a booming economy and property market, Shanghai presents international investors with a wide range of investment opportunities. The laws governing real estate investment are still regional and vary from province to city. Accordingly, the ease with which foreign investors can invest and extract their profits varies significantly. Investors are familiar with the process of investing and extracting profits in Shanghai, and it would likely take another 12–18 months to understand that process in another city. As such, China's secondary cities are generally overlooked by foreign investors as acceptable returns are rare.

EXHIBIT 3.16 Major Economic Indicators of Shanghai

Indicators	2004	2005	2006	2007	2008
GDP Growth	14.20%	11.10%	12.00%	14.30%	9.70%
Population Growth	2.40%	2.10%	2.10%	2.40%	1.60%
CPI	2.20%	1.00%	1.20%	3.20%	5.80%
Growth in Fixed Assets Investment	25.80%	14.80%	10.80%	13.60%	8.30%
Retail Sales Growth	10.50%	11.90%	13.00%	14.50%	17.90%
Growth in Real Estate Investment	30.40%	6.10%	2.30%	2.50%	4.50%
Disposable Income Growth of Urban Residents	12.20%	11.80%	10.80%	14.30%	12.90%

Source: National Bureau of Statistics of China (2009).

In 2005 alone, Shanghai (a city that already has 4,000 skyscrapers, almost double the number in New York) completed towers with more space for living and working than there was in all the office buildings in New York City.[13]

Office   Shanghai's office leasing market was vibrant, and was only challenged in late 2008 and early 2009 by contracted office demand and huge potential supply. Shanghai's office market elicits interest from foreign buyers, as many investors are keen to gain exposure to RMB-denominated assets. The total stock of Class A office is expected to be over 6 million sqm by the end of 2009.

The rent of Class A office kept rising from 1999 to 2007, and only started to decline from 2008, due to the large potential supply and the global economic recession. In the first quarter of 2009, average rent declined 5.2% compared with the previous quarter to US$33.7 per month per sqm. Rental levels in both Pudong and Puxi market segments decreased, too. The vacancy rate for Class A office has declined steadily since 1998 and started to rise again only in 2007. The vacancy rate was 16.9% in the first quarter of 2009, due to the global economic recession and the large amount of potential supply.

En-bloc sales of office in the first quarter of 2009 include the International Passenger Shipping Center and POS Plaza, which were purchased by Shanghai Construction Group and the consortium of Lujiazui Finance & Trade Zone Development Co., Ltd and Lujiazui Finance & Trade Zone United Development Co., Ltd. The price was US$8,175 and US$2,625 per sqm, respectively.

Approximately 716,092 square meters of new supply came on stream in 2009, one of the highest since 2000. This is over 10% of the total stock. In spite of the pressure brought by the large supply, Shanghai's position as the financial center of Mainland China has been confirmed by the central government, and the foreseeable booming financial industry would boost demand for prime office space. In addition, the monetary policy of the central bank will increase liquidity in the market, which will enhance investor confidence and ease market pressure to some extent.

Residential   The residential market in Shanghai remained relatively stable in the first quarter of 2009, although other property sectors were dampened by the global economic recession. Average rentals for luxury residential property declined slightly, partly due to budget cuts for expatriates in multinational companies in Shanghai. On the other hand, both price and transaction volume for the overall residential sales market in Shanghai experienced a pick up. In the first quarter of 2009, overall sales volume showed a solid increase of 23% quarter-over-quarter.

Luwan recorded the highest sales price for both overall residential and high-end residential markets, at US$6,211 and US$7,298 per square meter respectively due to its prime location in Shanghai city. Pudong, Changning, and Jing'an also claimed high rents for high-end residential properties.

Luxury residential properties showed signs of recovering, although in a more moderate manner. However, as developers offered few price discounts to entice buyers, the luxury residential sale market continued to see a low transaction volume. The declining number of new expatriates in Shanghai and the reduced housing packages for these expatriates negatively impacted high-end residential markets.

In addition, new town development is strongly encouraged by the government, particularly "sustainable development." Sustainable development and green building are increasingly emphasized given China's enormous and growing pollution and environmental quality problems. Five new town projects in Shanghai provide examples of China's approach to sustainable development:[14]

1. The World Expo 2010, a global centerpiece and a focus of Shanghai's efforts to achieve sustainable urbanization
2. Laotian New Town, part of the city's One City, Nine Towns program that seeks to shift growth to smaller urban areas outside the central city
3. Signup New City, one of the 11 satellite towns in the comprehensive plan for the Shanghai metropolitan region
4. Changing Island, planned as an ecological demonstration region
5. The Xuxi District, part of China's Agenda 21 program of sustainable communities

Retail   The retail sector has been very buoyant in Shanghai, fueled by year-over-year of astounding urban area growth, rising household incomes and corresponding disposable incomes, a growing wealthy class, an increasing number of expatriates, and a growing appetite for consumer goods of all kinds. Improving quality of design, merchandising, and tenant mix is also serving to attract consumers to Class A shopping centers.

The prime retail market continued to trend north. The market demand stimulated by the upgrading competition between foreign and local retailers, together with the scarcity of supply in top retail catchments, should push up the occupancy rate in the prime retail areas in the future.

The Shanghai municipal government included the retail planning of the Bund and Lujiazui area in its eleventh five-year plan. The sustainable growth of retail industry signals positively for the future trends of retail properties. More and more institutional investors recognized the growth potential of Shanghai's retail sector and have stepped up their efforts to identify opportunities in prime locations.

The retail market in Shanghai has seen a gradual rise in rents since its decline in 1997 because of the Asian financial crisis, and only started to fall since late 2008 due to the global economic recession. Even in recent months, the sustained positive performance of the Shanghai economy still drives corresponding growth in retail sales. In the first two months of 2009, the consolidated retail sales for Shanghai stood at 831 million RMB, up 15.2% year-over-year.

The average rent for retail spaces is forecasted to decline in the short term due to increased supply. However, high-end retail properties in favorable locations of the city are expected to maintain their rent levels or even experience a rent growth. In addition, some retail projects have started to readjust their trade mix in order to stay competitive in the market, which will enhance the overall quality of retail properties in Shanghai and drive up the average rent in the future.

Industrial   As mainland China's largest container port, Shanghai has developed a strong industrial base. Key industries include automobile, chemical production, and consumer goods manufacturing. Recently, a broad range of research and development centers related to these industries as well as telecommunications, pharmaceuticals, and biotechnology have been established in Shanghai. In the near future, the creation of the Yangshan deep water port and the expansion of Pudong International Airport will benefit future industrial expansion.

Industrial locations are increasingly focused on serving specific niches with the establishment of specialist zones targeting firms involved in similar sectors (e.g., Shanghai Microelectronics Industrial Base and Shanghai International Automobile Town). Modern logistics parks dedicated to air, land, or water transportation are becoming increasingly popular. Within these parks are multiple logistics operations and integrated service functions. It is becoming increasingly difficult to locate good quality industrial space close to Shanghai due to supply constraints and high land, utility, and labor costs.

The major industrial parks include Northwest Logistics Center, Pudong International Airport Logistics Center, Waigaioqaio Logistics Center, and Yangshan Deepwater Port.

Developers should be more cautious in building speculative developments, so build-to-suit projects appear to be a more attractive option. Five new projects with a total gross floor area (GFA) of 216,912 square meters are expected to be completed in 2009.

Guangzhou

As the heart of the Pearl River Delta, Guangzhou (GZ) has a significant export-oriented industrial base across a wide spectrum of manufacturing sectors. Key industries of Guangzhou include automobile, IT, telecommunications, pharmaceutical, petrochemical, and consumer electronics. High value-added activities in Guangzhou represent a much higher GDP per capita for the city compared to the overall figure for Southern China. Labor costs are rising in GZ, but the market still provides the necessary skills to meet the requirements of multinational manufacturers. Due to continued development of the manufacturing sector along the Pearl River Delta and the growing importance of GZ in the region on the back of improving infrastructure and services standard, demand for property in the GZ area will see healthy growth.

The proposed Hong Kong–Macau–Zhuhai Bridge to be completed in 2016 will significantly improve the regional infrastructure system. This will further enhance the overall attractiveness of GZ as a key manufacturing based for Southern China and will draw further investment to the area. Last year, industrial output for GZ increased 11.7%, and FDI grew by 10.3%.

Driven by a strong manufacturing cluster around the area and given the strategic location of GZ in the Pearl River Delta, large multinationals continue to set up and expand new industrial facilities in GZ including Toyota, Federal Express, Hitachi Lift, Nissan, and many more. Demand for industrial land and facilities should remain strong in the long run. Guangzhou recorded a GDP growth rate of 12.3% in 2008.

Office   The growing prominence of GZ as a major business node in Southern China is fueling the increase in take up of office space in the city by both local and foreign companies.

With significant development activity, overall vacancy still faces upward pressure. However, the subdued demand from multinational companies is partly offset by the upgrading demand of domestic companies into higher quality Class A office buildings, spurred by the low rent and the economic stimulus program of Chinese government. In the long run, as global economies emerge from the recession, strong growth in the office market is expected to resume.

Residential The residential market has benefited from China's entry into the WTO, increasing trade, general job growth, and the relocation of domestic and foreign managers to the area. The macroeconomic policies that came out in October 2008 boosted potential buyers' confidence, and residential transaction volume increased substantially during 2009. However, because of the global economic downturn, unusually high-priced residential projects, and reduced new supply, the transaction volume for high-end residential market saw a drop in the first half of 2009.

The majority of new development consisted mainly of two- or three-bedroom apartments with units smaller than 100 square meters representing 69% of the total. The highest residential price appeared in the Yuexiu and Tianhe submarkets.

Due to budget cuts in expatriates' housing packages, some high-end residential properties lowered rents to retain current tenants and attract potential new tenants. In light of the decreasing selling price, some owners of luxury residential properties put the properties on the leasing market instead of the sales market, which led to a rising vacancy rate of 30.6% and 17.6% for service apartments and villas.

Retail The retail market of GZ has continued to register steady growth in recent years. The lowering of the investment barriers for foreign investors in the sector has boosted growth as well. Retail demand for space driven by the food and beverage, banking, electric, and clothes sectors has been strong. Rising incomes and purchasing power are underpinning the growth. Foreign supermarkets and big box retail continue to expand actively.

The uncertain economic outlook will continue to affect the retail property market in the short term, and retailers are likely to remain cautious about expansion. New supply to be completed later in the year may cause vacancy rates to rise and keep downward pressure on rents, especially in nonprime retail catchments.

Industrial GZ is known as the "world's workshop." GZ has a significant export-oriented industrial base across a wide spectrum of manufacturing centers. Key industries include automobile, IT, telecommunications, pharmaceutical, petrochemical, and consumer electronics.

Continued development of the Pearl River Delta area and the growing importance of GZ in the region are resulting in growing demand for industrial facilities, particularly warehouse and logistics. Driven by a strong manufacturing cluster and the strategic location of GZ in the Pearl River Delta, key MNCs have been establishing industrial facilities including Federal Express, Hitachi, Toyota, and many others. The proposed Hong

Kong–Macao–Zhuhai Bridge (scheduled to be completed by 2016) will further improve the regional infrastructure system. Foreign enterprises have favored GZ in recent years. Owing to a shortage in supply of industrial space, leasing and sales are very active. New industrial complexes, in particular warehouse and logistics buildings with comprehensive facilities and future development potential, are highly sought after by institutional investors.

Shenzhen

The land-leasing system of China began in the city of Shenzhen (SZ), then extended to other coastal cities. Shenzhen, home to 8.8 million people, is located in the middle of Guangdong Province, contiguous to the New Territories of Hong Kong in the south. Shenzhen has jurisdiction over the six districts of Futian, Luohu, Nanshan, Longgang, Yantian, and Bao'an, with a total area of 1,953 square kilometers. The city remains the nearest gateway to Hong Kong from the mainland, is the earliest economic zone in China (1980), and is one of the most important open ports in China, with good communication facilities and convenient transportation. The annual disposable income per capita in Shenzhen is even higher than in Beijing and Shanghai in 2008.

- Foreign investment groups have focused their attention on the luxury residential sector.
- Shenzhen is the highest in China in terms of the population density at 4,506 persons per square kilometer. Numerous high-rises have sprung up in Futian District, with its population density topping 9,000 people per square kilometer.
- The proportion of people with college education or above is very high in Shenzhen.
- The high population density has brought heavy pressure on the environment.
- Situated on China's southern border, Shenzhen is separated only by a river from Hong Kong (its close proximity to Hong Kong being a factor in attracting business investment).
- In the past two decades, more than US$30 billion has been invested by outsiders in Shenzhen: building factories, forming joint ventures and hiring workers.

There is a large high-technology component to the economy boasting companies such as IBM, Seagate, Epson, HP, and many others.

Office   The office market has seen fast-growing demand over the last few years. With the rapid expansion of foreign banking, insurance, and logistics enterprises, demand for office has been strong. Overall demand for Class A space was strong with transactions by large MNCs driving the market, until 2008 when the growth rate of the economy slowed. The focus on the investment market has been on the Futian CBD.

In 2009, the financial service, external trade, international logistics, and manufacturing sectors were hit by the global economic recession, and office demand from these sectors was weak. However, since the beginning of 2010, demand for office space has shown signs of recovery. A number of enterprises postponed their relocation plans, while some enterprises even reduced their occupied office spaces or moved out from the grade A premises for cost savings.

Residential   The residential market has been hot in recent years as supply of new units has not kept pace with demand. The demand has been fueled by the expansion of the local economy, a tremendous level of in-migration of new residents into urban areas from all over China, foreign buyers, particularly from Hong Kong, and speculative activity. Rising per capita incomes of the city and relatively low mortgage rates have also been responsible for more residents upgrading into new housing.

During late 2008 and early 2009, the housing market cooled significantly with falling capital values. However, since then, the housing market has once again heated up, leading to a significant surge in the number of transactions and rising prices.

Industrial   SZ like GZ also possesses a strong industrial base centered on export-oriented manufacturing industries. Moreover, the government's support of hi-tech and emerging industries has spurred their rapid growth. An increasing number of MNCs are driving the demand for warehouse and logistics buildings at or near the port, major highways, and the airport. There is a growing market for turn-key/build-to-suit projects as export levels and the number of MNCs increases. Bao'an, Yantian Port, and Shekou all recorded strong demand in recent years. Supported by government policies and comprehensive facilities, the Shenzhen Greater Industrial Park and Guangming HiTech Park saw strong absorption.

The potential increasing value of the RMB and high investment returns have enabled Shenzhen's industrial and logistics parks to attract investment from foreign funds. These areas include Qianhaiwan Logistics Park, Shekou's Chiwan Area, and Futian Tax-Free Zone. There has been rising demand for higher standards and requirements from foreign firms for the industrial and logistics parks to match international standards. As the positive effects of recent economic growth stimulation policies are gradually reflected on the real economy, industrial demand is expected to recover following the revival of the macroeconomy.

SECONDARY MARKETS

While most real estate activity has been focused on the eastern coastal cities, secondary markets hold great promise. Many of the main secondary cities are growing rapidly, but they have not experienced the rampant (in some cases, speculative) capital value escalation in real estate assets and land as has occurred in the primary cities over the last several years.

Main secondary markets include Chengdu, Dalian, Wuhan, Chongqing, Tianjin, Hangzhou, Nanjing, Qingdao.

For space considerations, we highlight only the first three cities. Nevertheless, all of these cities possess considerable growth and investment potential. See map of China (Exhibit 3.1) for locations.

Most domestic and foreign companies would prefer to be in the primary cities of Beijing, Shanghai, and Guangzhou. However, the country is growing rapidly, and China is unusual in that it possesses a great many cities of significant size. In terms of size, its secondary cities would rank as primary cities in most other countries. Real estate in the choice areas of the primary cities has become overbought, pushing down cap rates to unreasonable levels. Even for development land, the best urban locations have been tied up and are extraordinarily expensive.

Secondary cities offer real estate markets that have not experienced the white hot popularity of the primary markets. Prices are more reasonable. Good urban development land is available. At the same time, many secondary cities are exhibiting strong growth. Domestic companies and MNCs are experiencing labor shortages and increasing labor costs in primary cities, compelling them to expand or relocate their manufacturing, logistics, and office functions to secondary cities. Finally, the government has been actively encouraging development of secondary cities, particularly those away from the coast in their "Go West" policy. This means that governments are much more accommodating about investment and development. Entitlements can be faster or even fast-tracked. Certain types of real estate, such as middle-tier housing and industrial are in short supply, and cities are rolling out the red carpet for international-standard developers to develop these products.

Chengdu

Chengdu has enjoyed growing interest from investors over the last few years. Some investment has bypassed Chongqing in favor of nearby Chengdu.

As the capital of Sichuan, China's most populous province (81 million people) (which formerly included Chongqing), Chengdu has been a government and cultural center for more than 2,000 years. Chengdu has natural advantages and is already the aviation hub for the area. It is a regional center for technology, commerce, finance, transportation, and communication in southwest China and has been promoted by the central government as a focus for FDI. Chengdu enjoys a pleasant temperate climate, a good industrial base, and fertile surrounding farm lands. Chengdu is situated far from the cities of China's east coast. Wages in Chengdu are approximately half of those in Shanghai and Beijing.[15]

Chengdu is fast becoming China's Silicon Valley, drawing smart young workers from all over the country. The Chengdu GDP maintained a double-digit growth rate for 18 consecutive years and was 12.1% in 2008, making it one of the fastest-growing cities in the country. Personal incomes have been rising as well with per capita GDP rising at 9.9% in 2008. Investment in real estate has grown by over 20% since 2001. Population growth is strong in the city mainly due to in-migration from the province, attracted by jobs and the favorable economic picture. The city is well planned with several radial ring roads and distinct land use districts. There are a number of Hong Kong and Singaporean developments underway.

The economic growth picture of Chengdu looks extremely favorable. With expansion of their service industry, a large supply of high-skilled and low-cost labor, good infrastructure, capable governance, and rising demand for all types of real estate, this market offers many investment and development options. An increasing number of MNCs are locating manufacturing and/or R&D in the city. Over 100 of the world's top 500 companies already have operations in Chengdu, including Intel, Microsoft, Dell, GE, Ericsson, Hutchison Whampoa, Toyota, Citibank, and HSBC, to name a few. The legal and regulatory regime of the city and province are considered to be fair and consistent.

The upcoming five-year plan, the official road map for governance in China, is expected to focus on the Chengdu-Chongqing corridor as the growth center for the region. The two cities are less than four hours apart by automobile, and the gap keeps narrowing as more infrastructure comes on line. The two cities can complement each other as parts of a megalopolis serving not only hundreds of millions of people in the Chinese hinterland, but also Central Asia, and eventually could come to rival Bangkok as a regional capital. The "Go West" policy, the natural economic momentum, and the national government's official plan should drive real estate values.

Dalian

Dalian features a strong industrial and IT-based economy. With close proximity to major urban centers, an abundance of colleges and universities, and a moderate climate, Dalian has been successful in attracting high-tech companies, particularly software companies, and vies with Chengdu for the distinction of being the Silicon Valley of China.

Dalian is 800 kilometers (500 miles) from Beijing, and is only a one-hour flight from Seoul and a three-hour flight from Tokyo. Dalian's overall incentive package includes a two-year tax holiday on profits, an 80% reduction in value-added taxes, and import tariff and VAT exemptions on equipment, software, and spare parts.

Dalian is one of the busiest tourist destinations in China, featuring attractive scenery and a pleasant environment. Dalian has a large Japanese-speaking population (more than 300,000), a byproduct of Dalian's 40-year occupation by Japan (1905 to 1945). The city government is also encouraging residents to study Japanese to win more software deals from Japan. All of these factors have made Dalian important to Japan's tech future.

The huge demand for embedded software from Japanese companies has provided Dalian with an opportunity to build up a large-scale software industry. Software exports have become an important part of Dalian's economy. Beijing still dominates China's IT sector, but Dalian is closing the gap fast, especially with the increasing cost of real estate in Beijing. Dalian is now honing its image as a software outsourcing center for North Asia. The Dalian city government forecasts exports of IT products to reach US$1.5 billion by 2012.

In order to stabilize economic growth and increase domestic demand, in 2009 Dalian actively improved fixed asset investment in the city. The planning committee intended to begin construction of 102 urban infrastructure projects with investment totaling RMB55.7 billion. Major projects under construction include Metro Line 1 and Line 2 and the Donglian Road project. The stimulus effect of these projects has already begun to emerge upon real estate projects located along these infrastructure projects.

Wuhan

Wuhan, the capital city of Hubei Province, is historically a trading hub centrally located in the heart of the country. Wuhan is a major commercial, distribution, and transport center on the Yangtze River waterway. Many of

China's rail lines go through Wuhan, and it is sometimes called "the Chicago of China." The city is a center of the automobile manufacturing industry, and hundreds of auto parts manufacturers, local or foreign, have emerged in Wuhan and surrounding cities.

Wuhan is the major destination of FDI in the province. In 2008, foreign investment amounted to US$2.6 billion. Hong Kong is a major investor with more than 2,000 enterprises in Wuhan. French investment in Wuhan mainly focused on the automobile industry.

Wuhan has been a major distribution center in central China. It attracts a number of retail enterprises from other Chinese provinces and overseas countries to set up their shops to tap the market potential of the region. Wuhan has played an important role in connecting the east with the west and, the south with the north in China. With an urban population of approximately 9 million, the city is one of the top 25 cities in the country and has favorable development potential.

Located at the middle reaches of the Yangtze River, Wuhan is a thoroughfare to nine provinces in China. The Beijing-Guangzhou Railway and the Yangtze River intersect in Wuhan City. The Beijing-Kowloon Railway and Wuhan-Guangzhou Railway also connect in the city. The Beijing-Zhuhai and Shanghai-Chengdu superhighway will cross at Wuhan City. In addition, a high-speed railway along the Yangtze River is in the process of being constructed. These high-speed road, railway, and river transportation methods will reinforce the status of Wuhan as China's major transportation hub.

Wuhan is the largest logistics and commercial center in inland China. Goods can easily be transported to five provinces around Wuhan: that is, Hunan, Jiangxi, Anhui, Henan, and Sichuan, which have a combined population of 345 million. There are presently more than 10,000 commercial organizations and 105,000 business branches in Wuhan City. As an important industrial base in China, Wuhan City has a very solid foundation in both high-tech industry and traditional manufacturing. Along the 88-kilometer ring of the city, a series of industrial zones have been established, such as China Optical Valley, Sino-Citroen Automobile City, Taiwan Business Zone, and Yangluo Development Zone. With 33 different sectors and more than 30,000 industrial enterprises, Wuhan City has businesses encompassing a wide range of industries, including iron and steel, automobile, machinery, petrochemical, optical telecom, Chinese and Western medicine, biology engineering, textile, garment, and food industries.

Wuhan is a technology research and education center, with its research and education capacity ranked among the top five in the country. There are 78 universities and colleges in the city, serving approximately 991,000 students. There are also 11 national labs in Wuhan City.

INVESTMENT STRATEGIES

This section examines commercial real estate business opportunities in the current market. The strategies are not ranked in order of investment attractiveness, but are simply arranged alphabetically. Potential investment and development strategies are discussed. Evaluative factors are intended to provide a relative, subjective discussion of the various investment alternatives.

Active Seniors Housing

Because of the large aging population, active seniors housing has great potential in China (Exhibit 3.17). Though a nascent concept in the country largely because of the affordability and culture, both factors are changing—per capita income is surging and attitudes about elderly care and the family are changing. The Chinese household is typically a multigenerational and

EXHIBIT 3.17 Active Seniors Housing

Factor	Comments
Risk Factors	It is difficult to estimate when exactly this market will take off. China's population is one of the fastest-aging in the world, but this strategy requires widespread cultural acceptance as well as sufficient disposable household income.
Execution and Implementation	Similar to issues with other ground-up development. Favorable aspect is that locations can be more flexible—urban infill, suburban, and even fringe.
Returns	It is difficult to estimate. This might also be a rental play.
Reg./Legal	No unusual issues here.
Market Size	The size of the aging Chinese population will be such that has never been seen in human history. There is an opportunity to build a brand in this niche. Foreign companies might be viewed with greater confidence.
Competition	There is no domestic or international competitor focused on this niche at present.
Barriers to Entry and Exit	In some ways, this strategy is a new concept in the Chinese market. It may take time and significant marketing dollars to sell the idea to consumers. Exit could either be through the sales route or hold for long-term income property.

extended family arrangement. Children have been traditionally expected to care for their aging parents or relatives. However, more people are choosing to live alone, and the elderly are encouraged to have more interests outside of minding the grandchildren. The biggest impetus for seniors housing, however, will be the one-child policy resulting in an *inverted age pyramid.* In many families there are four grandparents for every one child making the traditional form of elder care all but impossible. Thus there should be a growing demand for active seniors housing over the next two decades.

Buying Core Office

While the supply of Class A buildings or near–Class A assets is slim, there are still opportunities in both the primary and secondary markets. The investment banks have been the trailblazers in this strategy with the likes of Morgan Stanley, Goldman Sachs, Macquarie, and others buying core office, even value-added office. With fundamentals for office improving for nearly every Chinese city except Beijing, the timing for office seems opportune. Rents are rising, vacancies diminishing, and more and more foreign, creditworthy tenants are setting up or expanding offices in China. China is no longer a one-office location as is the case of other Asian countries such as Singapore, Hong Kong, and Taiwan. Because of its size and numerous market opportunities, China is becoming a multilocation office market for MNCs. Many of the acquisitions going forward will probably qualify as value-added office with improvements necessary in tenants, TI, design, and especially building management. Class A yields are roughly 7 to 8% in Shanghai and Beijing versus 5 to 6% in the United States, 5.5% in London, 4 to 5% in Hong Kong, or 4 to 5% in Tokyo. Is the additional risk in the Chinese market worth it? An increasing number of investors seem to think so. Would this strategy put the investors at odds with an office development program? These are questions that investors have to answer as they build on-the-ground knowledge of Chinese markets (Exhibit 3.18).

Buying Core Retail

Disposable incomes in China, especially in the eastern coastal cities are rising quickly. China is changing from the savings and subsistence consumer culture to a spending and lifestyle culture. Though this transition will take years (decades), the indications are already evident in the buoyant retail sector. Low-end (Carrefour, Metro, Walmart) as well as middle-tier retailers are registering brisk sales and growth. Luxury retailers have not quite hit their stride as only the very wealthy can afford their merchandise. Chinese

EXHIBIT 3.18 Buying Core Office

Factor	Comments
Risk Factors	Most Class A properties are held in strata title, making negotiations difficult and complicating exit strategies. Tenants have significantly more rights than in many more developed countries, including the ability to unilaterally terminate lease agreements. This presents additional risks as cash flows are not as certain as in some other countries. Long due diligence and negotiations periods translate into closing times that extend many months causing deals to fall through. Title and due diligence is spotty.
Execution and Implementation	Even bread and butter strategies such as core office require a significant amount of searching, negotiating, due diligence, and then much work to bring the asset up to international standard. All of this is management-intensive work.
Returns	Yields for stabilized office in large cities range from 6% to 8%. Those buying at low yields are betting on future rent increases, lowering the vacancy rate, and appreciation to improve returns. Also, Chinese banks are increasingly willing to lend to blue chip foreign companies on competitive terms.
Reg./Legal	The restrictions on foreign lending and investing for real estate have been relaxed. However, there are still the issues of taking profit in and initial capitalization. Some of these challenges can be avoided by forming a WFOE before investment.
Market Size	Assets exist in significant numbers in both primary and secondary markets. However, the number of investable core office assets is limited because of strata title and basic features of design and construction.
Competition	Several large international investment banks are in the market as well as many Hong Kong, Taiwan, and Singaporean players. Players are being bid up to unrealistically low cap levels.
Barriers to Entry and Exit	Expect a long prospecting, due diligence, and closing period. Barriers to exit are few for a single owner, Class A office in a good urban location. However, strata title ownership complicates exit.

EXHIBIT 3.19 Buying Core Retail

Factor	Comments
Risk Factors	Similar issues as core office. In addition, it is very difficult to obtain accurate rent rolls from buyers. Strata title properties predominate, but do not preclude deals. Much of the retail space will require new TI and much better asset management.
Execution and Implementation	There is a small inventory of investment Class Core retail. The same issues with due diligence, negotiations, and closing exist with retail as with office. Many of these properties will take quite a bit of work in cleaning them up and repositioning them. Strata title will be even more challenging.
Returns	Yields for stabilized retail in large cities range from 6% to 10%.
Reg./Legal	There are no unusual restrictions for this strategy. Foreign retailers face no exceptional barriers.
Market Size	China is one the single largest retail markets in the world by volume of customers. Eventually it will be the largest in terms of overall spend. There are significant opportunities to create and extend domestic and international brands.
Competition	There is relatively limited competition from foreign players in this space.
Barriers to Entry and Exit	Few barriers to entry or exit except as already noted.

retail environments tend to be poorly designed and merchandised. This is compounded by the fact that the great majority of retail properties are strata title. Such ownership complications make it difficult to maintain and upgrade property—upgrading and repositioning become nearly impossible. Retail foot traffic in the right location and with the appropriate tenant mix can be very high in China. As with office, there is significant competition in this space from other foreign real estate players. This has driven down cap rates and left a short supply of institutional-grade product (Exhibit 3.19).

Creating REITs

There is currently no REIT legislation on the books in China. However, two REITs (and several in the pipeline) have been formed, and REITs have gone public on the Hong Kong exchange. These have surpassed all investors' expectations in terms of returns and growth. Importantly these REITs need not consist of Class A properties alone. The general investor appetite for REITs is so strong and the market so new, that this level of segmentation is not yet necessary but will be as the market matures. Investors in Hong Kong want professionally managed, income-producing real estate in primary cities. Most investors are sanguine enough about the prospects of both income and capital value growth for Chinese properties that they are willing to pay a premium for Chinese REIT shares.

REITs are a potentially promising investment play in China. The China market is wide open and presents a full range of possible sectors—residential, office, retail, industrial, logistics, serviced apartments, and hospitality.

There are other advantages for overseas investors with a REIT strategy. First, one need not buy the properties and then take them public. Investors could first raise the money in the public markets and then acquire the properties. The second major advantage addresses one concern of many foreign investors for the China market—repatriating the profits. The REIT structure, through the sale of equity interests in the form of stock, allows a fast and potentially rapid return of the investment capital and returns. The REIT does this in a manner that ensures liquidity and flexibility. An investor need not sell entire properties, but can flexibly and quickly decide the level of preferred ownership by selling or buying shares in REITs. The risks associated with this strategy are the same as these of the China property market—dubious land titles, unpredictable laws and regulations, lack of transparency, complex tax issues, and rapid construction that can yield new, sometimes unwanted neighbors within a few months.

There are special risks associated with floating Chinese REITs in Hong Kong. There is the double taxation issue, which can adversely reduce income. Hong Kong is subject to property tax or profits tax if the property assets are held through a special-purpose vehicle (SPV). There is also a minimum real estate holding period of two years with a maximum gearing ratio of 35%. In addition, Chinese property markets can exhibit great volatility. Leases in China are typically shorter than in many markets. Thus security of income is not guaranteed. While rents have been going up, they could as easily decline with increasing supply coming online in many markets. Properties are also becoming more expensive to build as well as maintain, further potentially depressing NOI (Exhibit 3.20).

Developing Industrial and Logistics Parks and Buildings

Industrial investment is typically not a viable investment sector in most emerging markets. However, *China is a major exception.* The traditional current stock of industrial and logistics buildings is ill-suited to the requirements

EXHIBIT 3.20 Creating REITs

Factor	Comments
Risk Factors	Buying income-producing real estate suitable for institutional ownership that is producing a respectable yield is still not easy. There are too many buyers throughout China seeking the same kind of properties. Creating sufficient quantity and quality of properties may require value-added plays as well as development—lengthening the execution period for this strategy.
Execution and Implementation	There is quite a bit of legal work that needs to be done first. If this market gets too hot, the government could intervene and change the rule book, reducing returns or eliminating the market altogether.
Returns	Return on equity has been over 100%. Returns to investors in the REIT shares themselves have exceeded 30%. REIT IPOs floated on the Hong Kong exchange have been massively oversubscribed.
Reg./Legal	There is no REIT legislation in place, and double taxation applies.
Market Size	The demand for Chinese REITs is large, and the size of the Chinese market is large.
Competition	There are Chinese, Hong Kong, and Singaporean developers involved with this strategy. However, no large MNC has successfully launched a Chinese REIT, but several appear to be interested or in the process of developing.
Barriers to Entry and Exit	Planning, designing a REIT, jumping through the legal and regulatory hoops, acquiring a portfolio, marketing, and going public require significant front end costs and time. Exiting is fairly quick, liquid, and easy through sale of shares. The exit is one of the greatest attractions to the REIT play.

of an increasingly sophisticated, international supply chain. China is an industrial-based economy with production rapidly expanding, particularly in a handful of coastal cities with deep-water ports. These cities contain the industries that are seeing explosive growth year after year. Much of this production is export-oriented. There is an increasing need for modern logistics parks able to handle the volume and complexity of this export activity and modern warehouses that can accommodate efficient supply chain distribution demands—that is, multiple container trucks, rail, and refrigeration. There is far more demand than supply in most coastal markets forcing several exporting MNCs such as Walmart to build and operate their own warehouse/logistics centers (Exhibit 3.21).

Developing Middle-Income Residential in Downtowns

Most developers in China build high-density luxury units and target white-collar buyers, who have higher income levels and work and live in metropolitan areas. The greatest demand is actually in middle-income housing. For this bread and butter housing people wait in long lines outside of sales offices in the dead of winter just to have a chance to buy their own unit. The advantage of this product is that it can be developed potentially faster (more repetitive building elements and less cost in high end fixtures and finishes) and in a variety of nonprime locations, even fringe suburbs. Rapid population growth in the cities is being fueled by migrants from the countryside who move into the city for higher incomes. Annual population growth has averaged over 10% for the past 5 years in major Chinese cities, including the addition of more than 200,000 residents per year to cities such as Beijing, Shanghai, and Nanjing (Exhibit 3.22).

Developing New Luxury Residential in Urban Areas

For-sale luxury residential has been the preferred domain of local Chinese and Hong Kong developers and for good reason. With strong demand, most well-executed projects sell out before they are complete, boosting IRRs, and making financing unnecessary in many cases. While out of reach for most Chinese, a small percentage of wealthy Chinese on a large base still translates into more than sufficient demand for most projects. Moreover, many foreigners have gotten into the markets (some for the long-term, some for speculation). These buyers are mainly from Hong Kong or are overseas Chinese. There are some recently enacted restrictions on foreign ownership of residential real estate designed to cool speculative buying, but these should not significantly dampen the market as underlying demand remains strong. In fact Chinese banks willingly lend up to 80% loan-to-value (LTV) for foreigners to purchase residential properties. Some submarkets of Beijing and Shanghai are experiencing a high degree of supply overhang, but most of these are units in developments priced at the highest end of the luxury spectrum (Exhibit 3.23).

EXHIBIT 3.21 Developing Industrial and Logistics Parks

Factor	Comments
Risk Factors	Much of the land and existing assets for industrial real estate are owned and/or operated by the government. The industrial is still seen as a "strategic" sector to be closely controlled by the government. Working with the government this closely can slow the investment process and reduce returns.
Execution and Implementation	There are more private sites being allowed by the government for industrial development. However, many sites will have to be developed in partnership with the government. Industrial investment requires virtually all new greenfield development because of the poor quality of the existing asset base.
Returns	If properties can be preleased—build-to-suit, then returns can be quite high. Preleasing in the current market seems probable.
Reg./Legal	This strategy might involve some form of public and private partnership—always complex. Anything done in this strategy would undoubtedly face greater legal and regulatory hurdles. Many sites and some markets would be closed to the private investor.
Market Size	The industrial sector, particularly in the southern coastal cities is large and growing bigger each year and because increasing MNC demand will become more investment-grade over time.
Competition	Prologis, AMB, and a few others are making small forays into the market. Most competitors are domestic who produce noninvestment grade product.
Barriers to Entry and Exit	This strategy involves significant time to invest working with various levels of government. A beneficial aspect of industrial development, especially in China with its rapid construction practice, is that the *time-to-market is relatively fast*. The total development period (from deal close to product release) is rarely longer than a year for most assets. Entire industrial parks would require a longer period of time in part because they would be phased and involve significant infrastructure.

EXHIBIT 3.22 Develop Middle-Income Residential in Downtowns

Factor	Comments
Risk Factors	This strategy requires all greenfield development with the attendant risks involved. Interest rates are beginning to climb, potentially cooling demand. Some secondary cities lack sophisticated contractors and vendors.
Execution and Implementation	This would involve having some form of development capability on the ground in China. The Chinese partner would have to have large-scale housing production capability.
Returns	Difficult to estimate, but arguably the highest of any sector and strategy in China with the opportunity for profitability during the development phase because of presales.
Reg./Legal	No unusual legal or regulatory issues.
Market Size	Largest single real estate market segment in the country and perhaps the largest potential residential market in the world with hundreds of millions of people seeking new or upgraded housing.
Competition	There are many competitors, but most produce substandard product—subpar design, construction, marketing, and ongoing management.
Barriers to Entry and Exit	Significant time to invest working with various levels of government. The main entry barrier is the opportunity cost of our time vis-à-vis other investment opportunities taking far less time. Mixed use development would be likely.

Developing Urban and Suburban Retail Malls

Many Class A retail formats would be well received in China. The retail sector in China is quite buoyant and increasing steadily as incomes rise and as Chinese demand for noncommodity retail goods and international brands increases. China has a legacy of small, cramped, infill retail centers—the classic neighborhood retail shop format fronting streets. Currently the retail shopping experience tends to be bi-nodal—either incredibly high end, unaffordable to all but the very rich 1% or down-market with low quality goods and a lackluster if not downright unpleasant shopping experience. The growing middle class is demanding a shopping experience in between these two extremes. Given the rising rate of car ownership and the less expensive land in the urban fringes and suburbs, suburban malls anchored

EXHIBIT 3.23 Developing New Luxury Residential in Urban Areas

Factor	Comments
Risk Factors	The best sites for development are hotly contested. Investors should be careful to avoid bidding wars. Clear title must be a prerequisite as investors will be conveying title for individual owners within a short time after due diligence.
Execution and Implementation	Foreign investors need a Chinese development management team on the ground. Most importantly, development partners should have the willingness to learn international best practices and to not cut corners.
Returns	Developer profits for successful projects have been in the several hundred percent IRRs. Payback periods have been much less than projected because most projects are selling out during the design and construction phase.
Reg./Legal	Again land title is a major issue to clear before closing on any deal. Moreover, repatriating profits should be done through an offshore WOFE and an SPV.
Market Size	Housing is the biggest demand sector for the next 20 years. Luxury housing will enter the mainstream affordability range as incomes rise, further boosting demand.
Competition	The competition in this niche is the greatest as it is the preferred strategy of many domestic and now foreign developers and investors.
Barriers to Entry and Exit	Finding land, partners, and clear title are the main entry barriers. The exit, especially with an internationally branded product that meets the standards of true international class development, should be rapid.

with a large big box retailer are proving to be popular. With the likes of Morgan Stanley, Walmart, and Carrefour leading the way, their expansion has just begun. Lifestyle centers would do well in the country where people often use retail shopping as a form of recreation. Large, enclosed regional shopping malls have proven to be very popular (Exhibit 3.24).

Distressed Properties and Nonperforming Real Estate Loans

State-owned commercial banks have huge nonperforming loan (NPL) portfolios collateralized by a wide range of properties. With the commercial banks' trend of going public, one of the key requirements for them is to

EXHIBIT 3.24 Developing Urban and Suburban Retail Malls

Factor	Comments
Risk Factors	Investors would have to partner with a local developer. There are few retail developers with the experience and ability to successfully pull off a true Class A shopping mall. Development of this type will require significant expertise. The investment horizon would be long for a large retail project—perhaps three to six years until project stabilization.
Execution and Implementation	The typical issues with sourcing the best locations and structuring the best deals apply. Land sourcing and assembly is becoming more difficult in China with the rise in land values and the growing power of citizens in the face of eminent domain that is often required for large urban and suburban sites. The design of the center should reflect the changing and evolving spending patterns of the Chinese consumers.
Returns	Returns to retail development should easily exceed 30% IRR.
Reg./Legal	Restrictions against foreign retailers have been removed.
Market Size	The market size is immense. Chinese consumers are speeding up the retail value chain in their purchasing habits and disposable income.
Competition	There are a few foreign competitors teaming up with local development firms. However, these are few, and the market is large. If anything, these players are providing a degree of corroboration about this strategy.
Barriers to Entry and Exit	Securing the best urban sites will require a lot of looking and money. A series of established local partners will help in this regard. Exits include selling interests in the completed development, REITizing (even a single asset or a few assets can become a successful REIT), or selling strata title. The best bet is to hold for the long term and ride the Chinese retail spending boom. The rate of wealth creation growth for the average Chinese household promises to continue to be rapid.

eliminate bad debt and get as much money back on their books possible. In almost every city, there are stark reminders of these bad loans—large high-profile projects lie unfinished and abandoned. The government is keen to clean up the NPLs as well as finish these projects. There are opportunities to buy properties at below-market prices. Many of these are in excellent downtown locations. However, the complicated relationship between state-owned banks (the lenders) and their clients—state-owned enterprises (often the borrowers)—in some deals the ownership is unclear or the banks have only limited claims to ownership. Therefore it is difficult for the bank itself to clear the deal with prospective buyers without the cooperation of the borrowers or special authorization from the government. This aspect can hold up many deals (Exhibit 3.25).

EXHIBIT 3.25 Distressed Properties and Non-performing Real Estate Loans

Factor	Comments
Risk Factors	The greatest risk would perhaps be the fact that these assets are typically owned by some type of government agency (local, regional, federal). Most Chinese banks are government-owned to varying degrees. Thus the interactions with the government would be slow and political.
Execution and Implementation	Negotiating for distressed properties and real estate NPLs is like working within a black box. Terms, data points, and agreements can also change capriciously and without warning resulting in wasted work and investment.
Returns	Returns run the full range from zero to extremely high.
Reg./Legal	Government approvals would be required, slowing the deal timeline.
Market Size	Distressed properties and NPLs for real estate constitute a large number of assets in China.
Competition	Several large international investment banks have been focusing on this niche with varying degrees of success. The Chinese still prefer to work these deals out domestically.
Barriers to Entry and Exit	These deals can be complex and take a long time to work out. They can be highly political. The distressed properties themselves are often at various stages of completion, typically requiring significant capital investment and development/construction management/expertise to bring them to completion. Sometimes finishing an incomplete project can be more difficult and expensive than a new greenfield project.

EXHIBIT 3.26 Mezzanine Loans

Factor	Comments
Risk Factors	The main international partners would be Chinese developers who typically have nontransparent balance sheets. Due diligence would be difficult—long and expensive and inexact. Legal recourse would be virtually impossible.
Execution and Implementation	It would be necessary have to spend time learning and building relationships with the main players in the market. It is necessary to build guarantees and collateral into investments, and this would lead to complex and protracted regulations.
Returns	Participating in the promote structure of deals, returns especially in for-sale residential, retail, certain office buildings, could be quite high—exceeding 50% equity IRR. Investment horizons would be shorter than the entire development period. Mezzanine debt should be standard first in the promote (above preferred equity) that is first for returns and first to return the original investment.
Reg./Legal	The restrictions on foreign lending and investing for real estate have been relaxed. However, there are still the issues of taking profit in and initial capitalization. Some of these challenges can be avoided by forming a WFOE before investment.
Market Size	The market size is enormous. There are over 25,000 developers in China with thousands of investment projects in need of mezzanine financing. Many of these developers are financially strapped or in financial distress. Many more cannot begin projects without some form of mezzanine financing. A mezzanine strategy would allow us to enter prime projects at critical junctures—that is, when projects are in the home stretch of their completion time frames—allowing us to reduce our development/construction risk.
Competition	There is no domestic or international competitor focused on this niche at present. There is a huge gap in this market. Macquarie Bank and Morgan Stanley are apparently considering entering this business.
Barriers to Entry and Exit	It is important to know the leading developers. This business is built on trust. Local banks and investment companies might perceive us to be a competitive threat and move to enact legislation limiting our business.

EXHIBIT 3.27 Mixed-Use Development

Factor	Comments
Risk Factors	Mixed-use projects are very complex, large, and extend over a long period of time.
Execution and Implementation	Large mixed-use requires a great deal of skill, management, and good relationships with local government.
Returns	Because of the various sectors and product type, and the duration of such projects—three to six years is the typical range—returns are difficult to estimate. However, investors can lay off some risk and harvest returns along the way by phasing and selling portions or interests in the project.
Reg./Legal	This strategy might involve some form of public and private partnership—always complex. Anything investors did in this strategy would undoubtedly face greater legal and regulatory hurdles.
Market Size	Immense. Retail and residential, which would be the primary components of such projects and demand in China for these sectors, is infinite at this stage.
Competition	Many domestic and a few overseas Chinese firms are active. The most ambitious projects yet are now on the drawing boards.
Barriers to Entry and Exit	Significant time would have to be devoted to working with various levels of government. The approval process would be long and complex. It is necessary to consider the opportunity cost of our time vis-á-vis other investment opportunities taking far less time.

Mezzanine Financing

Recent government measures to control credit, restrict presale arrangements, and reduce the portfolio of nonperforming loans in China's banks have led to a shortage of capital for many investors. This has created an opportunity for offshore mezzanine financing. The offshore mezzanine financing can be done through a cooperative joint venture structure, which provides some measure of security to the lender and assures compliance with lending laws in China. Mezzanine financing makes broad-scale investment easier, facilitating investment in a greater number of deals. The investor could substitute equity for the mezzanine debt for more attractive deals (Exhibit 3.26).

Mixed-Use Development

China has a voracious appetite for Class A mixed-use developments incorporating housing, retail, entertainment, and office. This is a new product type for the country and one that has been met with very strong demand. China is starved for world-class design and construction for public places. There are several potential developers with whom investors could partner to produce these types of projects. Risk could be mitigated by phasing, preselling, selling shares, and selling strata title in the project. These projects would be especially suitable at transit hubs to take advantage of pedestrian traffic, access, and visibility. Some investors may have a core competency and competitive advantage in this product type. In fact, few players internationally can undertake these large and complex projects successfully. Regional and local governments are also encouraging these types of projects, as they are high profile and can showcase cutting-edge design, and they are often seen as economic development catalysts for marginal urban areas (Exhibit 3.27).

NOTES

1. Economist Intelligence Unit, *China Country Report* (January 2008).
2. Economist Intelligence Unit, *China Country Report* (January 2009).
3. Transparency International, *Global Corruption Report* (2008).
4. National Bureau of Statistics of China, *Communiqué on 2004 Rural Poverty Monitoring of China* (2005).
5. World Bank, Urban Development and China, http://go.worldbank.org/ LHTNOP9GU0.
6. DTZ Debenham Tie Leung, *Asia-Pacific Property Investment Guide* (2007/ 2008).
7. *China Commerce Yearbook 2008.*
8. "New Policies Affecting Foreign Investment in Chinese Real Estate," *Xinhua News*, July 31, 2006.
9. World Bank, *China's Rapid Urbanization: Benefits, Challenges & Strategies* (2008).
10. Ministry of Construction of China, *The Real Estate Market Supervision Statistics* (2004).
11. World Tourism Organization, *Tourism 2020 Vision—East Asia & Pacific* (2001).
12. The population is estimated at 12.30 million.

13. "China Builds Its Dreams, and Some Fear a Bubble," *New York Times*, October 18, 2005.
14. Alexander E. Kalamaros, *Shanghai's Sustainable New Towns* (Urban Land Institute, 2005).
15. China Trade in Services, Chengdu, "China: a Growing Software and Outsourcing Hub," April 22, 2009.

CHAPTER 4

India

INTRODUCTION

The Indian property market differs significantly from many other markets in the world, and investment strategy and decisions must be adjusted accordingly. The Indian market is extremely large, diverse, complex, fragmented, and experiencing rapid growth. It is also rather undeveloped, with issues of low transparency, corruption, and bureaucratic laws and governance.

The Indian market offers a variety of potential opportunities. The economy is growing, and demand for many types of real estate is strong around the country, albeit concentrated in a handful of cities. This chapter explores investment opportunities and outlines potential approaches to pursue these opportunities.

The playing field appears open for a variety of investment and development strategies. There are relatively few major foreign players in the office space, retail (shopping centers/malls), hospitality (hotels/serviced apartments), IT/business parks, and industrial/logistics/warehousing sectors, and limited foreign presence in for-sale residential.

The fundamental growth factors that drive real estate are strong. GDP growth, exports (current account), foreign direct investment (FDI), urban growth, population growth, income growth (particularly the middle class), increasing disposable incomes, all portend greater real estate demand and increasing market segmentation. Moreover, the market has been rather artificially constrained because the many regulatory barriers that had been erected for so long greatly limited foreign competition. These have only recently been reduced or removed or are in the process of being scaled back. There is pent-up, unfulfilled demand in several sectors that the domestic real estate market alone had not been able to fulfill.

With the change in FDI regulation, the continuing strength of the Indian economy, and the ongoing improvements to infrastructure, India could be entering a phase of even stronger, deeper, and more diversified growth in the real estate industry. In fact, the real estate sector is booming, growing at a rate of around 30% per year.

The sectors with the greatest opportunity currently seem to be residential, hotel/hospitality, and office/R&D. In all three sectors foreign investors would enjoy advantages in expertise, development standards, and capital strength.

OVERVIEW OF THE MARKET ENVIRONMENT

India is an enormously large, diverse, and complex country. English is widely spoken and is the lingua franca, though Hindi is the official national language. The system of government is a parliamentary democracy consisting of 29 states and 6 union territories. The annual GDP was US$1,296 billion in 2009, making it the eleventh-largest economy in the world. FDI in 2009 reached US$27.09 billion, compared with US$3.58 billion in 2000. Over US$17 billion worth of property stock is created annually. India seems to have demonstrated that it can stay on a high growth trajectory for the long-term. *The Economist* summed up the potential opportunity in this way—"think back to China a decade ago, and a prosperous India is not such an impossible dream."[1]

India is noteworthy in many respects, including its prodigious population. In 2009, India's population was 1.16 billion and with its rate of growth (1.3%) will surpass China's population by 2030. More than two-thirds of the population lives in rural areas, with over 60% living in villages with populations of 5,000 or less. By 2010, India's urban population is forecast to increase to one-third of the total population.

According to the 2001 census, there were 35 cities with over one million inhabitants and at least 15 more with populations between 800,000 and 990,000. India's rapid urbanization follows a familiar pattern of many emerging market countries. In 1991, there were 23 cities with populations over one million, in 1981, only 12 cities, and in 1971, only 7. The number is estimated to rise to 70 by 2025, when they will contain about one-half of the country's urban inhabitants.

Most of this increase in urban population is due to a massive and ongoing rural-urban migration. The cities are seen by the populace as places of opportunity. Rural areas tend to have the greatest concentrations of poverty. The agriculture sector still employs a disproportionate amount of the working population; in 2005–2006, 56% of the country's workers were employed in the agricultural sector, which contributes only 18% to GDP. Most of the farming is done at subsistence level with the great majority of farm workers living well below the poverty line. As a result, India's GDP per capita in

2007–2008 was only 33,299 rupees (Rs), which ranked 113th by World Bank in 2008.

Most growth and real estate investment has occurred in the six leading major urban agglomerations:

1. Greater Mumbai (Greater Bombay), population 16.4 million
2. Kolkata (Calcutta) population 13.2 million
3. Delhi, population 12.8 million
4. Chennai (Madras), population 6.4 million
5. Bangalore, population 5.7 million
6. Hyderabad, population 5.5 million

India's national performance in many aspects masks considerable interstate variation in terms of economic growth, economic policy, population, and human development (Exhibit 4.1). Since 1991, Gujarat and Maharashtra have been the fastest-growing states, enjoying rates of growth around 6 to 8%, comparable with the East Asian economies. High growth private-sector industries are concentrated around Mumbai in Maharashtra and parts of Gujarat; around Delhi, including Haryana and western Uttar Pradesh; and in the corridor from Bangalore in Karnataka to Chennai in Tamil Nadu.

Delhi is the political capital and a key tourist gateway city. Bangalore is the Information Technology/IT-Enabled Services/Business Process Outsourcing (IT/ITES/BPO) hub where 40% of the new office is absorbed. Mumbai is the financial capital and the center of the media entertainment industry, "Bollywood" and corporate headquarters. Chennai, Pune, and Hyderabad are also key IT destinations.

India's population is extremely diverse, differentiated by language, religion, caste, and class. A significant political divide exists between Hindus (83% of the population) and the other religious groups, including Muslims (11%), Sikhs, and Christians.

The Economy

Agriculture dominates the economy and accounts for 56% of the labor force and near 20% of GDP. India has some of the lowest human development indicators in the world, particularly in rural areas. At the other end of the scale, India has a large number of qualified professionals, as well as several internationally established industrial groups. The services sector has proved to be India's most dynamic sector in recent years, with telecoms and IT registering particularly rapid growth. Services, including airlines, banks, construction, and small-scale private traders, as well as the public sector,

EXHIBIT 4.1 India Gross State Product and Incomes

	GSP (US Dollar in Billions)	%age of Total GDP	Per-Capita Income in INR	Per-Capita Income in USD
Maharashtra	$147.27	14.83%	47,051	$1,172
Uttar Pradesh	$85.81	8.64%	16,060	$400
Andhra Pradesh	$81.37	8.19%	35,600	$887
Gujarat	$76.45	7.70%	32,065	$799
Tamil Nadu	$76.00	7.65%	45,773	$1,140
West Bengal	$76.72	7.73%	40,757	$1,016
Karnataka	$59.39	5.98%	36,266	$904
Rajasthan	$43.96	4.43%	23,986	$598
Kerala	$41.30	4.16%	43,104	$1,074
Haryana	$38.43	3.87%	59,008	$1,470
Delhi	$35.86	3.61%	78,690	$1,961
Madhya Pradesh	$35.51	3.58%	18,051	$450
Punjab	$35.96	3.62%	46,686	$1,163
Bihar	$28.56	2.88%	11,074	$276
Orrisa	$29.67	2.99%	26,654	$664
Chattisgarh	$19.79	1.99%	29,776	$742
Assam	$17.85	1.80%	21,991	$548
Jharkhand	$17.26	1.74%	19,928	$497
Uttrakhand	$8.87	0.89%	32,884	$819
Himachal Pradesh	$8.03	0.81%	40,107	$999
Jammu & Kashmir	$7.92	0.80%	24,214	$603
Goa	$4.29	0.43%	105,582	$2,631
Chandigarh	$3.53	0.36%	110,728	$2,759
Tripura	$2.70	0.27%	28,806	$718
Pondicherry	$2.57	0.26%	78,302	$1,951
Meghalaya	$2.11	0.21%	29,811	$743
Nagaland	$1.56	0.16%	21,822	$544
Manipur	$1.46	0.15%	19,780	$493
Arunachal Pradesh	$0.97	0.10%	28,945	$721
Mizoram	$0.82	0.08%	27,501	$685
Sikkim	$0.57	0.06%	33,349	$831
Andaman & Nicobar Islands	$0.54	0.05%	44,304	$1,104

1 USD = 40.1346 R
Source: VMW Analytics, 2009.

accounted for 52.8% of GDP in 2007–2008. While some privatization of state-owned-enterprises has occurred in this sector, the predominance of inefficient state-owned enterprises, particularly in the banking sector, remains a drag on faster economic growth.

Economic Policy

The adoption of the command economy (essentially a form of quasi-socialism) after India's independence from Great Britain, created severe restrictions on the private sector, and led to the growth of large and inefficient state-owned enterprises (SOEs) unaccustomed to competition. Moves to open up India's economy have met opposition from vested interests including politicians, unions, bureaucrats, and some industrialists.

India still, in some ways, suffers from this legacy, with its excessive regulation and economic controls, which have only been scaled back in the last decade or so. India has made good progress in reducing its fiscal deficit. The fiscal deficit improved from 6.6% of GDP in 1991–1992 to 0.1% in 2006–2007. The objective of the Reserve Bank of India is to maintain price stability and ensure an adequate flow of credit to the economy. In recent years, inflation has fallen to around 4.5%, down from double-digit inflation in the first half of the 1990s. The policy of price stability has gained further importance following the opening up of the economy and far-reaching reform in the financial sector.

Economic Performance

India's economy expanded considerably during the 1980s to reach an annual rate of GDP growth of around 5.5% at the end of the decade. Following a slowdown in the early 1990s, currency devaluation, import liberalization, and industrial delicensing (a form of privatization of state-owned enterprises), it rapidly rose to over 5% by the mid-1990s, peaking at 7.8% in 1995–1996.

Real GDP growth was 5.2% in the five-year period from 1997–1998 to 2002–2003. The slowdown was mainly the result of a significant fall in industrial and agricultural growth, whereas services growth continued its rapid expansion and had become the main engine of economic growth. However, afterward its GDP maintained strong growth again. In 2007–2008, its GDP growth reached 9.0%. The global financial crisis diminished India's GDP growth in 2008–2009; however, it was one of the few major economies to see positive growth for that period (Exhibit 4.2).

Inflation was an issue earlier in the 1990s when it averaged close to 10%. In 1997–2003 the rate averaged around 6% due to improved

EXHIBIT 4.2 Key Economic Indicators

	2004–05	2005–06	2006–07	2007–08	2008–09[1] Proj.	2009–10[2] Proj.
Growth (y/y percent change)[1]						
Real GDP (at factor cost)	7.5	9.4	9.6	9.0	6.3	5.3
Nonagricultural sector	9.5	10.3	11.0	10.0	7.1	5.9
Industrial production	8.4	8.2	11.5	8.5	…	…
Saving and investment (percent of GDP)						
Gross saving[3]	31.8	34.3	34.8	36.0	34.6	34.9
Gross investment[3]	32.2	35.5	35.9	37.5	37.6	36.4
External trade[4]						
Merchandise exports (US$ billions)	85.2	105.2	128.9	166.2	186.4	169.0
y/y percent change	28.5	23.4	22.6	28.9	12.2	−9.4
Merchandise imports (US$ billions)	118.9	157.1	190.7	257.8	298.0	265.5
y/y percent change	48.6	32.1	21.4	35.2	15.6	−10.9

Sources: IMF 2009 Article IV Consultation with India. Data provided by the Indian authorities; CEIC Data Company Ltd; Bloomberg L.P.; World Development Indicators; and Fund staff estimates and projections.
[1]Data are for April–March fiscal years.
[2]Current staff projections.
[3]Differs from official data, calculated with gross investment and current account. Gross investment includes errors and omissions.
[4]Annual data are on balance of payments basis.

EXHIBIT 4.3 Key Economic Indicators

No.	Description	China	India
1	Population (billion) (2008)	1.33	1.19
2	Urban Population (%) (2005)	43	29
3	GDP Per Capita (PPP,US$) (2008)	5,963	2,762
4	Exports (billion US$) (2008)	1,429	166
5	Inflation (%) (2008)	5.9	8.3
6	Savings (% of GDP) (2000–2003)	43	22
7	Labor Laws	More flexible	Less flexible
8	Corporate Tax (%) (2008)	25	42.2
9	Double Taxation	No	Yes
10	Value-Added Tax (VAT)	Yes	No
11	Internet Users (millions) (2007)	210	80

Source: IMF, Ministry of Statistics and Programme Implementation, India and National Bureau of Statistics of China.

productivity, an appreciating currency, and improved monetary management by the central bank. In recent years it was further lowered to 4.5%. Exports have surged in the past years. Merchandise exports rose 28.9% year-over-year in fiscal year 2007–2008, and 171.1% in 2003–2004.

The last decade saw faster improvements in human development indicators, especially in literacy and life expectancy. Generally, fertility and mortality are lower in southern and western states compared with most of the northern and eastern states. As trade has been liberalized and industry gives greater latitude to relocate more freely, industrial development has become more concentrated in the south and along the west coast. The northern states have fallen further behind. The software export boom has largely been concentrated in the southern and western cities of Chennai, Bangalore, Mumbai, and Hyderabad.

India is often compared to China in terms of economic performance and as a model of potential investment opportunities and economic development. As Exhibit 4.3 indicates, India still lags behind China in most key areas. China had been favored for manufacturing and has developed only a limited business process outsourcing (BPO) industry.

Capital Flows and Foreign Debt

India's improving economic condition has attracted rising international confidence as reflected by the surge in portfolio investment and revision of international credit ratings to investment grade. Net portfolio flows amounted to

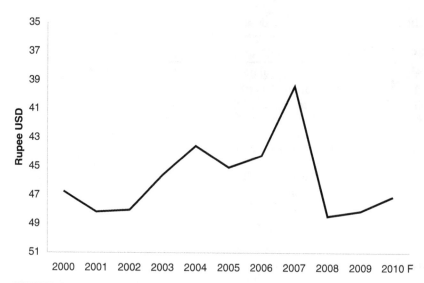

EXHIBIT 4.4 Average Yearly Rupee Exchange Rate vs. U.S. Dollar
Source: Economist Intelligence Unit.

US$12.7 billion in 2007, up from US$11.9 billion in the previous year. Foreign direct investment stood at a record US$41.2 billion in 2008, up from US$25.1 billion in 2007. The fast-growing services sector was the largest recipient of FDI flows. Worker's remittances grew to US$26 billion in 2007, from US$24 billion in the prior year.

India's total external debt rose from US$112.1 billion at the end of December 2003 to US$237.3 billion at the end of 2008. However the ratio of debt to GDP fell from 20.2% to 19.3% over the same period. Commercial finance is increasingly replacing foreign aid. India is still the World Bank's biggest borrower, but nearly one-half of the funds are lent on near commercial terms. India's current debt stock and foreign payment obligations are manageable. Restrictions on external commercial borrowing have been changed to include overseas direct investment in joint ventures in order to allow Indian corporations to diversify into international markets.

India has never defaulted on its external debt, and its external risk assessment is now fairly positive. The rupee has generally been stable against world currencies, including the U.S. dollar, as shown by Exhibit 4.4. It is expected that the rupee will continue its gradual appreciation against the U.S. dollar as its strong economic performance continues. Accordingly, this will tend to create positive appreciation of capital investments made in U.S. dollars (Exhibit 4.4).

The currency remained roughly constant in terms of the government's real effective exchange rate calculation, which takes into account the trade-weighted changes in the nominal rate against a basket of currencies and also relative inflation. The exchange-rate policy focused on maintaining India's external competitiveness.

The Global Outsourcing Trend and India's Human Capital Advantage

India has been one of the major recipients of the growing global outsourcing trend. IT-enabled services (ITES) in India generated revenues of US$40 billion in FY 2006–2007. This industry is expected to be a US$77 billion industry by 2010, growing by 25% annually.

The call center industry has changed from the days of pure low-value-added call handling and transcription services to outbound services, e-CRM (customer relationship management), marketing, credit cards, claims processing, and technical help desk functions. India is moving up the value chain to more mission critical and core outsourcing services of all kinds.

India is well positioned to increase its share of the IT/ITES/BPO global market and become a hub for these services. India's low labor costs; large, and skilled English speaking workforce; conducive policy environment; and government support have given it all of the advantages needed to grow. Some of the major cities and corporate players include:

- Mumbai: E Serve, Efunds, Datametrics Technologies, Amex Information Technologies, IDLX, Spectramind, ICICI
- Delhi: GE-CIS, Convergys, Spectramind, EXL-Conseco, British Airways
- Bangalore: IQ Infotech, iSeva Service, 24/7 Services, Firstring, Msource, HSBC
- Hyderabad: GE Capital, HSBC, Customer Asset
- Chennai: Citibank, Brigade Solutions, World Bank, EDS, Standard and Chartered, ABN Amro
- Pune: Mphasis-BPL, Infinity Data Technologies, WNS

It is likely that India will continue to be an attractive location for more IT outsourced activities, and possibly new industries such as biomedical, health care, and more research and development for a wide variety of industries. India is a country with extraordinary human capital resources with 7 million fresh graduates annually including 350,000 engineering and IT professionals. The human capital pool is said to offer both quality and quantity. India possesses 11,594 colleges and 247 universities. These higher learning institutions are geographically distributed around the country, ensuring a regional distribution of human capital.

Infrastructure

The poor condition of India's infrastructure is a widely acknowledged hindrance to growth. Although the government has made infrastructure a priority, real progress has only been made in the "new economy" telecommunications sector, and recently in road construction.

The poor state of India's infrastructure has negatively impacted GDP and has been one of the ongoing problems for sustaining India's domestic growth as well as attracting and increasing FDI. Inadequate infrastructure in India includes substandard roads, highways, power, water, sewer, rail, metro systems, and airports. Because of lack of planning and large federal and state budget deficits, India's infrastructure suffered from chronic neglect for decades.

India has the most extensive rail network in the world at 63,100 kilometers of rail. The national railway company employs 1.5 million staff. The railways suffer from chronic underinvestment and underpricing, though there is progress on regulatory reform and unsound cross-subsidization policies. Alternative means of raising revenue have been employed, including public and private partnerships, but the option of privatization was opposed by industry unions. The road network has received renewed emphasis in recent years. There are three million kilometers of roads in the country, most of which are badly maintained. National highways comprise just 57,700 kilometers of that total. The National Highways Development Project seeks to expand more than 13,000 kilometers of highway with four and six lanes between India's four metropolitan centers—Delhi, Mumbai, Chennai, and Kolkata as well as the north-south and east-west corridors.

India has 13 major ports, seven on the east coast and six on the west, which are managed by the Port Trust of India. India's ports are plagued by inefficiency. The average turnaround times are around 3.85 days and pre-berth waiting times are around 9.59 hours in 2008–2009. Poor port governance and inefficient customs clearing translate into high costs. The government has attempted to increase private sector participation to boost efficiency and to introduce investment capital.

Economic Summary

India remains challenged by its somewhat weak fiscal position and large agricultural sector, both of which are in need of significant reform. The estimated GDP growth in fiscal year 2009–2010 has been revised downward to

5.9%, reflecting weak monsoons, which depressed agricultural growth. GDP growth was fueled by robust technology and manufacturing exports, but imports grew even faster, leaving an estimated US$4.2billion current account deficit for 2009. Nonresident Indians (NRI) capital flows, although lighter due to the weakening dollar, kept international reserves strong (US$254 billion in 2008). GDP growth is expected to remain high. The pace of economic growth slowed considerably over 2008 and 2009, but remained positive. According to the EIU, all components of India's GDP should expand sharply in 2010. For example, both imports and exports of goods and services declined by about 10% in 2009, but are expected to grow by about 12% and 26%, respectively, in 2010. Private consumption, which grew by just 2% in 2009, is forecast to increase by 18% in 2010.

Weather still affects GDP. A bad monsoon could have a substantial material impact. Essentially, the agricultural sector has been overlooked in India's structural reform efforts, depriving it of the productivity increases experienced by the modernizing manufacturing and service industries.

THE REAL ESTATE MARKET

Market Growth Rate

The market is growing rapidly in all sectors, particularly residential and retail. The last few years have witnessed revenue and profit growth in the residential sector of some submarkets. Though slowing over the past year, strong growth rates may return due to pent-up demand in residential, office, retail, and hospitality.

Industry Potential

The real estate industry has been a laggard until the last few years. There is significant pent-up demand in all sectors, both from domestic and international sources. The fact that the industry has low productivity is a substantial component of potential growth. Real estate and construction appear to be one of the fastest-growing sectors in an economy that shows no sign of slowing in the near term. The real estate market, relative to population and economy size, is an unusually small percentage of GDP.

Breadth of Product Lines

The market is emerging, and there is relatively little product segmentation. As the market matures with the growth of corporate demand, the expansion of the middle class and concomitant buying power, and increasing exposure to international standards, there will be increasing product segmentation in all sectors. One only has to look at the increasing diversity of various types of automobiles over the last five years to imagine a similar product proliferation in real estate.

Number of Competitors

There are relatively few domestic or international competitors relative to the size of the market. The market is young and competitors are relatively unsophisticated. However, both international and domestic competitors are rapidly increasing.

Market Share Stability

The regional and national markets are up for grabs with no major domestic or international player establishing a dominant market area or line of business. There are only a few real estate players attempting to compete at the national level. There are indications of more intense competition on the horizon as competitors are increasingly confident about the sector and their ability to grow and capture market share.

Purchasing Patterns

Domestic consumers are beginning to want and demand international-standard housing, office, and retail space. Many Indians have traveled and lived abroad as is indicated by the large number of non-resident Indians (NRIs). Indians have been overly characterized as "price sensitive." This notwithstanding, the next phase of domestic demand is additionally likely to be characterized by a demand for higher quality and variety, with less emphasis on lowest price. Nearly all Indians desire to own their own residence. Due to increasing population (and households) and the scarcity and cost of urban land, the only feasible possibility for international-class housing will be in the stacked flat, high-density format, much like the housing of Singapore and Hong Kong.

Ease of Entry

The market appears to offer a variety of entry vehicles. The main challenge will be in structuring investments. Real estate FDI is now seen by the government as highly beneficial to the economic development of the country. Therefore, laws will continue to change to favor the attraction of more foreign real estate investment. The trend in investment laws has been to require lower thresholds of capital investment and project size. Thus a broader range of deals will be feasible. There is no securitized (liquid) real estate market open for foreigners. The main avenue is through direct development and partnership with domestic firms.

Ease of Exit

While there is no secondary or securitized market, the number of buyers for Class A, international-standard product far outnumbers the sellers of such assets. In this stage, exiting should not be problematic. However, the range of exit options found in mature markets, such as selling of shares (REITs), IPOs, and limited partnerships is more limited.

Real estate markets continue to gather momentum in all major areas of the country. Mumbai, Delhi, Bangalore, Chennai, and Hyderabad continue to attract interest from IT and high-tech (domestic and multinational) companies who are either establishing a base in these places or are looking for expansion. Driven by the IT/ITES/BPO demand, the suburban locations are witnessing the most development: the suburban business districts (SBDs) of Mumbai, Delhi, Bangalore, and Chennai are all seeing brisk development activity due to easier availability of land, construction of larger floor plates, and offers of build-to-suit (BTS) facilities.

India lags far behind other developing countries in terms of its share contribution of real estate (development and construction) to its GDP. Very low labor productivity in the residential sector reflects low capital investment and a marginalized sector with little international competition. In proportion to the size of its economy, its record of strong economic growth, domestic and international demand, the real estate sector appears to have significant potential for growth. In fact, over half the FDI inflows into China are in the real estate sector compared to less than one-tenth of 1% for India.

Although India has 35 cities with a population in excess of 1 million, most of the investment in real estate is concentrated in five cities (see Exhibit 4.5):

1. Delhi—more popularly known as NCR or the National Capital Region, includes the surrounding rapidly growing townships of Gurgaon and Noida.
2. Mumbai—the commercial and financial capital of India, contributing more than 4% of India's GDP.
3. Bangalore—the emerging software hub of Asia.
4. Chennai (Madras)—a key port and commercial town on the east coast and also referred to as the Mumbai of the south.

EXHIBIT 4.5 Map of India
Source: © Map Resources, www.mapresources.com.

5. Hyderabad—actively promoted as the next-generation tech city by a proactive government and currently plays host to many leading global brands in software and BPO services.

This chapter examines all five cities and the major property sectors within them. More emphasis is given to Delhi, Mumbai, and Bangalore as these are the major metro areas and the leading destinations for real estate FDI.

Real estate has traditionally been viewed by the government as a sector that should be protected from international competition and one that would benefit little from FDI. These views have changed considerably with the passage of real estate FDI legislation in February 2005. Real estate has since been given priority as a means for economic development. The government believes that the real estate sector has a multiplier effect throughout the economy.

PROPERTY SECTORS

This section reviews the main real estate sectors—office, residential, retail, industrial and hospitality—at the national level, with a general discussion of characteristics and trends. Most of the information and data is derived from the primary and secondary market areas of Delhi, Mumbai, Bangalore, Chennai, and Hyderabad.

For the office, residential, and the currently planned, newer-format retail centers, the design, quality, floor plate, materials, and now even property maintenance, are near Class A, international standard. In particular, for office, the level of Class A office is high because this is the most mature sector due to the fact that demand and space requirements have been largely driven by large multinational corporations (MNCs). Residential developments largely borrow heavily from new high-density developments undertaken in the cities of Singapore and Hong Kong. In fact, several of the new residential developments are by firms from these countries.

Office

As much as 50% of commercial space in Delhi, Mumbai, Chennai, and Bangalore was being absorbed by IT companies during 2008–2009. The IT sector growth has led to the emergence of Suburban Business Districts (SBDs) in the suburbs of each Indian Metropolitan city. The Central Business Districts (CBDs) are losing out to SBDs that offer high-quality buildings at lower costs. Specifically designed build-to-suit multitenanted buildings are being developed for such clients.

Properties are usually turned over to the tenant in "cold shell" form— that is, no tenant improvements (TIs), carpet, furniture, and sometimes even without HVAC systems and lighting. Recently, more and more tenants are not only desiring a warm shell—all of the above including TIs but also cubicles for a "plug and play" move in.

The trend for rents for Class A office space has been a gradual decline in per square foot rents in all of the major markets from their highs in the late 1990s. The heights of the 1990s are in many ways artificial because the Indian real estate market was characterized by virtually a complete lack of modern office product anywhere in the nation and sudden, growing demand. As the global economy recovers and more investment capital flows into the sector, these yields are expected to decline in the medium term.

With IT companies targeting less expensive SBD locations, little supply is planned in the CBDs of Delhi, Mumbai, Chennai, and Bangalore. This is marginally strengthening the rental values and causing a fall in the vacancy levels in CBDs. Bangalore is the clear leader in both the current and projected demand for space. However, Mumbai's rate of demand growth is also noteworthy.

At the same time, rental values in the SBDs have remained stable and may come under pressure due to significant supply. Actual gross yields on commercial real estate across metros ranges from 9 to 11%.

Exhibit 4.6 summarizes the salient investment attributes and business opportunities of the office sector nationally. Importantly, the demand for high quality, low-cost office space at the periphery is expected to grow. Secondary cities such as Pune, Chandigarh, and Cochin are likely to see spillover growth.

As the exhibit indicates, demand for Class A office is strong, but supply will no doubt be attracted by high returns. There is an opportunity to ride this expanding tide of demand for international-class office space in the primary markets. The center cores of Mumbai and Delhi offer supply-constrained markets for high rise, Class A office. These conditions and the short supply could spell opportunity as the CBD locations gradually become more attractive given more urban residential development and the increase in outsourced higher-value-added services. However, developing in the CBD is fraught with many challenges in India.

Residential

On the residential front, prices in the SBDs of major metros have been surging in both the luxury apartment segment, due to scarce availability, and mid-market condominium market, which has been driven by lowered housing interest rates. In some cases, the appreciation has been bubble-like as submarkets such as Gurgaon (a popular suburb of Delhi) have seen a 20 to 30% appreciation in capital values in 2008. In the wake of strong economic growth, real estate markets should continue to gain steam. This could result in falling vacancies in the CBD areas and more development in the suburbs.

EXHIBIT 4.6 Office Market Overview

Market Factor	Market Characteristics	Drivers	Future Trends	Business Opportunity
Demand for New Development	Mainly for large BTS developments in suburban locations.	ITES and BPO led growth mainly.	Demand is likely to move towards cheaper locations. Cities such as Chennai, Pune, and Chandigarh to benefit.	Growing demand for Class A, state of the art office buildings in suburban office locations around major cities. Leverage international development and operational experience.
Supply of New Development	Large floor plates, no basements, suburban location.	Capital support and demand for new spaces.	Scalable development concepts to continue, speculative developments would be limited.	Look for more supply-constrained locations such as prime SBDs and infill CBD locations.
Investment Market Support	Insufficient transactions to derive meaningful return data.	Most capital grows from traditional fixed income investments.	Gradual movement towards entity-level investments, vis-à-vis asset-level investments.	Channel U.S. fixed income investment for higher core returns in India. Office demand stronger than most U.S. or foreign markets.
Debt Market	Debt availability is limited relative to recent years.	Abundant liquidity. Less risky lending.	Interest rates could firm up by about 25–50 Bp, putting pressure on asset yields.	Leverage lower cost U.S. and international debt.

India has an acute housing shortage. Under a Special Action Plan on housing, 2 million units will need to be constructed each year—700,000 in urban areas and 1.3 million in rural areas.[2] The government estimates approximately 50 million people in urban areas live in what are officially designated as slums and this number is greatly under reported. Rural housing conditions are also poor.

The growth in the commercial sector has stimulated the residential markets of Indian cities. Essentially IT/ITES/BPO job creation has created demand for high-density housing closer to suburban job centers. This is a new and growing market. Traditionally Indians preferred to live in their own detached bungalow in or near the city center. This is becoming increasingly difficult.

Moreover, there are easily available home loans offering much lower interest rates than have historically been available. Residential developments featuring integrated townships with in-house recreation facilities have greatly spurred demand. The shift toward mid and high-end apartments, with larger floor plate areas means that most of the existing housing stock is defunct for current demand standards. Luxury apartments are found to have nearly unprecedented demand with numerous project launches and complete bookings before launch.

The demand is being fueled not only by India's surging economy, but also because of significant pent-up demand. The existing housing stock across the nation tends to be old and unsuited to the needs of modern living. Moreover, because of the moribund economy prior to the mid-1990s and rent control laws dampening the returns to housing development and property management, very little new housing stock was added (see Exhibit 4.7).

There are concerns that the rapid escalation in housing values will price many out of the market. In the United States, on average, it takes approximately 6 years of median annual income to equal to the value of a single-family house. In Gurgaon, it would take 15 years of median annual income. Ironically the housing price increases and decreasing affordability have been behind the rise and expansion of the residential mortgage market, which, in turn has been a factor boosting residential capital values and demand even higher. Long-term mortgages allow buyers to afford more expensive housing. Mortgages also make it easier to buy a house with only a small down payment. Now it is not necessary to have the full cash payment required to buy a house. This is a dramatic change in the house buying environment, and it is a change that is still transforming the market.

The prime center city areas are witnessing huge demand for land sites for developing high-end apartments. These are generally in the three-bedroom category, targeted towards wealthy occupants or senior executives. With

EXHIBIT 4.7 Residential Market Overview

Market Factor	Market Characteristics	Drivers	Future Trends	Business Opportunity
Demand for New Housing Stock	Mainly in primary and secondary cities. Home ownership on the rise.	Ready availability of housing finance. Mortgages are becoming commonly accepted.	Demand to be mainly restricted in the 1,000–2,000 square feet apartments. In suburban locations.	Development of international standard housing in SBDs and CBDs meeting with exceptionally strong demand. Insufficient supply and development capability. Demand for Class A apartments could be addressed.
Supply of New Housing Stock	Located in suburban locations and redevelopment of CBD properties.	Increased home ownership and take up of housing finance.	To be located next to workplaces in suburban locations of cities. Oversupply not likely soon given the difficulty in finding land and entitling it.	Supply is inadequate. There is an opportunity for further product segmentation. Market is characterized by copycat projects.

(Continued)

119

EXHIBIT 4.7 (*Continued*)

Market Factor	Market Characteristics	Drivers	Future Trends	Business Opportunity
Investment/Developer Market	Short project cycle and abundant capital support first mover advantage to existing players.	Cheap construction finance available to homeowner for purchase of property.	Should be increased domestic and international competition in residential development. Competition for the best deals and development partners to heighten. Look for increased regulation because of unscrupulous developers.	Entry-level equity investment in housing development companies/housing projects likely. Opportunity for lower-cost debt. Flexible mortgage financing not yet widespread. Mortgage industry is fragmented. Branding opportunity and the realization of scale and scope through technological and managerial centralization.
Debt Market	For homeowners: 8% interest rates for a 15-year mortgage.	Construction finance scarce.	Interest rates likely to firm up for housing finance due to hardening of primary lending rates and inflationary pressure in the next year.	More flexible debt structures, higher LTV ratios are possibilities are competitive advantage.

land prices soaring, there has been a rise in the capital and rental values of such apartments. In the leasing segment, landlords are expecting higher rentals for independent bungalows or apartments with a view.

The relatively short development cycle and strong domestic demand are key elements of the attractiveness of the residential market. A clear investment strategy here is to invest in a number of regional residential developers. Demand is so strong that many projects are "self-financing." That is, the deposits and purchases made by buyers completely and in many cases quickly (within months) cover the project costs to create a "negative working capital" situation—unheard of in most markets of the world. In fact, profit can be harvested within a few months of project announcement, leading to some unscrupulous behavior on the part of rogue developers, but presenting an opportunity for a team with a strong domestic and international reputation.

A segment of the residential market almost completely neglected is the Class A rental market. While small, there is no organized, corporate management of apartments in the country. This is an opportunity for an international or domestic firm to create efficiencies and economies of scale in this industry.

The key driver in the residential market from 2005 to 2008 was the drop in the mortgage rate from 14% to 11% in 2005. This was part of a longer-term trend going back to the late 1990s for lower long-term mortgage rates and the expansion of consumer and mortgage credit in the country (Exhibit 4.8). The housing finance institutions were aggressive with loan policies and disbursements due to excess liquidity. This trend reversed, and lending rates are now elevated above 13%, which in addition to inflated housing values, has put severe downward pressure on housing prices.

However, the mortgage market remains small in relative terms and represents only 2% of GDP as contrasted with Malaysia at 23%, Singapore at 36%, and the United States at 52%. The housing sector owes part of its growth to tax concessions (housing loan interest tax write-offs), increasingly important as incomes rise. The residential market is characterized by sales of apartments and developed land plots by the state government agencies and private developers. Across all cities, developers do not lease out apartments; instead all leasing transactions are done through the individual apartment owners.

The residential market has witnessed intense construction activity in recent years due mainly to the premium in condominiums. Developers in Mumbai, Delhi, Bangalore, and Chennai are recording brisk sales. The development of new residential apartments is being driven by the services sector—IT, banking, finance, and retail with most of the new investment clustering around the cities of Delhi, Bangalore, Mumbai, and Chennai.

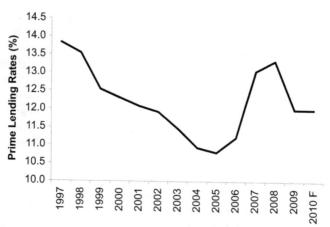

EXHIBIT 4.8   Prime Lending Rates (%)
Source: Economist Intelligence Unit.

The prime residential locations have also seen a slight increase in leasing activity in the suburban locations of Delhi and Mumbai and in Bangalore. Since expatriates prefer leasing independent bungalows and semi-detached houses in Delhi, Bangalore, Mumbai, and Chennai, there has been an increase in rental values for these properties in prime space in the suburbs of Delhi and Mumbai, Chennai, and Bangalore by business executives, which has led buyers to consider suburban locations.

The Retail Sector

The retail sector has been booming in the last few years. India was ranked thirteenth in the world in private consumption expenditure in 2008, at approximately US$675 billion. A very small percentage of retail is organized in a corporate fashion—most shopping areas consist of small neighborhood retail (shopkeepers). The retail sector has been growing quickly, and the organized retail sector is anticipated to grow at a faster rate and to represent a much greater share of the total. Most of the rapid growth will be in the large metropolitan cities. India has been one of the last Asian economies to liberalize its retail sector. The entry of multinational firms is beginning to transform the sector. The retail supply chain and the consumer interest in branded products have grown from scratch.

Global retail players have begun to enter the market, indirectly via the licensee/franchisee route, since FDI is not allowed in the retail sector. All major Indian cities have recently completed infill malls (within the last two to three years) and/or have several malls underway. The retail sector is providing a boost to the commercial sector by increasing the demand from front-office personnel (managers and technical professionals) to back-office workers (clerical, fulfillment, and bookkeeping). The retail sector is also gaining acceptance in the job market and more business schools are focusing on it. The sector is expected to create 50,000 jobs per year over the next several years.

The large Indian retail players include Shopper's Stop, Foodworld, Vivek's, Nilgirls, Pantaloon, Subhiksha, Ebony, Lifestyle, Globus, Barista, Qwicky's, Café Coffee Day, Willis Lifestyle, Raymond, Bata, and Westside. The international players include McDonald's, Dominos, Gautier, Spencer's, Levis, Lee, Nike, Adidas, TGIF, Benetton, Swarovski's, Sony, Sharp, Kodak, and the Shoppe. Most of the foreign companies have to depend on shopping malls for the locations of their outlets, and have had to pay a premium for these locations. There is speculation about whether the government will liberalize the retail sector in the future, allowing direct access by large retailers. If this occurs, the entire retail landscape can change rapidly. Already Walmart is making plans to enter the market.

The Indian consumer is split into three main categories: (1) the high-income urban consumers, (2) the middle-class urban consumer, and the (3) low-income urban and rural consumer. The high-income consumers are willing to pay for choice in quality and selection and desire a complete shopping experience found in larger retail department stores. The middle-income–class shopper prefers quality and competitive pricing. The low-income urban and rural consumer is very price-sensitive and is less concerned about quality and choice and often frequents the local shops. As awareness and disposable incomes rise, the three categories will gradually become less distinct. The larger players will have a growing advantage in the urban areas, where price, quality selection, presentation, economies of scale, efficient operations, and regional and global supply chains are key competitive advantages (see Exhibit 4.9).

Opportunities abound for the foreign investor to create a higher-quality shopping environment and increased retail segmentation—regional malls (large-scale and more horizontal), lifestyle centers, and power centers. Like the residential sector, there is an opportunity to agglomerate operating companies and properties, and fashion them into more organized and corporate operating entities.

The country has gained significant purchasing power with the growth of the middle class, which ranges, depending upon the economic income definition used, between 100 and 200 million persons. The market environment has been steadily improving. The markets in Mumbai, Delhi, Bangalore, and Chennai are booming and undergoing a defining change. A large number of

EXHIBIT 4.9 Retail Market Overview

Market Factor	Market Characteristics	Drivers	Future Trends	Business Opportunity
Demand of New Retail	Rapid growth of retail malls across metros in India. Most of these are vertical, "infill malls."	Higher disposable incomes and growth of food and beverage, retail market.	Demand likely to stabilize with the glut in the initial phases.	Opportunity to segment the market, to improve the quality of the shopping experience and design of centers. Larger, international-class malls and lifestyle centers are lacking.
Supply of New Malls	Largely in suburban towns or new residential hubs.	Speculative developments on the rise. Heavy reliance on attracting foottraffic. Average spend by consumer still low by international standards.	Consolidation likely for mall spaces. Supply could be retarded to address the glut in the market.	Supply does not appear to be constrained in most urban areas.
Investment/ Developer Market	Largely speculative investments tied up at the construction stage. Few investments by institutions on greenfield projects	Supply of malls has spurred interest. Strata title sales on the rise.	Investment will continue to flow to the sector as new markets open up particularly in secondary and tertiary cities.	Investment in mall development companies recommended, and asset level investment to be avoided because of potential oversupply and industry consolidation.
Debt Market	For buy-out of spaces: largely restricted for large anchor tenant, multiplexes and a few well known brands.	Debt less readily available as compared to commercial office space and restricted to anchor tenants and few mall development companies.	Rent discounting for retail malls is likely to be available for short term tenants (<5 years) to tide over risk perception against lending to retail spaces.	Potential opportunity to purchase retail distressed debt if current mall performance worsens.

malls, ranging in size from 50,000 to 400,000 sf are under development in various parts of these cities, including suburbs.

Many prominent retailers believe that increasing disposable income and purchasing power in the middle class is resulting in increased purchasing activity. They also indicate that technology advancement, such as enterprise resource planning software, has allowed them to streamline processes, thereby lowering operating costs and increasing profitability. In addition the entry of international retailers (albeit slowly and primarily as joint venture partners or franchisers) is providing competition to existing players as well as increased choice and awareness for consumers.

However, the retail sector is not without its challenges. Many of the existing shopping malls (albeit poorly designed, located, and merchandised) are failing to attract buying consumers. Shoppers are spending a lot of time, but not much money in the malls, and profits are beginning to fall. Much of the initial success of the first-generation malls is attributable to the novelty of a Western shopping experience. As one shopper quipped, "A lot of people come here just for the air-conditioning. If it looks crowded, it's just because there are a lot of people roaming around aimlessly—not many are shopping."

At the consumer level, attitudes and wants of the consumer are changing with increased awareness levels of products through media (television and the internet are ubiquitous among the middle class) and exposure to Western trends. At the same time, consumers have easier access to consumer credit. Credit cards are now commonly accepted, and many younger professionals have at least one in their wallets. The change is accelerated by increasing numbers of self-employed people (as opposed to salaried workers) both in urban and rural areas, who demand and adapt quickly to new products such as cell phones. Consumers are becoming more sophisticated, demanding higher value and increased differentiation. Consumers are also looking outside the home more and more for entertainment. They are focusing on a combination of convenience and quality of the shopping experience, which requires a diverse product range as well as recreation and entertainment facilities.

Larger formats are being introduced, and a number of malls offering services and facilities to enhance the shopping experience—multiplexes, food and beverage, and apparel—are in the pipeline. Thus far, developers have been fairly successful in leasing/selling space to potential retailers, and therefore construction activity has continued. One of the challenges is that many of the malls are concentrated in specific areas of cities and tend to look alike with similar stores and amenities. Mall developers will have to differentiate themselves in terms of different concepts and target customers, and in new locations.

The Industrial Sector

The industrial market in India is controlled and guided by the state governments, greatly dampening the vitality of the sector, with the exception of the new Special Economic Zones (SEZs)—a sort of free trade zone promulgated by the national government. Transactions primarily consist of direct land procurement from the state and central governments under land disposal schemes launched by the respective agencies. Most of these government "industrial estates" are located in the outskirts of major cities or in the rural areas that are categorized as "backward areas" by the state government as part of the policy to promote investments in these locations.

The key clusters for the manufacture and assembly of automobile and consumer goods are located in Chennai, Mumbai, and Delhi. High-tech assembly and testing operations of leading hardware and peripherals manufacturing firms are clustered in Bangalore and Delhi. Recently, more IT and software firms have been moving into industrial areas in order to take advantage of the significantly lower cost of land. Most state governments have allowed these services to operate from designated industrial parks as part of their overall policy to promote the growth of software in their states.

These industrial locations can be ideal for these back-office processing and call centers. Most of the companies use retrofitted industrial buildings or new premises constructed on the design-and-build approach. The government is also promoting SEZs in the hope that they will boost offshore manufacturing and trading activities (see Exhibit 4.10).

The Hotel and Hospitality Sector

The hotel and hospitality sector displays perhaps the strongest fundamentals of any sector other than residential. Arrival growth, room rate growth, and RevPAR growth rank India's largest cities ahead of all other Asian metros. Moreover, international-class supply is surprisingly low—the hospitality and hotel sector ranked the lowest in FDI. From 1991 to 2004, hotel and hospitality projects amounted to only 0.92% of the total FDI inflow into the country during this period. The serviced apartment market segment has seen strong demand and very little supply.

The hotel market has seen steadily increasing visitor arrivals over the decade. The ratio of the number of rooms versus international arrivals is one of the lowest in Asia.

The Indian tourism industry has performed poorly over the last 18 months, due to a combination of global recession and the Mumbai

EXHIBIT 4.10 Industrial Market Overview

Market Factor	Market Characteristics	Drivers	Future Trends	Business Opportunity
Demand for New Development	Demand is muted as India remains an agricultural and services-based economy.	New manufacturing facilities and distribution facilities, especially for higher-value agricultural products.	Proximity to rail, air, roads increasingly important. Refrigerated warehouse and vertical manufacturing facilities on the horizon.	The Mumbai SEZ offers promise as it is large, mixed-use, and close to congested Mumbai. SEZs offer reduced or no income and property taxes and fast tracked development approvals. Existing assets can be had for low prices given the disorganized state of the sector.
Supply of New Development	Lack of modern, large floor plate facilities.	MNCs, even those in services, will increasingly require modern industrial if only for logistics and storage.	More SEZs are being created, integrated with transportation infrastructure.	There are no major developers involved in industrial development. There is opportunity to sponsor one to cater to future demand.
Investment Market Support	Insufficient Class A space to derive meaningful return data.	Significant international capital sources, such as Hines, are being attracted to these sites.	This should be an important investment sector with India's ongoing economic development.	There could be significant financial interest in the sector if there were more investable assets and companies.
Debt Market	Relatively conservative underwriting terms are used in common practice.	Abundant liquidity. Less risky lending.	Interest rates could firm up by about 2.5–50 Bps by year end, putting pressure on asset yields.	Leverage lower-cost U.S. and international debt.

terrorist attacks. Foreign tourist arrivals had averaged about 5 million per year until 2007, then fell in 2008 and 2009. The premium-tier hotels saw average occupancy levels decline by 10 to 15% over the last year.

The increased service of Indian private airlines across the globe coupled with improved airports will further strengthen the long term bullish trend in the hospitality industry. This will raise the demand for hotel room nights. With only 95,000 rooms in the entire country (Beijing alone contains that number); the size of the hotel industry represents a very small figure for India's size and growth prospects. Based on the forecasted growth in demand, it is expected that another 75,000 to 80,000 rooms will be needed across the country during the next five years to meet the demand (see Exhibit 4.11).

PRIMARY MARKETS

This chapter focuses on the top five urban markets of Mumbai, Bangalore, Delhi (considered primary markets), and Chennai, and Hyderabad (considered secondary markets) to a limited extent.

Mumbai

Mumbai is the largest metropolis in India and the sixth-largest in the world. The city is a major business destination and is the commercial capital of India. Mumbai is the largest port in India, handling the largest tonnage of foreign trade in the country, and it is also the hub for national and international business. It is the headquarters capital of the country, and the city accounts for 70% of business transactions in the country.

Mumbai's population is primarily (about two-thirds) concentrated on Mumbai Island making it one of the most densely populated places in the world, reaching up to 600,000 persons per square mile. With one of the best urban transportation systems in the country, Mumbai is well connected to other major cities in India. Commuting within the city is made possible by the suburban train service that connects south Mumbai with the northern suburbs.

Office   Mumbai recorded the highest level of absorption among all the Indian cities over the last several years. In the Malad and Powai (districts of Mumbai), developers are constructing a large supply of commercial space, catering to the demand of IT and computer companies. In comparison, Bandra-Kurla and Andheri-Kurla Complex have witnessed relatively lower

EXHIBIT 4.11 Hotel Market Overview

Attribute	Market Characteristics	Growth Drivers	Future Trends	Business Opportunity
Demand for Hotel Rooms	High demand, increased leisure and business travel.	Increased travel within the country. Increasing business and tourist arrivals.	Demand likely to increase for the next 2–3 years.	Development of Class A hotels in primary and secondary cities as well as business class hotels is dictated by strong and increasing demand.
Supply of Rooms	Higher occupancy (68%) was recorded in 2008 (an increase of 2.8% over the previous year). Supply of 5D/5/4 star rooms is expected to be about 55,000 in 2012.	Growth of travelers to major cities such as Mumbai, Delhi, and Bangalore.	Supply is expected to pick up due to completion of major projects across India.	The Indian market remains supply-constrained because of regulatory, institutional, legal, and land assembly issues. Most hotel sites are urban infill—the most difficult type of new development sites in the country. Moreover, first class hotels typically require five or more acres. Land prices in India for prime urban sites are among the highest in the world.
Investment/ Developer Market	Restricted to government led disinvestment.	Limited investments market.	Transaction activity may increase in the short term. However, development activity is expected to slow.	New development as well as purchasing and adding value to existing assets, chains, and operating hotel companies are viable strategies to investigate.
Debt Support	Restricted to development of hotel projects. Balance sheet–based project funding.	Leverage for investment buyouts absent. Debt for development projects available.	Look for more debt to compete for project development and recapitalizations.	Lower-cost debt could fund development projects and hotel chain buyouts.

levels of construction activity and will contribute approximately one-third of the total expected supply.

In terms of demand, the IT, ITES, and technology sector have been the main drivers for demand for office space in Mumbai in recent years, especially in the secondary business districts of Malad and Powai. This is due to the lower rental/capital values, superior social infrastructure, and campus-like environments available in these suburbs.

Retail   There is a trend towards occupiers preferring mall space in the city to traditional main street locations. Preconstruction leasing resulted in three anchor transactions in "Inorbit" mall in Malad. Total mall stock in the city has now crossed the 1 million sf mark.

Absorption levels in the retail segment continue to be strong, and rental values are displaying stability, although the escalation in retail values has now ceased. There are several new malls under construction in various parts of Mumbai—a majority are planned in the suburbs. Retail rental and capital values in Mumbai have also remained stable—both in the traditional retail areas (Linking Road, Colaba, etc.) and the suburbs. Yields on retail property have been between 10 to 12%.

Residential   The majority of the demand for leased residential property in the prime locations south of South Mumbai is from executives in multinational firms. The central and western suburban residential belts have also witnessed a significant increase in demand—in part due to continuous relocation of companies south of Mumbai to the northern suburbs. Most of the new supply of good-quality residential space has been in the suburbs such as Gorgaon-Kandivali-Borvali belt and Mulund-Thane-Bhandup belt. In addition, an increasing number of mill lands are becoming available for redevelopment.

Central Mumbai is likely to witness new residential developments. The residential sector in the city continues to grow in terms of supply and absorption levels. This supply, mostly in the middle market, is gearing to meet the high demand from the middle-class population for such housing. Developers such as the Evershine builders and the Ajmera Group are at the forefront of the development of mid-market apartments for the city.

Prominent upper-middle to luxury-class developments are also being constructed in South Mumbai by developers such as Tata Housing and Shapoorji Palloonji. Demand for residential properties in the suburbs has picked up, and values have stabilized during the last years. Yields of residential property in prime residential areas of South Mumbai have been in the range of 6% to 8% for existing stock. If one includes capital appreciation, then yields in recent years for Class A developments in the suburbs of Mumbai have often exceeded 100%.

The suburban locations of Mumbai witnessed strong growth over the last several years. In particular the submarkets of Lower Parel/Parel in the Central belt and Powai, Kandivali (East), Malad, and Gurgaon in the northern suburbs. The demand is fueled by accelerating suburbanization trends among corporations and consequent demand in the surrounding precincts. The quality of apartment developments has increased, and some of the best rank with any high density development anywhere in the world.

Bangalore

Bangalore is the capital of Karnataka State and the fifth-largest city in the country. Situated 5,000 feet above sea level, the city enjoys a good year-round climate and boasts many parks and tree-lined streets. Bangalore is the undisputed leader in software exports. The boom in the Indian IT industry has resulted in Bangalore being designated as the "Silicon Valley" of the Indian IT industry. The city actively promotes and enhances its high-tech status. The city recently completed ring roads and peripheral roads as well as an IT township off Hosue Road.

A major challenge for the city has to do with its own success in economic growth and creating jobs. The city has a boom town atmosphere. Bangalore is one of the leading cities for high-quality and high-paying jobs in the country. It is informally reported that over 1,000 new people migrate to live in Bangalore every day! As a result, the city's infrastructure is greatly overburdened. The traffic at most times moves at a snail's pace. There is no metro rail within the center of the city, which further exacerbates the nearly impossible grid lock traffic most of the day. A new airport, Bengaluru International, opened in 2008, which should help to some degree.

Office The Bangalore commercial market comprises the central area CBD—Brigade Road and Richmond Road, and SBD commercial supply continues to be governed by its ever-growing IT industry. New supply is concentrated in the suburban IT industry centers such as Whitefield, Airport Road, Koramangala, Hosur Road, and Banerghatta Road. The Outer Ring Road is also gaining popularity as a destination for new commercial development—largely due to the easy availability of large land parcels for build-to-suit buildings, easy accessibility, and proximity to IT industry locations.

The areas north of Bangalore between Yalahanka and Devanahalli are also attracting attention due to the recent opening of the international airport at Devanahalli.

The office market in Bangalore has enjoyed stabilized values and absorption rates. Developers maintain their optimism for the future. The quoted rental values have remained stable for Class A buildings in the CBD in spite of significant supply.

In terms of the prime office market, the CBD is a reaching saturation point in terms of fresh development opportunities, and the focus has now shifted towards the secondary locations in the east and south. Investment yields have trended downward and range from 10% to 12%. They have been driven south by increasing supply by developers able to complete a building, from design to final occupancy within a breathtaking eight months. Also there is abundant capital increasingly willing to accept lower returns to have a stake in the Bangalore suburban office market.

The IT and computer, R&D product development centers, and call centers have been the main demand drivers. These companies prefer Class A space with higher ceilings, easy broadband connectivity, and larger floor plates of 35,000 to 50,000 sf. As the IT industry in India is anticipated to grow steadily, Bangalore should continue to be in the lead—demand for international-class office space near IT locations is likely to continue.

Due to the steady demand for smaller leased offices in the CBD, rental values are expected to remain stable in the next two quarters. Capital values are also expected to remain stable over the next year as developers refurbish old buildings in the CBD, creating higher-quality supply. Office space rentals in the suburbs should see upward pressure due to the growing demand for large offices.

The Outer Ring Road area is also gaining popularity as a destination for new commercial developments—largely due to the easy availability of large land parcels for build-to-suit buildings, easy accessibility, and proximity to the IT industry locations. IT companies, R&D product development centers, and call centers have all been the main demand drivers.

Yields on commercial property in the CBD range between 10 and 12%. Capital and rental values have remained steady in the suburbs due to a match in supply and demand. Due to steady demand for smaller leased offices in the CBD, rental values are expected to remain stable due to developers refurbishing old buildings in the CBD and creating high quality supply. Office-space rentals in the suburbs are expected to face upward pressure due to the growing demand for large offices.

Retail Bangalore retail properties had been limited to the main-street locations, but there has been increasing interest in other locations. The reason has been the increase in commercial and residential developments in secondary locations. Retailers of prominent brands are capitalizing on the lower rents and growing catchment areas of these locations. Developers are optimistic about the outlook due to the visible shift in retailer preferences towards malls. Prominent developers are now viewing malls as commercially viable development options. A number of new malls have been developed, and many more are on the way. The demand for these malls, especially the ones located at the Outer Ring Road, IT Corridor, and Whitefield, is expected to grow due to their proximity to office locations.

The traditional retail areas—Brigade Road (CBD), Commercial Street, Jaya Nagar block IV (residential area), and Malleswaram (residential area) have witnessed demand primarily from restaurants (Pizza Hut, Pizza Corner, etc.), departmental stores, and branded super stores. Some demand for smaller leased office space by new companies has been seen in the CBD.

Residential The residential market continues to witness sustained interest from mid-market segment buyers. Responding to this demand, new projects have been launched in Koramangala, Bannerghatta Road, and the surrounding areas. These locations have the largest concentrations of software and computer firms. The area is seeing mixed-use developments with commercial and retail space.

There are a large number of prime residential projects under construction at Sarjapur Road, HSR layout, Whitefield, Kanakapura Road, and Banerghatta Road—residential areas in the outskirts of Bangalore. These projects comprise good-quality residential apartments with amenities such as clubhouses, swimming pools, gyms, indoor games, and so on. Lower interest rates on housing loans have increased the demand, especially in areas such as Banerghatta Road, Whitefield, and Sarjapur Road. Most buyers are young IT professionals who prefer these areas due to the close proximity of their work places, as they are relatively cheaper when compared to accommodation around CBD. Demand for leased residential property in prime residential areas (Central Bangalore) has remained steady.

Delhi

Delhi is more than the political capital of India. In the Indian context, it is the center of national governance, international commerce, education, tourism, and culture. Delhi is a mixture of culture and civilizations.

The city can roughly be split into three major groupings: (1) established commercial, residential, governmental districts of Delhi and the old city of Shahjehandabad (CBD), (2) new commercial districts (NCDs), and (3) the suburban districts of Noida and Gurgaon.

The established commercial, residential, and government district in Delhi is the traditional center of the city and where most of the city's five-star hotels are located.

New commercial districts are now being developed around the periphery of Delhi, principally in the suburbs of Gurgoan in the southwest and Noida to the southeast.

The old city or the walled city of Shahjehanabad is the oldest commercial hub of the city and was the heart of the city until Connaught Place was developed. The region is the location of wholesale commodities, especially in spices, herbal medicines, electrical goods, shoes, and so on. The traditional urban form of narrow alleys and mixed-use developments still commands the highest rental values, but with no new development potential.

Office   The Delhi office market largely comprises the central CBD and suburban business districts SBDs of Delhi, Gurgaon, and Noida. SBDs of Gurgaon and Noida are leading in the supply of high-quality commercial space. The CBD of Connaught Place has practically no new supply—largely constrained due to the unavailability of land, which is in stark contrast to the abundant supply in Gurgaon.

Developers in Gurgaon are responding to the preferences of IT companies by designing buildings with large floor plates (greater than 15,000 sf). Noida on the other hand has new supply and relatively smaller buildings built on industrial and institutional lands. The general congestion of Delhi, parking problems, and poor maintenance of existing buildings have made the CBD relatively less desirable, though rents are considerably higher due to the lack of supply. The recent ongoing construction work on the metro rail and corresponding traffic problems, have contributed to this.

Based on the current estimated and stated timelines, just over 1 million sf of office space is slated to be completed in the National Capital Region (NCR) in 2009. The majority of construction is taking place in the suburban submarkets of Gurgaon and Noida.

Rising vacancy levels and stagnant demand for Grade A space have led to a vacancy rate in the SBD of about 15% for Class A. Yields have been rising and average between 10 and 12% in the NCR area.

The NCR real estate market has seen robust suburban activity that has primarily been supported by strong developments undertaken by several large developers. There has been significant office space absorption, and this momentum is expected to see an upswing only in the NCR region. Significant growth of 25% is expected, the bulk of which would be due to the second-stage growth from the tech firms already established in the NCR. The supply of prime properties by contrast is low. Consequently, there is substantial value-added activity in the form of redevelopment and remodeling of existing Grade B buildings across the NCR.

Gurgaon is expected to continue to outperform Noida due to superior infrastructure, scalability, number of options, and quality of buildings.

Retail   Established retail districts of central and south Delhi are witnessing increased competition from new malls on the outskirts of the city. Mall development continues unabated in Gurgaon, raising the specter of possible glut and inability of infrastructure to cope with traffic. Ghaziabad and Noida in the east also witnessed fast growth in supply and demand of retail space. In Delhi the development authorities have taken a number of positive steps to develop large-format organized retailing areas. Consequently, a number of malls are being constructed in parts of the west and east of Delhi. Over two million sf of additional shopping mall space is planned in the next two years.

Residential   Expatriate demand continues to drive residential leasing markets in the prime areas of Delhi (Vasant, Vihar, Malcha, Marg, Westend, Shanti Niketan, etc.). Increasingly, landlords in the prime areas are redeveloping their independent houses into apartments—often a joint venture with developers who then also take on the responsibility of marketing. This is currently the source of most of the new supply of well-built apartments in the preferred areas of the city.

Although supply in Gurgaon continues to increase with a number of developers putting new projects in the market, real estate values have seen a significant upward movement in the last year.

The supply of good-quality space (both independent houses and apartments) is low, falling behind demand, and thereby increasing the rental values in the prime areas of Delhi. Residential capital values, especially in Gurgaon, appear to be at the beginning of an upward cycle led by speculative and end user demand.

One of the key trends is the new supply of high-end residential properties in the suburbs. Demand was spurred by both end users and investors. There has been increased appetite for suburban properties in the middle-tier price range in Noida and Gurgaon. Leading residential developers are Unitech, Omaxe, and Eldeco.

Both central and south Delhi have witnessed a huge spurt in activity, which was followed by an unprecedented rise in capital values. The increase in demand has given rise to additional apartment development. This trend reflects an increasing standard of living and strong consumer confidence.

SECONDARY MARKETS

The secondary cities offer IT/ITES/BPO firms the opportunity to expand while allowing them to reduce operational costs and maintain diversity in regional skill sets. The secondary markets are touted for their higher growth and greater returns potential than that of primary markets, as they have more to grow, they are less expensive labor markets, and the government tends to be more inclined to grant concessions such as free land and tax holidays.

Chennai

Chennai (formerly known as Madras) is the fourth-largest city of India. The city is well connected to most major cities in India by air, rail, and road. Chennai is also a major port and several passenger vessels dock at Chennai Harbor. The infrastructure of this city is easily superior to all other primary and secondary market cities. The city's government has reputation for being efficient and business friendly.

Office   The market is responding to the demand for high-quality supply. As opposed to many other high-growth cities, Chennai is witnessing a large amount of construction activity within the city limits as well as the suburbs.

The suburbs and industrial estates have large land parcels that can be developed into modern office buildings and also provide ample parking in a less congested environment. The IT high-tech sector continues to be the main demand driver, and companies in these sectors have tended to locate in the suburbs due to the availability of office space with large floor plates and a relatively lower cost, when compared to the CBD.

Infrastructure improvements like the six-lane expressway and the Outer Ring Road in the city are likely to increase the area of development activity in the SBD and in the city. These infrastructure improvements could also accelerate the development of more secondary business micromarkets in the city.

Retail The majority of supply is largely located in the ground and first floor of office complexes or in the form of markets in residential neighborhoods—Anna Nagar, Adyar, and Besant Nagar (with notable exceptions of Spencer Plaza, etc.).

Demand drivers continue to be food chains, apparel stores, and jewelers, and although these retailers have traditionally preferred established retail locations, they are now indicating a preference for spaces in exclusive shopping malls. Unlike other cities, mall development in Chennai has not yet caught up, and it is likely that the market will respond in the medium term. Demand in traditional retail areas has been steady, and rentals have remained stable.

Residential Demand for suburban leased residential property has increased during the last year, primarily due to the increasing numbers of IT/high-tech professionals working in the IT corridor and the falling housing interest loan rates. The suburban residential areas of Velacherry and Mogappair are emerging as residential options, primarily due to their affordability when compared to areas within the city and, to some extent, the proximity of certain sectors to the IT corridor. Expatriates have continued to prefer the traditional areas of Boat Club, Bishop Garden, and Kotturpuram.

There are a number of apartment complexes under construction in various parts of the city. These complexes typically have 8 to 24 apartments and are built on land where old bungalows previously existed. A number of developers are responding to increasing demand for larger complexes with integrated recreation facilities. Many of these tend to be developed in the suburbs where larger land parcels are available. There appears to be an equilibrium of supply and demand in the center of the city; however, in the suburbs, the supply of residential property is expected to outstrip demand, and prices could face downward pressure.

Hyderabad

Hyderabad, located in the state of Andhra Pradesh, promotes itself as the next Bangalore, only better because it is smaller and less expensive. Software exports from the city have grown at a phenomenal rate over the last several years. The city has been known for a progressive stance on economic development. Microsoft Corporation recently completed a major R&D campus in the suburb of the city, hiring more than 3,000 IT professionals to do new software programming.

The government is leading the development of a high-tech business park called INFOCITY. Spread over 175 acres and with complete road, utilities, and IT infrastructure, the park is expected to cost about US$209 million and to create 4.5 million sf of space.

Hyderabad has been experiencing an upward trend in both CBD and SBD rents over the last several years. This is mainly due to the fact that there is virtually no supply of Class A office in the CBD. While nearly all new office development takes place in the SBD, supply volume has been relatively small.

The IT/ITES/BPO sector is expected to continue to be the main driver of commercial space in Hyderabad over the next year. There is a large demand for commercial space in the peripheral areas of Hyderabad. This demand will mainly emanate from the call-center or back-office segment. However, supply continues to match demand, as a number of developers produce high-quality buildings on the market. Yields for Class A range between 12 and 14%.

Kolkata (Calcutta)

Though the second-largest city in the country, Kolkata has lagged behind other major Indian cities in terms of economic development and attracting investment capital, both domestic and foreign. This situation has created a lackluster real estate market with unexciting current and medium-term opportunities. The government has been aggressively marketing Kolkata to attract IT investments.

The real estate sector has certainly lagged other major markets, putting it last in terms of attractiveness vis-à-vis other major Indian real estate markets. The development of the IT parks could provide the impetus for attracting investments in Kolkata in the form of technology companies looking for even less expensive labor. State and city government incentives such as low land prices, investments into campus developments, and build-to-suit facilities all promise to lift the real estate market. But right now they are only plans and promises—more marketing than substance.

Rajarhat is witnessing some infrastructure improvement. A new direct road from the airport to Rajarhat has been constructed. The state government has plans to improve accessibility to the Salt Lake area by connecting it with the underground rail network. CBD rental and capital values from Class A office are high due to very low supply.

Tertiary Cities

These cities are often cited as offering significant investment potential due to the fact they have been heretofore largely bypassed for the larger primary markets. Moreover, their quality of life is relatively high, they have significant numbers of university graduates, and they are lower cost centers—labor, real estate, and the cost of doing business are all lower. A number of leading Indian developers have already identified these cities as priorities, and a few have already made investments there.

Pune   Pune is located about 130 miles from Mumbai. It is known as a university town and is sometimes referred to as the Oxford of India. Its economy is witnessing a transition from industrial activities to increased business in IT, ITES, and BPO. The government is acting as a promoter of this transition. For example, the government of Maharashtra was behind the development of a 238-acre Software Technology Park (STP), operational for the last four years.

The biotech sector has become a new area of focus for the state government. A 43-acre biotech park is being developed by MIDC as Phase II of the STP. Many builders have commenced IT/ITES projects in the eastern suburbs. This area is taking off and caters mainly to build-to-suit developments. For example, the Ozone office project is spread over 80 acres, provides 100% power backup, state of the art telecommunications systems, and ample security.

IT/ITES appears to be the main driver for Pune real estate into the future, Manufacturing along with agriculture will continue to comprise important components of the economy. Capital appreciation is expected to continue as there is a lack of quality supply entering the market. IT/ITES users have to go the build-to-suit option to meet their real estate needs.

Chandigarh   This city of about 1 million lies in the foothills of the Himalayas at the confluence of the states of Punjab, Haryana, and Himachal Pradesh. It is ranked number one in the country in terms of the Human Development Index and the Best City in India in which to live by *Outlook Magazine*. By general consensus, it is the cleanest and best-planned city in India with excellent urban infrastructure and amenities. This is an early market, but it shows considerable promise. The city is attracting attention as a IT/ITES/BPO destination.

Cochin   Cochin is a port city in the state of Kerala on the southwest coast of the peninsula. The city is well known for its high quality of life, scenic beauty, and its highly educated workforce, boasting a literacy rate of nearly 100%. Cochin has well established connections via national highways and railways. It is a major port of the country, located close to main global shipping routes linking Asia with Europe. The airport is one of the newest and most efficient in the country and serves a large nonresident Indian community.

Cochin is beginning to receive IT/ITES investment. There are two major office parks being planned. Both the Port Authority and the Airport Authority have launched special economic zones. The airport site will offer retail, industrial, and residential development sites. The Port will offer residential, commercial, and infrastructure development sites. The port sites will be competitively tendered while the airport sited can be negotiated.

INVESTMENT STRATEGIES

Core Stabilized Office Investment

This strategy entails making equity investments in existing core stabilized office properties in the CBDs of primary urban markets.

This is perhaps the lowest risk and lowest returning strategy. It is attractive in that investments can be executed fairly quickly and easily. There are supply risks, particularly as new Class A office is built in the SBDs surrounding most Indian cities. However, the CBDs remain extremely supply-constrained due to the paucity of developable parcels, excessive regulation, and politics surrounding urban redevelopment. Real estate development can be extremely politicized in India. Upon expiration of their leases, international tenants happily vacate these older urban office buildings for newer true Class A buildings, both within the CBD and the SBD. A value-added play—renovating existing office buildings—is certainly worth exploring (see Exhibit 4.12).

For-Lease Residential Development (Apartments and Serviced Apartments)

There is no organized for-lease residential market in the country. This market could be developed for luxury apartments or serviced apartments.

There appears to be strong demand for professionally designed and managed apartment housing, as well as serviced apartment housing. With the increasing incomes and mobility of urban populations, particularly the increasing trend of young professionals moving to new urban areas, apartments would be a logical real estate need. The increasing number of foreign expatriates from many countries as well as Indian business professionals on assignment has been behind the demand for serviced apartments (see Exhibit 4.13).

EXHIBIT 4.12 Core Stabilized Office Investment

Factor	Comments
Risk Factors	The risk is perhaps the lowest of any investment strategy as there are fewer unknowns. Properties are stabilized—there is no construction risk and there should be few legal or regulatory issues. A drawback is the fact that lease terms in India are much shorter, where 3–5 year leases are the norm, not the exception. However, most tenants tend to renew with the average *effective* corporate tenant occupancy being about 10 years.
Execution and Implementation	India's main nonfarm economic expansion is in the growth of the service sector, particularly BPO, IT, and ITES. However, the outsourcing boom has not been focused on the CBD with core stabilized assets.
Returns	Current returns reflect falling capitalization rates, primarily as a result of rising investor demand. Returns for Class A office in core locations for stabilized office properties range between 10% and 12%. Returns are likely to drop with increasing investor interest.
Reg./Legal	As an existing asset, there should be few if any issues in this area. An important caveat in India, however, is that clear title can sometimes be an issue even on existing, stabilized assets.
Market Size	Large market with opportunities throughout the country.
Competition	This sector faces a fair amount of competition as it has a disproportional number of foreign investors. However, the market can accommodate many more players. The main competition will be from domestic individual and institutional buyers.
Barriers to Entry and Exit	Sourcing of these types of deals can be done easily through direct contact with owners as well as the brokerage community. Exit options are flexible as properties can be held and managed over the long term, can be sold wholly, or sold in pieces in the form of strata title transactions.

EXHIBIT 4.13 For-Lease Residential Development (Apartments and Serviced-Apartments)

Factor	Comments
Risk Factors	While Indian renters tend to be price sensitive, renting may be the only alternative in cities in which affordability is an issue such as Mumbai and Delhi. Factors such as increasing population, surging household formation, and the rural to urban migration spell strong residential demand for some time to come. Increasing housing unaffordability will force many new house seekers to rent, perhaps for many years if current trends continue.
Execution and Implementation	Running a successful rental housing operation will undoubtedly involve a learning curve where trained personnel and market infrastructure are scarce.
Returns	Returns are in excess of 10% for new development.
Reg./Legal	Clear land title, especially when buying from private owners, can be an issue. Tenant rights are a problem in India. Rent increases and evictions might prove difficult.
Market Size	Apartment demand is unproven at this point because this sector does not exist currently in the Indian market. There might be an adoption curve for the domestic population. Serviced apartments are beginning to be built in larger urban areas and are experiencing strong demand.
Competition	There are no organized apartment competitors and only a handful of players engaged in serviced apartment development and operations.
Barriers to Entry and Exit	Exit barriers are extremely low given the strong demand. A stabilized, international-class apartment complex is likely to be in strong demand by a wide range of potential buyers.

For-Sale Residential Development

This strategy entails developing new for-sale residential developments in major urban areas.

This strategy offers potentially high returns. The demand for international Class A for-sale residential far outstrips supply in most urban areas. The greatest demand is for the middle segment of the market. The combination of a buoyant economy, an expanding middle class, historically low interest rates, and a developing residential mortgage market continue to spur strong demand. Middle-class workers in urban areas desire to buy existing bungalow housing; however, it is becoming too expensive or simply unavailable. This investment strategy offers a highly attractive feature of negative working capital and self-financing projects in many cases currently. Risk is low as most projects sell out before construction commences. Unlike the U.S. condominium market, there is very little product defect liability risk (see Exhibit 4.14).

EXHIBIT 4.14 For-Sale Residential Development

Factor	Comments
Risk Factors	Risk is low, as projects typically sell out before construction. Little risk of product liability. Rising sales prices more than cover construction materials price increases.
Execution and Implementation	None for foreigners, except for minimum project size. The preferred strategy would be to partner with a local development firm.
Returns	This is the highest returning strategy today, both in percentage returns and absolute cash returns. Strong demand and rising sales prices have boosted returns in 2004. Yields in excess of 80% are common, and equity IRRs can exceed several hundred percent. In some cases, no project equity is required.
Reg./Legal	Clear land title, especially when buying from private owners, can be an issue. So far, construction remains relatively unregulated with virtually no unions.
Market Size	The market size is immense, especially considering the fact that there is still unmet pent-up demand built up over the last decade. This is the single largest real estate sector in the Indian market. Factors such as increasing population, surging household formation, and the rural to urban migration spell strong residential demand for some time to come.
Competition	There are relatively few competitors and only a handful of national players.
Barriers to Entry and Exit	Exit barriers are extremely low given the strong demand.

Hospitality—Five-Star Luxury Hotels and Business-Class Hotels

Demand is strong due to increased business and leisure travel both from domestic and international customers. New international-class hotel demand is strong with occupancies exceeding 90% for quality product in some large metros.

Demand is likely to increase substantially in line with the continued expansion of the economy and as international arrivals increase. Currently there is a relatively low supply of new hotel rooms. In particular, the demand factors for five-star hotels *and* mid-tier business hotels appear strong.

The domestic Indian business traveler has long suffered with the deplorable state of most domestic Indian hotels. With his increased sophistication and exposure to global standards, the domestic Indian traveler is demanding an international-standard quality for a reasonable price (see Exhibit 4.15).

Land Investment/Land Banking

This strategy would entail buying or optioning (undeveloped or with some improvements) land and holding for a period of three to five years and then either selling and/or developing portions of the site.

The greatest real estate capital appreciation in the country in recent years has been in land—not just any land, but urban land in high-demand locations. Land that is income producing, that is improved but below highest and best use, would help pay for the cost of carry. The attractions of this strategy are numerous. Land prices in many locations around India have been escalating faster than improved real estate. This strategic option is attractive because it is the simplest. As the real estate and construction markets continue to grow, it is likely that appreciation will continue to be robust (Exhibit 4.16).

Mortgage Industry

This strategy would involve an investment in a growing Indian mortgage company.

The mortgage industry is nascent and growing quickly. The volume of mortgages as a percentage of GDP is among the lowest in Asia. With the expanding middle class, the growth of consumer credit, and the demand for international-standard housing, the mortgage industry is estimated to be

EXHIBIT 4.15 Develop Luxury and Business-Class Hotels

Factor	Comments
Risk Factors	Hotels are a sector closely tied with the current economy and political situation. An economic or political shock could adversely and immediately affect this sector. One only need recall the effect of 9/11 on the American hospitality industry, the effects of which were felt for nearly two years. A recent Indian example is the 2008 terrorist attack on the famous Oberoi Hotel in Mumbai.
Execution and Implementation	No unusual risks.
Returns	IRR returns could exceed 30%.
Reg./Legal	No unusual risks.
Market Size	As FDI is well below relative per capita adjusted levels of other countries, business as well as tourism travel should increase rapidly. Business and tourism travel for a country of India's size are remarkably low. If India's growth rate continues to be robust, then hospitality will be in great demand.
Competition	There are existing domestic and international chains, but with relatively few hotels. There is no competition currently in the business-class hotel strategy.
Barriers to Entry and Exit	No unusual barriers.

one of the largest in the world in five to eight years. Mortgage finance is undergoing a revolution in domestic finance, where heretofore the pattern has been to pay cash for most real estate transactions. There is growing popularity and acceptance of home mortgages. There is room for additional product development and segmentation. Currently, most mortgages only offer a LTV ratio not exceeding 70% with mostly fixed rates (usually no better than 7.5%) and a relatively short term from between 15 and 20 years (see Exhibit 4.17). Demand continues to grow from India's young population (forming separate households from their extended families in increasing rates), rising incomes, cultural goals for home ownership (especially for the nuclear family), growing home prices, and low affordability (obviating cash purchases in many cases).

EXHIBIT 4.16   Land Investment and Land Banking

Factor	Comments
Risk Factors	The main risks for land banking are essentially twofold. First, land title, especially for privately purchased land in the country, can be murky. There is no title insurance industry. There are lawsuits regarding land title constantly reported in the daily press. Second, government regulations for real estate FDI require some degree of development progress to be made. In other words, they discourage and prohibit land banking and land speculation. However, entitlement and approvals (planning, zoning, design clearance) can take years—sufficient time for this strategy to be executed.
Execution and Implementation	There are relatively few barriers to entry.
Returns	Returns could be several hundred percent.
Reg./Legal	Clear title and laws requiring development (discouraging speculation) are the main barriers. Squatters during the investment period could also be a problem. They would have to be removed at disposition or lease.
Market Size	The market is quite large. Indian cities are rapidly urbanizing. The rural-to-urban migration trend is likely to further accelerate with the growth of urban economies and the continued decline of the agricultural economy. Urban land will become increasingly scarce.
Competition	Many local players engage in land investment. It is a competitive market, no doubt. A foreign investor could enjoy a capital and scale advantage over most of these players.
Barriers to Entry and Exit	The barriers to exit include market timing. There have been two cycles over the last 13 years.

Office Development for Lease

This strategy involves the development of Class A office and R&D and the leasing and management of space long term.

The demand for office space in the SBDs of the major urban areas will continue to grow as outsourcing grows. The nature of demand is also changing. Increasingly, office users prefer to lease their spaces, not to own. In fact, as is typical in the United States, users would prefer a "plug and play"

EXHIBIT 4.17 Mortgage Industry

Factor	Comments
Risk Factors	The right partner company would be key. There is considerable interest rate risk as the Indian economy is prone to oil, inflation, and monetary supply shocks.
Execution and Implementation	Finding the right partner, conducting extensive due diligence, and monitoring the terms of the partnership going forward.
Returns	High. Difficult to estimate.
Reg./Legal	There would have to be government clearance to invest in the home mortgage industry.
Market Size	Enormous, perhaps growing to a several hundred US$ billion market within the next five years. It may be the single largest market in the world after China.
Competition	There is no domestic or international competitor focusing on this niche at present.
Barriers to Entry and Exit	Few.

model in which they take relatively short-term leases of fully-fitted-out space (see Exhibit 4.18).

Office/R&D New Development for Sale

This would involve the development of new or the purchase of existing office/R&D assets and their sale to domestic and international buyers.

The demand for office and R&D space is being fueled by the continued expansion of IT/ITES/BPO. With growing outsourcing by MNCs and the cost advantage of the Indian service sector, office demand will grow. At the same time, much of the existing office and R&D supply is largely outdated and defunct. Users, whether MNCs or domestic (Infosys, Satyam, TCS) are demanding international-standard space. Chennai, Pune, and Hyderabad, or even tertiary cities such as Chandigarh and Cochin are likely to benefit further due to their comparative cost advantages. There is also likely to be more appreciation in these markets as they have not moved as high as the primary office markets. This sector offers the advantage of having a large market of ready buyers or users (see Exhibit 4.19).

EXHIBIT 4.18 Office Development for Lease

Factor	Comments
Risk Factors	Market risk, construction costs, development timing.
Execution and Implementation	Many projects are begun without being fully leased up. The safest strategy would be a build to suit with a credit MNC. This may not be possible in every case, and it may be undesirable to have a single tenant occupying the majority of the space.
Returns	IRRs tend to be in the 20s. The major component of return will be through capital appreciation and realized at the sale of the building.
Reg./Legal	Office buildings and parks tend to be encouraged by local governments as they are seen as job creators. Thus entitlements are likely to be fast-tracked and incentives such as low-cost or free land, income and property tax holidays are widely available, particularly in secondary cities eager to attract new job-creating investment in high tech and BPO.
Market Size	The market size is large, given that BPO/ITES is the main driver of economic growth in the country and the growth of domestic demand.
Competition	There are relatively few competitors and only a handful of national players.
Barriers to Entry and Exit	A class A, fully leased building will likely have many buyers upon stabilization.

Special Economic Zone Developments

This strategy poses a very interesting set of rewards and risks. The rewards consist of the opportunity to control a large amount of developable urban land, reaping the enormous capital appreciation of land values in urban areas. The risks are that the project could be a black hole, drawing capital and resources for an excessively long investment period without economic return. Many of these projects require significant horizontal development before vertical development can commence.

These projects are immense, requiring, typically, hundreds of millions of dollars and very long investment horizons—often exceeding five years. Because of the large scale, capital-intensive, and open-ended nature of these projects, there are many unmanageable and unknown risks. However, these projects can be highly successful as well (see Exhibit 4.20).

EXHIBIT 4.19 Office and R&D Development For Sale

Factor	Comments
Risk Factors	First-class office and R&D is experiencing strong demand, which is expected to continue.
Execution and Implementation	Few risks, except for minimum project size and investment.
Returns	Returns tend to range between 18% and 35%.
Reg./Legal	Clear land title, especially when buying from private owners, can be an issue. So far, construction remains relatively unregulated with virtually no unions.
Market Size	Large and expected to grow. The largest market demand is for large floor plate, Class A office in the SBDs.
Competition	Several regional and only a few national developers.
Barriers to Entry and Exit	Exit barriers are extremely low given the strong demand. Assets can be sold in whole or in pieces via strata title.

EXHIBIT 4.20 Special Economic Zone Developments

Factor	Comments
Risk Factors	Risks are high because of many unknowns. Not just in the large size of the projects, but in their high-profile nature, their political implications, and the fact that significant horizontal development must be put in place before any vertical development can be done. Many of these projects require the displacement of poor squatters.
Execution and Implementation	These are complex investments with many deal parameters to negotiate. Huge capital requirements, technical and financial capability needed.
Returns	Indicated returns are in the range of 30% for the Mumbai SEZ for example. Because India's cities are choked with congestion and infrastructure grossly underdeveloped, SEZs offer a special opportunity for an integrated, planned working and living environment. However, cost overruns can be extreme and could wipe out all returns.
Reg./Legal	These projects are highly visible and political. Entitlements could take many years.
Market Size	There are relatively few SEZs in the country. Like the Mumbai SEZ, they tend to be very large and capital intensive.
Competition	Relatively limited because of enormous size of these projects and their complexity. Only the largest investors and developers can undertake them.
Barriers to Entry and Exit	These are not single assets, but campuses or even new townships. Exiting is no simple, one-time transaction.

EXHIBIT 4.21 Retail Development

Factor	Comments
Risk Factors	Risk is high as there have been very few successful retail ventures in the country to date. There is a paucity of international expertise in the planning, design, and management of first-rate retail malls.
Execution and Implementation	Finding suitable parcels large enough to accommodate regional and lifestyle centers is challenging. Direct foreign retailers are precluded from the market. Domestic anchors cannot pay high rents.
Returns	Reported returns are in the mid teens, but actual return numbers are virtually nonexistent.
Reg./Legal	Direct foreign investment by retailers is still precluded, but this is likely to change. Sales (VAT) tax is low.
Market Size	The Indian market is quite large—one of the largest in the world due to a substantial middle class estimated at 100 million and growing. Buying power, while low, is expanding with growing incomes and the development of widespread consumer credit. The demand for international goods and brands is growing.
Competition	This sector is dominated by local developers who have produced subpar developments—not international class centers.
Barriers to Entry and Exit	Unless developments are executed to a high international standard, there is the possibility of being superseded by the next generation of retail development, which is undoubtedly around the corner when direct retail FDI is allowed.

Retail Development

This strategy would involve investing in new retail development in urban areas. Most of this new development would be retail malls.

The retail sector has been viewed as the most challenging of the primary real estate investment sectors. There has been much development activity, but mixed financial returns. It is widely recognized that the Indian consumer has been starved for modern retail. In recent years, there have been a large number of "mall" developments in the major metros. These are vertical infill developments, most of which are ill-planned and poorly executed. As a result, retail development has a dubious reputation. Sales are slow, and most

EXHIBIT 4.22 Transit Oriented Development (TOD)

Factor	Comments
Risk Factors	The greatest risk would perhaps be the fact that these sites are typically owned by some type of government agency (local, regional, federal). Thus the interactions with the government would be slow and political.
Execution and Implementation	Significant time to invest working with various levels of government. The main barrier is the opportunity cost of time vis-à-vis other investment opportunities taking far less time.
Returns	Difficult to estimate.
Reg./Legal	This strategy would involve some form of public and private partnership—always complex. These transactions would also fall under the category of privatization—politically sensitive, especially in the case of railroads—considered an essential public good in India.
Market Size	There are thousands of TOD sites in India.
Competition	There is no domestic or international competitor focused on this niche at present.
Barriers to Entry and Exit	Could be a messy collection of diverse assets, including diverse operating businesses.

Indians go to the mall to walk around in the air conditioning, not to shop. There is a perception that malls are overbuilt. This may or may not be true depending how one views the effectiveness of existing retail developments in meeting demand (see Exhibit 4.21).

Transit-Oriented Development (TOD)

Transit-oriented development would seem to offer significant potential in a country were the most heavily trafficked sites are transit-oriented.

The roadway system is highly congested in most urban areas. It will be difficult to increase the number of roads because of the system of property rights, high land costs, and the general contentiousness of most large-scale public initiatives that involve relocation. Indian cities are some of the most densely populated in the world. Rail systems will increasingly be the most viable way to get around cities. The rail sites are often some of the most prime locations in Indian cities. Many of these sites are government-owned and are grossly underutilized both in terms of physical coverage as well as their economic use. TOD sites could be developed for retail, office residential, and industrial uses (see Exhibit 4.22).

NOTES

1. *The Economist*, February 21, 2005. "Let it Shine," *The Economist*, February 19, 2004.
2. Government of India, Special Action Plan on Housing (2008).

CHAPTER 5

Brazil

INTRODUCTION

Brazil benefits from a large and growing economy, a growing urban population and youthful demographic profile, expanding real estate market capitalization, lessened levels of systemic market risk, and proven political and financial stability. Furthermore, strong capital appreciation and high rental growth rates were recorded in real estate markets of the country during its economic recovery from 2004 through the middle of 2008. Going forward, we believe that this robust performance will likely continue despite a temporary slowdown brought on by the global recession. The case for Brazil is very strong relative to other South American countries, and to emerging countries elsewhere in the world, given its favorable ranking on all major indices of market attractiveness (such as market capitalization, economic size and growth rates, level of urbanization, and market risk). Although in the short-term real estate pricing has suffered along with other asset classes worldwide, 2010 may provide a very good window of opportunity for market entry.

Brazil is the world's fifth-largest country both in terms of area and population. It is currently the world's eighth-largest economy,[1] and is expected to be the world's fifth-largest economy by 2050.[2] Brazil's enormous size and sharp regional disparities require a more nuanced view of investment potential (see Exhibit 5.1). The aim of this chapter is to analyze the market and to discuss investment strategies for each of the four main property types, considering local drivers as well as the outlook for supply and demand.

OVERVIEW OF THE MARKET ENVIRONMENT

As with China and India, Brazil's stock of real estate has not kept up with the quantity and quality required by businesses and households, given the strong pace of economic growth, job expansion, and buoyant consumer demand. It has most certainly not kept up with the considerable pent-up demand for new housing. The upgrade of its sovereign long-term debt—by all key ratings agencies—to investment grade, bodes very well for investment conditions. The mid-to-long-term trajectory of development and growth continues to portend strong growth. Forecasts from a range of sources suggest Brazil's economic growth rate was less affected than most countries in the world, and the effects of the global recession will likely be mild.

In spite of the global economic slowdown in 2009, Brazil's performance to date proves it has weathered the storm well. Its economy is broad and balanced and not overly dependent on exports to any one other country. Indeed, exports as a percentage of GDP are very low by world standards. For the past year or more, a heightened rerating of risk has been a feature of the new world of investment. Inflationary risks, which had challenged many developed and emerging countries around the world, have currently abated. We believe the fundamentals of Brazil's economic and fiscal management appear very strong—both relative to its own history and relative to peer emerging countries and, increasingly, compared to the world's mature and developed markets.

The country has enormous catch-up potential relative to the developed global economies; with vast natural resources, sizable pools of labor, and high prospective investment rates. Its debt position is vastly improved, having moved from being the world's largest emerging-market debtor, to a net foreign creditor by January 2008. Brazil's fiscal policy is strict and responsible, and its political environment is stable. A large foreign exchange reserve is expected to continue to cushion Brazil in further global volatility while its relatively underdeveloped credit market has, to date, been less affected by the current problems plaguing global credit markets.

The Economic and Institutional Environment

We believe that there is a strong macroeconomic case for investment in Brazil over both the long term and the short term, given its size and growth momentum. Despite the negative growth recorded in early 2009, Brazil's economy rebounded strongly with many output indicators at or approaching pre-crisis levels by the end of the year.

GDP   Global growth slowed in 2008 and contracted further in 2009, in the deepest global fall since the Great Depression of the 1930s. During

EXHIBIT 5.1 Map of Brazil
Source: © Map Resources, www.mapresources.com.

the third quarter of 2009, forecasts stabilized, and, due to some upward revisions for some of the major developed economies, the world GDP growth rate for 2009 was revised up by 0.5%. Brazil's economic resiliency was proven during the recent global recession whereby it recorded just two consecutive quarters of negative growth (4Q 2008 and 1Q 2009). It was one of the last major economies to enter recession and one of the first to return to growth, while the decline in output was relatively mild. Compared to other major economies, Brazil and Japan are the major global economies forecast to rapidly equal or surpass their long-term average, as early as 2010 (Exhibit 5.2).

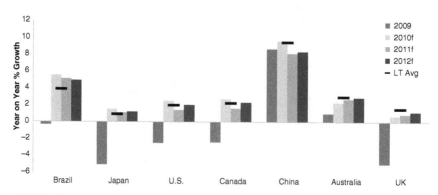

EXHIBIT 5.2 Global Economic Growth Forecast
Sources: Thomson Financial Datastream /EIU, ING Real Estate Research & Strategy, as of October 15, 2009.
Note: Geographies ranked, left to right, by the difference between their forecast GDP growth rate of 2010 and their average long-term GDP growth rate ("LT Avg" stands for the "long-term average," a blended simple average of 10-year historic data and the 5-year forecast: 1999–2013f); "f" refers to forecast numbers.

Even though it slowed down due to the global downturn, Brazil's average economic growth rate remains impressive for several reasons. Of the 15 largest economies in the world, only China and India are forecast to have higher growth rates than Brazil from 2010 to 2012. Notably, it must be highlighted that China and India are lower-middle income countries, while Brazil is already an upper-middle income country with lower natural growth rates.[3]

The average rate of real GDP growth per annum between 2000 and 2007 was 3.4%, higher than the 2.6% rate of the 1990s or the 1.6% rate of "the lost decade" of the 1980s, in which GDP per capita declined. Per capita income may likely decline in 2009 as a consequence of the downturn (Exhibit 5.3), but is forecast to regain the upward trend by 2010.

Brazil weathered the global macroeconomic and financial crisis due to its relatively small credit markets, a diversified economy, a large domestic sector, and a fiscally responsible administration.

Brazil has been generally less affected than other markets for several reasons:

- Credit markets form a tiny proportion of the Brazilian economy compared to the U.S. and European markets, and other places currently beset by the credit crunch.

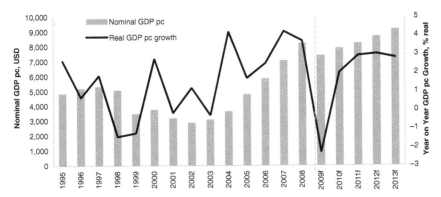

EXHIBIT 5.3 Brazil's GDP/Capita and GDP/Capita Rates of Growth
Source: Economist Intelligence Unit, ING Real Estate Research & Strategy, as of September 28, 2009.

- Brazil's administration is proving to be fiscally responsible.
- It is becoming politically and financially less risky for international investors on a number of indicators explored below.
- It is a net exporter of both food and petroleum.
- It has a wide range of trading partners globally.
- It draws upon a broad economic base, while rising domestic consumption will likely be a key growth engine beginning in 2010 (EIU, as of September 2009).

Trade and Commodities The Brazilian economy has been significantly transformed in the past few decades. Traditionally, agriculture and mining have been important contributors to economic growth, and although both sectors have recently reaped record high prices on global markets, the primary products in the first eight months of the year composed around 43% of Brazil's exports compared to 45% from manufacturing and 13% from semimanufacturing.[4] As the economic crisis hit developed markets and depressed demand for foreign products, Brazilian exports of goods initially fell, but have since staged a solid recovery. The decline in manufacturing exports (cumulative 12 months figure as of August 2009 was −20%), was much larger than the decline in primary products (−2% for the cumulative 12 months figure).[5] Even so, manufacturing still represents the highest share of Brazilian exports of goods.

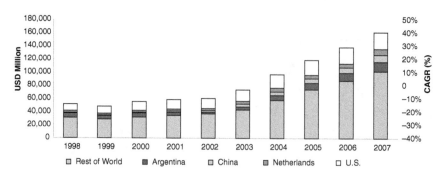

EXHIBIT 5.4 Main Markets for Brazilian Exports
Source: Thomson Financial Datastream/OECD/IMF Direction of Trade Statistics, ING Real Estate Research & Strategy, as of June 9, 2009.
Note: "CAGR" refers to "compound annual growth rate." "Rest of World" refers to other countries not elsewhere mentioned on the graph.

Brazil's trade surplus was the twelfth-largest in the world in 2007 but the current account deficit is estimated to have been –1.8% of GDP in 2008 and will likely remain negative (although smaller) for the coming years. Brazil exports its goods to a diversified group of markets (Exhibit 5.4), and the United States has traditionally been its major trading partner, although representing less than 14% of total exports of goods in 2008.[6] Despite the traditionally closer trade links to the United States, Europe, and to a lesser extent, Japan, trade links with Asia are growing. In fact, China (including Hong Kong) is now the leading destination for Brazilian exports, with a 15% share of the total exports for the first half of 2009. Although part of this effect might be temporary, due to subdued demand from the United States, which was harder hit by the economic crisis, and a boosted demand for commodities from China, there has been an effort to strengthen economic links with China.

In the past few years, Brazil has moved from a net importer of oil to a net exporter and if recent announcements by Petrobras (the state oil company) of major offshore oil discoveries prove true, Brazil may rank among the world's leading oil-producing nations within the coming decade.[7] In 2007 and in 2008, oil accumulations were found in several exploratory blocks in the Santos Basin off the southeast coastline. These accumulations were named Tupi, Bem-te-vi, Carioca, Parati, Caramba, and Jupiter. The large oil deposits found near the Tupi field could have 8 billion barrels of recoverable oil equivalent, according to Petrobras.[8] The company has announced that some of the fields in the Santos Basin exceed previous estimates. Forecasts

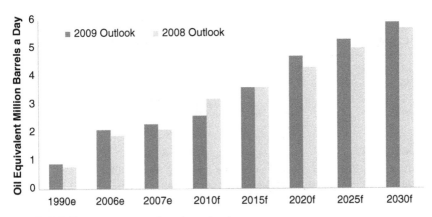

EXHIBIT 5.5 Brazil's Liquid Fuel Production
Source: U.S. Energy Information Administration, International Energy Outlook May 2009, ING Real Estate Research & Strategy, as of September 28, 2009.

by the U.S. Energy Administration forecast that Brazilian fuel production will grow steadily for the next two decades (Exhibit 5.5), and the long-term outlook as of 2009 has improved even further compared to the 2008 outlook.

Economic growth through the 1980s had been highly correlated with trade with both the UK and the United States (Exhibit 5.6). More recently, trade links with China have been especially strong. As a consequence, Brazil currently has no significant economic correlation with the Europe 15, the UK, or the United States, broadly suggesting that diversification benefits may be achieved from investment exposure to Brazil.[9] By contrast, the stronger trade links have shifted the relationship towards China, and Brazilian economic growth now appears strongly correlated to Chinese growth. Whereas export growth to the United States and to other Latin American countries has been growing by around 10% each year, exports to China (from a smaller base) have been growing at almost 30% per year.

Foreign Direct Investment   Quite aside from the export sector, the Brazilian economy benefits from other strong sectors. Brazil's gross fixed investment (GFI) as a percentage of GDP is still low compared to most emerging markets; thus there is considerable further potential for GFI to improve. Now that investment-grade status has been attained for Brazil's sovereign debt (by S&P and Fitch as of April and May 2008, and by Moody's in

EXHIBIT 5.6 Brazil's Economic Growth Correlation with Selected World Markets

1981–1992	Brazil	1993–2008	Brazil
Brazil	1.00	Brazil	1.00
China	0.41	China	0.66
Europe 15	−0.23	Europe 15	−0.08
India	0.34	India	0.09
UK	0.65	UK	−0.13
U.S.	0.53	U.S.	−0.13

Sources: ING Real Estate Research & Strategy, as of April 2008.
Highlighted coefficients indicate significant correlations assumed at 90% (1.645/√12 for 1981–1992 and > 1.645/√15 for 1993–2008).

September 2009), foreign investment volumes may improve over earlier forecasts (Exhibit 5.7). This is because many funds have a mandate to only invest in markets with the investment-grade rating. This may bode well for demand in the real estate sector.

Inflation Spiraling high inflation rates have frequently marred periods of strong growth in Brazil. Inflation is expected to have peaked in 2008, with the subdued economic activity and relatively low energy and commodity

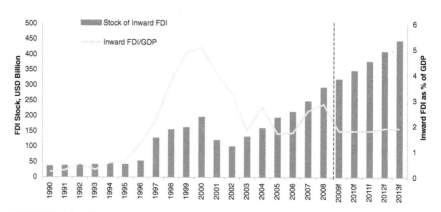

EXHIBIT 5.7 Foreign Direct Investment (FDI) in Brazil
Source: Economist Intelligence Unit, ING Real Estate Research & Strategy, as of September 30, 2009.

prices taking pressure off the inflation rate in the short term. Although a rebound in the global economy may spur increased inflationary pressures, we believe the risks of extremely high inflation are minimal compared to earlier periods.

The current administration in Brazil continues to demonstrate a highly responsible policy, which bolsters its credentials as one that is serious about targeting inflation. The administration appears to be firmly committed to the Fiscal Responsibility Law, and this has served to strengthen investor confidence. Brazil's Central Bank raised the benchmark policy rate (the SELIC rate) in April 2008, ending a period of over two-and-a-half years where it had been cut 18 times. The rate was raised again several times to reach 13.75% in September 2008. The trend changed again in January 2009, when the Central Bank began a series of sharp cuts in an aggressive attempt to support economic activity. The previous period of rate rising allowed room to cut rates as needed, unlike in most other major economies (Exhibit 5.8).

Currency   Brazil introduced a free-floating exchange rate in 1999. Although there is no official target for the exchange rate level, the Central Bank of Brazil actively intervened in the markets to contain appreciation

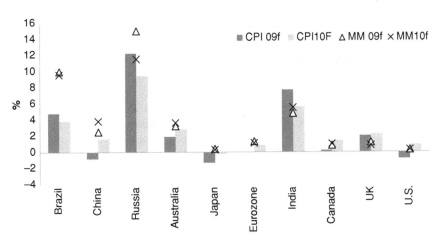

EXHIBIT 5.8   Consumer Price Index ("CPI") and Money Market Rate in Selected Markets
Source: EIU, ING Real Estate Research & Strategy, as of September 30, 2009. Countries are ranked by the higher spread between the money market rate and the CPI rate for 2009.

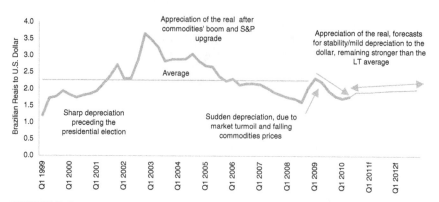

EXHIBIT 5.9 Brazilian Real to USD spot exchange rate
Source: Thomson Financial Datastream, ING Economics forecasts as of September 14, 2009, ING Real Estate Research & Strategy, as of September 15, 2009.

during 2007 and 2008. However, the interventions were limited, and the Real strengthened against the U.S. dollar by 20% during 2007 and continued to strengthen until the end of August 2008, in part because of high commodity prices and the widening spread between Brazil's policy interest rate, the SELIC, and policy rates of most developed countries. The Real then started a trend of depreciation in which it devalued almost 60% until December 2008, when the depreciation trend finished and the real started appreciating again. We believe that the outlook for the real depends on the extent of weakening of global growth and the success of the measures taken by the Brazilian government. The long-term outlook may also depend on global commodity prices, as the real appears to be historically correlated with these prices. Many forecasters anticipate a broadly stable path through 2010 and 2011, with risks to the upside. In the base case, the Real might remain stable or depreciate only slightly to the U.S. Dollar, due mainly to the general strengthening of the U.S. dollar against many of the major currencies (Exhibit 5.9).

Political Risk   President Lula has governed since the end of 2002, after easily winning a second term in 2007. Polls through 2009 have given him very high approval rates.

With the economic recovery, we believe that risks of social discontent have eased and the era of political stability will likely continue. Aside from strong political leadership, deeper structural and institutional changes have been put in place, which have been secured by an expanded middle class. This suggests that regardless of political leadership in future decades, institutions should have sufficient strength to maintain stability. Therefore, although the current crisis might take a toll on the governing party and the next elections might bring a change of party, we believe that political stability is likely to be maintained.

Population and Demographics   The population of Brazil is estimated at more than 191 million.[10] It is a highly urbanized country with some 86% of Brazilians living in cities, a proportion that rose from 75% in 1990. This equates to circa 165 million urban dwellers in 2009, and both the number and proportion of urbanized Brazilians continues to grow. Brazil has the fourth-largest urban population in the world.[11] Current forecasts have the total Brazilian population surpassing 200 million in the year 2012 (Exhibit 5.10).[12]

Brazil's youthful demographic profile is a tremendous asset for its real estate investment potential. The median age in Brazil is currently 28.6, and this will increase to 32.2 by 2020. The median age is not forecast to surpass 40 before 2050.[13] Brazil is aging at a much slower pace than Europe, Japan, North America, or emerging markets such as China or Russia. As of 2009, there are over 96 million Brazilians aged between 15 and 44, and this is forecast to stabilize at over 100 million in 2020.

Exhibit 5.11 illustrates the young population profile of Brazil, especially relative to North America (which in turn has a young profile relative to Europe and Japan), for 2009 and 2020. An important indicator of Brazil's

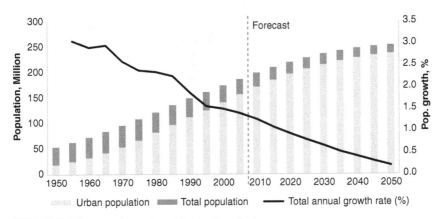

EXHIBIT 5.10   Brazil Total and Urban Population
Source: UN population division, as of May 2008.
Note: Size and annual growth rate are calculated for five-year periods.

BRAZIL

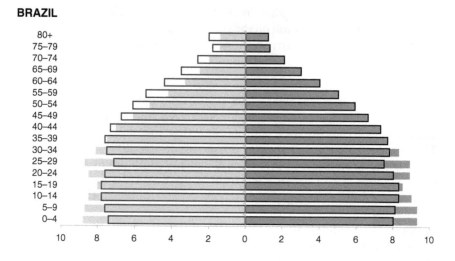

U.S.

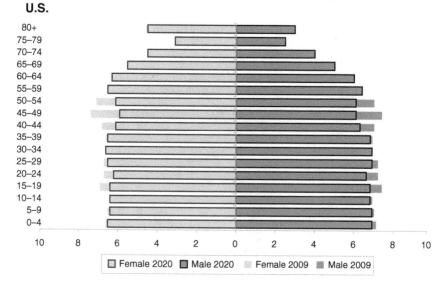

☐ Female 2020   ☐ Male 2020   ☐ Female 2009   ☐ Male 2009

EXHIBIT 5.11   Population Profiles Estimated for 2009 and 2020: Brazil and the United States

Source: U.S. Census Bureau; ING Real Estate Research & Strategy, as of February 3, 2009.

potential is that demographic, demand-driven growth—notably in urban areas—should be a feature of the country for several decades to come. The total dependency ratio in 2008 is estimated at 49%; with children rather than the elderly comprising the vast majority (81%) of dependants.[14] This ratio is below those observed in developed countries, but above other developing countries like China.[15] However, the Brazilian ratio is expected to lower through the coming years and to peak towards 2050 at 56%, around when that demographic transition should have completed.[16]

Brazil is divided into 27 federal units or states, which includes the federal district where Brasilia, the capital, is located. The states are grouped into five broad geographic regions, and they vary enormously in their size and characteristics. Several Northern states (those in the Amazon Basin) are very new, having formed only in the past few decades with migration into those areas. The Northern states are rapidly growing yet remain very small, underdeveloped, and remote. In contrast, São Paulo state alone would be the second-largest economy in all of Latin America (after only Mexico) if it were a separate country. The state of São Paulo contributes over a third of Brazil's GDP (Exhibit 5.12) and nearby states in the south and southeast are also among the largest economically. The states of the southeast and south also contain 58% of Brazil's total population and a considerably higher share of the country's wealthier households (see Exhibit 5.13).[17]

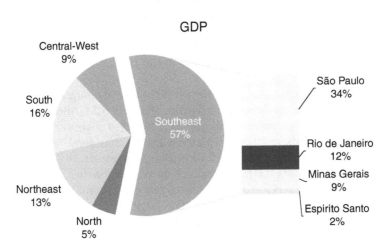

EXHIBIT 5.12 Comparative Economic Size (GDP) of Brazil's Regions/States (% of total)
Source: IBGE, ING Real Estate Research & Strategy, as of January 22, 2009.

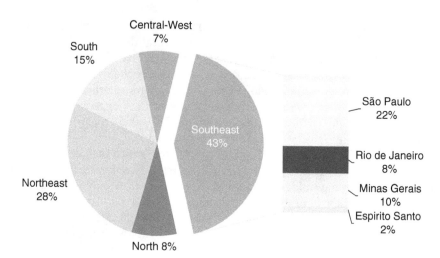

EXHIBIT 5.13 Population Size by Brazil's Regions/States (% of total)
Source: IBGE, ING Real Estate Research & Strategy, as of January 22, 2009. Data refers to year end 2006.

Brazil is further divided into over 5,500 municipios. Fourteen of them have populations greater than one million, another 23 have populations greater than half a million but less than one million, and a further 62 municipalities have populations between 250,000 to 500,000.[18] Indeed two of the world's most populous metropolitan areas are located in Brazil. As of mid-2008, the greater São Paulo metro had an estimated population of almost 20 million, while Rio de Janeiro's total metro area is home to more than 11.5 million inhabitants, according to the June 2009 population data from IBGE.

When Brazil's pattern of urbanization is compared alongside that of the United States, there are several similarities (Exhibit 5.14). Both countries have a few very large cities in the top tier, but also a sizable number of second-tier and third-tier cities, which must also be considered as potentially investable markets for international institutional investors.

Exhibit 5.15 ranks the municipalities by the size of their GDPs. It can be observed that the services sector is the largest contributor to the economy of most of the richest municipalities. The large economies of São Paulo and Rio de Janeiro are underestimated here, as the municipalities which border them—and which compose the broader metropolitan area—are also sizable and add to the economic might of the overall metropolitan region. For example, the large and comparatively wealthy municipalities of Barueri, Guarulhos, São Bernardo do Campo, and Osasco are all located on the

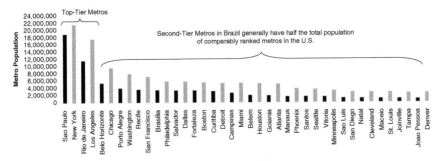

EXHIBIT 5.14   Urban Systems of the United States and Brazil Compared
Sources: Moody's economy.com, citypopulation.com compiled from various sources, as of February 2008.
Note: Brazilian metros are coded black and U.S. metros are coded gray.

borders of São Paulo municipality and together comprise the São Paulo metropolitan area.

Income   Income inequality is a negative feature of Brazilian society and has been entrenched in the country for centuries. Brazil exhibits one of the world's highest Gini coefficients, a statistical measure of income inequality within countries. On the positive side, the current administration has done much to improve the uneven distribution of wealth. Broad policy changes of benefit to the entire population have been combined with policy interventions targeting the poorest strata and those among the working poor most at risk of falling into poverty. To date, these policies have been very successful and have gained sufficient traction to ensure that the great gulf between rich and poor is not widened and that the middle classes continue to expand.

The middle class has expanded rapidly in the last few years, and as of 2009 it comprised 52% of the total population in the country. In the period 2002–2008, the middle class expanded considerably, and the lower segments have decreased even more, from 43% of the total in 2002 to 32.5% in 2008 (Exhibit 5.16).[19] Additionally, the middle class has not only expanded and inequality has diminished, but the total income level of the middle class has increased as well. Such a positive development in Brazil contrasts with the erosion of the middle classes in some developed countries where high debt burdens, job insecurity, and falling values of household assets are translating into weaker real estate demand.

Relative to the national distribution of household income, the states and metropolitan regions of the south and southeast, along with the capital Brasilia (Distrito Federal) in the central west, have a far higher

EXHIBIT 5.15 Office Market Overview

Rank 2006	Rank 2005	Municipality	State	GDP (000s USD)	% Services	GDP pc (USD)
1	1	São Paulo	São Paulo	129,751,755	64%	11,778
2	2	Rio de Janeiro	Rio de Janeiro	58,696,794	66%	9,565
3	3	Brasília	Distrito Federal	41,115,672	83%	17,248
4	5	Belo Horizonte	Minas Gerais	15,011,978	69%	6,255
5	4	Curitiba	Paraná	14,749,562	64%	8,247
6	7	Manaus	Amazonas	14,640,821	38%	8,671
7	6	Porto Alegre	Rio Grande do Sul	13,814,997	70%	9,587
8	10	Guarulhos	São Paulo	11,772,612	56%	9,174
9	8	Barueri	São Paulo	11,690,022	69%	44,022
10	9	Salvador	Bahia	11,042,639	65%	4,069
11	11	Campinas	São Paulo	10,837,337	55%	10,230
12	16	Campos dos Goytacazes	Rio de Janeiro	10,603,336	15%	24,678
13	15	Duque de Caxias	Rio de Janeiro	10,351,284	52%	12,107
14	12	Fortaleza	Ceará	10,338,639	67%	4,278
15	13	São Bernardo do Campo	São Paulo	9,436,952	46%	11,739

Source: IBGE, ING Real Estate Research & Strategy, as of January 2009. Data as of end 2006. 1USD = 2.18 BRA.
Note: "% services" refers to the service sector share of GDP and "GDP pc (USD)" refers to GDP per capita in USD.

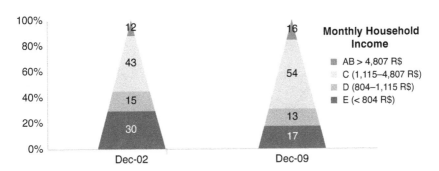

EXHIBIT 5.16 Income Distribution
Source: Getulio Vargas Foundation, as published in *Epoca*, ING Real Estate Research & Strategy, as of February 18, 2009.

proportion of households earning above the minimum salary.[20] According to the Instituto Brasileiro de Geografia e Estatística (IBGE), the northern and northeastern states have high proportions of households earning less than the minimum salary. These regional distinctions are sharp and suggest that investment in the south and southeastern states and metros may be more compelling.

Two important indicators of the purchasing power of Brazilian households are (1) personal credit and credit delinquencies, and (2) motor vehicle sales. Both indicators have proved to be sensitive to economic downturn in other parts of the world.

Brazilian car sales rose dramatically in the mid-2000s based on strong household income growth and the wider availability of credit. The growth in domestic vehicle sales is a logical outcome of relatively low fuel prices, public transport systems under pressure in all cities, and real rising household incomes, often as a result of dual incomes being earned. Brazilian vehicle manufacturers have also recorded strong production and export figures. However, motor vehicle sales slumped in the final months of 2008, partly due to the weaker foreign demand and partly due to the worsened internal economic outlook and the first negative employment figures.

The volume of personal credit outstanding in Brazil expanded from R93 million in July 2007 to more than R140 million by May 2009. Delinquency rates (including payments more than 15 days behind) have been little changed since July 2007 (Exhibit 5.17). Figures for the business sector show a slight increase in the delinquency rate, but still a very low rate of 3.9%, which we believe (together with the increased lending and declining interest rates) points to a strengthening of the credit markets.

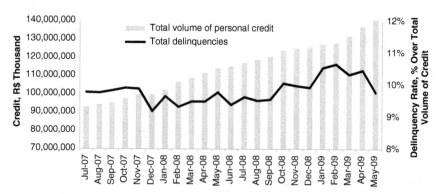

EXHIBIT 5.17 Personal Credit Delinquencies in Brazil
Sources: Banco Central do Brasil and ACREFI (Associacao Nacional das Instituicoes de Credito, Financiamento e Investimento), as of September 30, 2009.

Employment The economically active population has grown impressively in Brazil over the past few years (Exhibit 5.18), and the rate of unemployment in Brazil's major cities has trended downwards (Exhibit 5.19). In stark contrast to the high and still rising unemployment rates of most other G20 countries in late 2009, Brazil's economy generated positive job growth and the unemployment rate began moving down.

Economic growth in all sectors of the Brazilian economy from 2003 to 2007 generated upwards of 2.2 million jobs.[21] Labor force participation rates in the large Brazilian cities are quite high, and they were stable in 2008

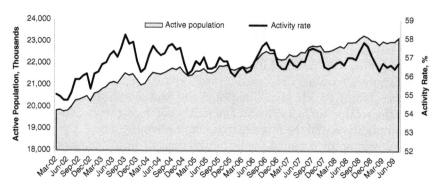

EXHIBIT 5.18 Economically Active Population in Urban Brazil
Source: IBGE, ING Real Estate Research & Strategy, as of September 30, 2009. Data up to July 2009. "Data" refers to the six largest urban areas in Brazil: São Paulo, Rio de Janeiro, Belo Horizonte, Porto Alegre, Salvador, and Recife.

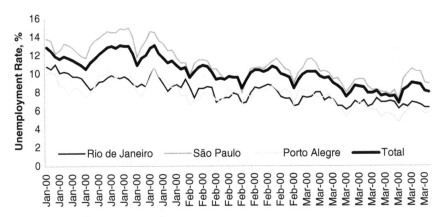

EXHIBIT 5.19 Urban Unemployment in Brazil
Source: IBGE (SIDRA), ING Real Estate Research & Strategy, as of September 15, 2009. Data up to July 2009.

after a general upward trend. The average participation rate in the country as of July 2009 was 56.7%.[22]

THE REAL ESTATE MARKET

Brazil can be characterized as a growth-oriented market. There is ample opportunity to innovate and to build market share. The inherent returns in many strategies can be very high. The country represents an enormous opportunity; however, there are many risks having to do with market strategy, location, and timing.

The for-sale residential industry has boomed in recent years and should continue to enjoy healthy fundamentals as demand continues to outstrip supply. Mass housing development in the for-sale category should continue to do well as Brazilians have little propensity to participate in the rental market. We believe that home builders targeting developments in well-located submarkets of first- and second-tier cities should continue to do well in the coming years.[23]

The industrial sector is dominated by owner-occupiers. Build-to-suit and sale-leaseback are potential opportunities, especially when credit-worthy tenants present opportunities to outsource the management of their buildings. New infrastructure—ports, airports, and ring roads—is being developed/planned throughout Brazil on a massive scale. The development of distribution facilities at strategic locations relative to this new infrastructure will likely be necessary. Despite the short-term slump in foreign trade caused by the global economic downturn, exports and imports are expected to continue growing at a very fast pace once the downturn is over. Given the increasing volume of imports expected (partly due to a wealthier population and rising consumption levels), logistics facilities near the main centers of population and located on key infrastructure should respond well to demand. São Paulo's industrial rental growth in 2007 at 30% (the sixth-highest in the world for the year) and 46% in 2008 for Rio de Janeiro (the highest rental growth that year). Rental growth for 2009 has eased from those strong rates of growth, as the economic downturn has hit demand. But there remains a shortage of good stock.

For the office sector, strong rental growth and capital appreciation characterized the main markets over the period 2006 to 2008. The global economic downturn has put a damper on rental growth and capital appreciation in the short term, and with rents remaining stable in São Paulo. Supply and demand fundamentals vary widely by submarket and must be considered closely. We expect the weakened rates of absorption due to economic deceleration to pick up now that employment is expanding together with the recovery of growth in the services sector. Currently, vacancy rates are at relatively low levels in Rio de Janeiro and São Paulo but will likely edge higher, and rental growth will likely be more modest than in the past few years. Nonetheless, Brazilian office occupancy costs are still relatively cheap by global standards. Prime properties with credit worthy tenants are likely to perform well in the medium and long term. Retrofitted buildings, especially in the highly constrained markets with out-of-date supply, may provide good opportunities. The market could be entered through codevelopment and retrofit strategies. For European or North American multinational tenants (where environmental considerations may matter in home jurisdictions), there may be a premium to be paid for a "greener" building in Brazil as there are very few of these currently.

Retail confidence and sales continue to be much more robust in Brazil than in other major markets, despite a slowdown in the first months of 2009. Brazil still has an overall shopping center penetration ratio (gross lettable area per capita) that is quite low considering the average purchasing power of its consumers. Those municipalities and states that have low current shopping center penetration relative to their size and wealth have been identified for development through joint venture with local partners. Additionally, the middle class is growing and becoming wealthier, which will likely expand the consumer base of shopping centers. Smaller malls, anchored with grocery chains or department stores, could do well in smaller, second-tier cities, which are currently underserved. We believe the continued expansion of the middle class and the home-building boom suggests that shopping centers located near areas of high population growth, and with the appropriate tenant mix serving new household formation, might do well.

Characterizing the Real Estate Market

The market growth rate is high and seemingly sustainable. Investment has been largely focused in the primary markets of Rio de Janeiro and São Paulo; however, secondary markets also offer compelling growth dynamics. Growth in Brazil is underpinned by surging global and local demand—GDP growth, incomes, population, urbanization, demand for higher quality product, and other factors are strong and will continue to fuel real estate.

Industry Potential

The real estate industry holds enormous potential. Primary and secondary markets are expanding at a considerable rate. Brazil is an agricultural, commodities, and industrial juggernaut. The growth in these three areas is creating a gigantic demand for all sorts of real estate—residential (for-sale, service apartment, and rental), office (CBD and R&D), retail (malls, power centers, shops), hotel (luxury and business class), and industrial (warehouse and logistics, particularly at the ports), with double-digit GDP growth on a large base, and much of this growth is concentrated in the large cities.

Breadth of Product Lines

Product lines are still emerging, and some do not exist at all. There is significant pent-up demand for many different types of real estate product. There exists a large potential for significant product segmentation in both the luxury segment for the middle tier to respond to the growing wealth and quality-seeking middle-class population. There is also significant demand for affordable housing.

Number and Quality of Competitors

The competitive field is not overly crowded, though there has been increasing interest from institutional investors in Brazil over the past decade. The quality of the competition ranges considerably. Most are new companies lured to the high returns and the perceived glamour of real estate development. Most of these companies are inefficient, have little knowledge of best practices, and produce dubious-quality product. There are few regional players and national firms. Many firms are relatively unsophisticated with most personnel having limited real estate experience.

Ease of Entry and Exit

Entry and exit are rather easy in contrast to comparable emerging market countries. Nevertheless, market entry into this large and complex country should be carefully planned. The market is not completely transparent. It is relationships-driven. Relationships must be developed with business partners as well as with local, regional, and national government officials initiating major investments in the country. A wrong early misstep could be costly.

Technology and Productivity

In general, building technology and productivity are only slightly below international standards. However, by and large, the real estate and construction industries are characterized by inefficient techniques and technology resulting in sub–Class A product. São Paulo and Rio de Janeiro tend to have the best developers and construction capabilities, and are attracting the vast majority of foreign investors and developers.

PROPERTY SECTORS

Office

Office demand has been driven by a general expansion of the Brazilian economy (see Exhibit 5.20). The performance of the broader Brazilian economy led to strong demand in the financial and business services sector in recent years. Accounting, consulting, insurance, legal, and other business services benefitted from the growth in manufacturing, agribusiness, and mining. An increasing number of multinational and domestic firms have absorbed this space. Global events of 2008 and 2009 led to much greater caution in any expansion plans. But with some stronger confidence levels returning, looser monetary policy, and the rebound in the overall Brazilian economy boosting employment numbers in the second half of 2009 (as discussed in the previous chapters), the forecast for 2010 may see stronger absorption of space in the main office markets.

The finance sector in Brazil had been growing rapidly until the Global Financial Crisis. Banking activity thrived under what were more favorable credit conditions, although credit still represented a much smaller role in the economy relative to more developed economies. The strong performance of the equities sector in 2006 and 2007 also spurred expansion of office occupiers. According to data from the *World Federation of Exchanges*, São Paulo's Stock Exchange had the sixth-greatest expansion of domestic market capitalization in the world between December 2006 and December 2007—at

EXHIBIT 5.20 Office Market Overview

Market Factor	Market Characteristics	Drivers	Future Trends	Business Opportunity
Demand for New Development	Strong demand for office space, particularly in major cities.	Rapid growth in urban population and service sector, expanding white collar employment.	Demand is likely to grow even stronger as the market continues to mature.	Growing demand for Class A, state of the art office buildings in primary markets.
Supply of New Development	Concentration in primary markets, improving design and quality.	Macro trends including demographic growth, urbanization, and increasing commodity demand fueling strong GDP growth.	Scalable development concepts to continue, speculative developments will be limited until end of global recession.	Institutional-grade investment will be concentrated in primary markets of Sao Paolo and Rio de Janeiro, though opportunities exist in secondary markets as well.
Investment Market Support	Increasing interest from institutional investors, including a growing number of country-focused investment vehicles.	Most capital flows from traditional fixed-income investments.	Gradual movement towards entity level investments, vis-à-vis asset-level investments.	Channel U.S. fixed-income investment for higher core returns. Office demand stronger than most U.S. or foreign markets.
Debt Market	Debt availability is limited relative to recent years, and the cost is higher than in more developed countries.	Higher interest rate environment than many mature markets.	Expanding FDI may bring new debt providers as well.	Leverage lower cost U.S. and international debt.

over 90%.[24] Brazil's was also the world's ninth-best-performing broad market index (local currency terms, % change 2006–2007) with almost 44% growth, according to the *World Federation of Exchanges*. Figures turned negative in 2008, and the Brazilian stock exchange fell by 44% in local currency, in line with most markets around the world (which was a better performance than the main indices of the other "BRIC" countries). In 2009, this trend changed, and the BOVESPA index has recorded positive returns staging a strong year-to-date rebound.

White collar employment has been increasing in its share of total employment over the past several years—from just over 12% in 1Q 2002 to roughly 15% by mid 2009 (IBGE, June 2009). The share of white collar employment has remained stable through recent months despite the economic downturn, suggesting the "business" sector has been less hit by the crisis to date. One broad indicator of the expansion of Brazil's corporate sector is the number of firms that have made the "Forbes Global 2000"—those 2,000 companies worldwide that are the largest in terms of market cap. As seen in Exhibit 5.21, only 13 Brazilian firms made this list in the year 2003; however, the 2008 listing identified 34. Although these firms cover a range of industry sectors, all occupy some office space and furthermore have the need for related financial and business services in order to compete in domestic and global markets. Such healthy medium-term expansion of the corporate sector bodes well for ongoing need of modern and efficient office space.

São Paulo is by far the most sizable office market in the country; not surprising given that almost 1.5 million employees in the office sector (financial, real estate, other office services) work in the metropolitan region of São Paulo, around 45% of the total in the country.[25] It is firmly established as the country's commercial center and places in the ranks of the world's top 20 financial centers. Rio de Janeiro ranks next with almost 800,000 office sector employees in the metropolitan region. Both São Paulo and Rio have a number of office submarkets with quite specific characteristics (noted further below). At this point these two cities appear to be the only office markets of sufficient size to be of interest for most international institutional investors.

Second-tier cities with less important office markets include Belo Horizonte, Curitiba, and Porto Alegre. Belo Horizonte has the largest total office employment of the three, with more than 330,000 people, as of May 2009. The strictly financial services employees are a relatively minor share of the total (each city has between 20,000 and 25,000 financial services employees).[26] Brasilia is a distinct market in Brazil due to the predominance of public sector employment within its services sector. Among the first- and second-tier municipalities mentioned above, the public sector composes less than 13% of services sector employment.[27] For Brasilia, however, as the national capital, the proportion is much higher at 49%. There are, nonetheless,

EXHIBIT 5.21 Brazilian Companies in the Forbes Global 2000

2010 Rank	Company	Industry	Assets (US$ Billions)	Market Value (US$ Billions)
18	Petrobras-Petróleo Brasil	Oil & Gas Operations	198.26	190.34
51	Banco Bradesco	Banking	281.4	54.5
52	Banco do Brasil	Banking	406.46	42.78
80	Vale	Materials	100.81	145.14
82	Itaúsa	Conglomerates	342.63	28.74
235	Eletrobrás	Utilities	58	15.95
478	CSN-Cia Siderurgica	Materials	16.74	25.3
620	Usiminas	Materials	14.78	14.26
658	Tele Norte Leste	Telecommunications Services	16.73	7.99
698	JBS	Food, Drink, & Tobacco	24.37	12.18
701	CBD-Brasil Distribuição	Food Markets	10.33	9.54
732	Metalurgica Gerdau	Materials	26.23	7.42
782	Cemig	Utilities	10.44	9.25
864	CPFL Energia	Utilities	7.02	10.16
919	Braskem	Chemicals	12.68	3.58
930	BM&F Bovespa	Diversified Financials	12.17	13.17
942	Redecard	Business Services & Supplies	10.01	10.2
953	BRF-Brasil Foods	Food, Drink, & Tobacco	14.76	10.75
980	Fibria Celulose	Materials	16.25	8.72
1102	Cielo	Business Services & Supplies	1.61	11.03
1190	Ultrapar Participacoes	Oil & Gas Operations	6.37	3.87
1316	Sabesp-Saneamento Basico	Utilities	11.61	3.89
1335	Bradespar	Diversified Financials	5.08	7.67
1380	CCR	Transportation	5.22	9.31
1399	Natura Cosmeticos	Household & Personal Products	1.57	8.22
1432	Banrisul	Banking	16.41	3.38
1461	OGX	Oil & Gas Operations	4.18	29.3
1472	Copel	Utilities	5.51	5.66
1486	Embraer	Aerospace & Defense	9.04	3.96
1648	WEG	Capital Goods	2.49	6.04
1680	Net Serviços	Media	4.78	4.31
1705	Fosfertil	Chemicals	1.79	4.81
1813	Sul America	Insurance	7.14	2.47

Source: Forbes, April 21, 2010.
Note: The Forbes 2000 list refers to the world's largest 2000 public companies ranked by a composite score based on sales, profits, assets, and market value.

almost 33,000 financial services employees there, although much of the office-occupying workforce is employed by the government, and much of that is believed to be in government-owned buildings. Thus, although it is Brazil's third-largest city in terms of GDP, size of its services sector, and finance employees, Brasilia is a special category because of the heavy influence of the federal government functions concentrated there. As most government departments have tended to own the buildings they occupy, opportunities in Brasilia are not expected to be as attractive to international investors as the deeper and higher-grade markets of São Paulo or Rio.

Following continued economic development and increasing investment activity, office yields have experienced a notable and steady compression in Brazil since 2003, and further compression is anticipated over the medium to longer terms, especially if Brazil retains the investment-grade status achieved in 2008, as we expect it to do.

Retail

The first shopping centers were built in Brazil's largest cities in the 1960s. An important wave of shopping center development took place in the 1990s and the share of all retail sales transacting in shopping centers is now close to 20%. There were 385 shopping centers in Brazil as of June 2009, according to the national retail organization.[28] This is up from around 150 shopping centers barely a decade ago. This figure is much lower than in Mexico—with a little over half the population of Brazil—where there are over 1,000 shopping centers and malls. New construction and consolidation of ownership is anticipated in the coming years. We believe that favorable socio-demographic trends suggest the demand-side fundamentals are strong, and with shopping center rental default rates and vacancy rates both around 2%, the property type appears to be well positioned (Exhibit 5.22).

Though the pace of increase has decelerated amid the recent economic downturn, retail sales have generally been surging in Brazil over the past decade (Exhibit 5.23). The economic recovery has been quick, strong, and based largely on private consumption, but a more cautious environment globally remains, so we expect modest retail expansion plans in Brazil to return gradually and remain below the relatively strong growth rates of the past few years.

The strength of retail sales in Brazil during most of 2008 and the quick recovery was unsurprising considering the bullish results of retail confidence surveys. Strong consumer confidence indicators bode well for continued rental growth for new retail formats in the medium term, except in places with supply-demand imbalances. As seen in Exhibit 5.24, the index survey from Brazil declined in the final months of 2008, but has recovered quick and strong, ahead of the other selected countries of the Americas

EXHIBIT 5.22 Retail Market Overview

Market Factor	Market Characteristics	Drivers	Future Trends	Business Opportunity
Demand for New Development	Rapid growth of retail malls across major and secondary metros.	Real income driven by higher wages and increased productivity; change in consumer behavior. Expanding consumer credit.	Growth of consumer class with discretionary consumption.	Larger, international-class malls and lifestyle centers are expanding. Opportunity to segment the market, to improve the quality of the shopping experience and design of centers.
Supply of New Development	Mainly in primary cities and expanding in secondary markets.	Surging middle class and rising household income. Low retail supply relative to other emerging markets.	Consolidation likely for mall spaces. Emergence of national and international players in the market.	Supply is constrained in primary market core areas. Additional development potential in outer edges and in secondary markets.
Investment Market Support	Short project cycle and abundant capital support first mover advantage to existing players.	Supply of malls has spurred interest.	Investment will continue to flow to the sector as new markets open up particularly in secondary and tertiary cities.	Opportunities in both regional retail malls and grocery-anchored community and neighborhood centers.
Debt Market	Plenty of commercial lending from domestic banks for now.	Increased development activity will drive construction lending.	Increasing international presence may bring additional lenders to market. Rates will likely rise as inflationary pressures increase.	Opportunities exist if Brazilian government and domestic banks curtail lending.

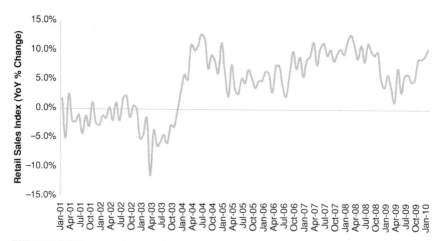

EXHIBIT 5.23 Brazil's Retail Sales Index Growth (2003 = 100)
Source: Thomson Financial Datastream/IBGE; ING Real Estate Research & Strategy.
Data up to August 2009, as of October 2009.
Note: "YoY" refers to year-over-year.

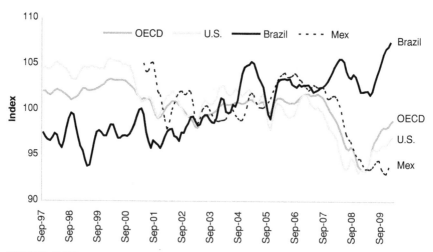

EXHIBIT 5.24 Brazilian Retail Consumer Confidence
Sources: Thomson Financial Datastream; Organization for Economic Cooperation
and Development (OECD); ING Real Estate Research & Strategy, as of October 15,
2009.

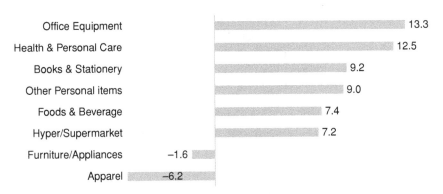

EXHIBIT 5.25   Retail Sales Year-over-Year Growth by Category (year to date as of August 2009 over August 2008)
Source: Thomson Financial Datastream/IBGE; ING Real Estate Research & Strategy, as of October 15, 2009.
Figures on the graphic are percentage growth figures.

and the OECD, and reaching levels close to the all-time highs of 2005 and early 2008.

Additionally, the "Fundaçao Getulio Vargas" has published consumer confidence data up to September 2009, and indices for current and future conditions show a positive evolution, far from the bottom in April and very close to levels of one year ago.

Sales have been strong in most categories and in most states. Exhibit 5.25 shows growth in retail sales by broad product classification up to August 2009. Food and beverages and supermarket sales recorded 7% growth, which is stronger than previous months. Books and stationery and other personal care items grew by a strong 9% and 12% respectively, but it is still the retail sale of office equipment—which includes computers and communication equipment—that continues to consistently be the best performing retail category over the past year. For that category, there was a 13% growth in cumulative sales as of August 2009 over August 2008.

Since the end of 2003, almost all year-over-year changes to the monthly supermarket retail sales index have been positive, and the most recent readings of this indicator continue this trend. Major supermarket anchors in Brazilian retail include the following:

- **Carrefour.** This French chain became the country's number one supermarket chain following their early 2007 acquisition of local chain Atacadao, which had operated 34 discount hypermarkets across the country (17 located in São Paulo state) and thereafter brought its total to 109 hypermarkets in addition to a portfolio of other retail formats. Plans for future expansion include 70 new stores in 2009 and more than R$1 billion invested in 2009–2010.

- **Pao de Acucar** ("Sugar Loaf"). This chain has at least 551 stores across Brazil: 496 were super/hypermarkets retailing foodstuffs; many of the remainder sell home appliances. São Paulo state represents over half of the company's net sales in recent years.
- **Walmart.** In 2004 it bought 116 stores of the local Bompreco supermarket chain located through the northeast of Brazil. Its subsequent acquisitions are Nacionale and Mercadorama, the chain leaders in Rio Grande do Sul and Parana respectively. The aggressive expansion plans announced in January 2008 by Walmart for Brazil are indicative of this sentiment. The company announced in 2007 its intention to invest US$649 million across the country in various formats in 2008, focusing on lower-income consumers.[29] The chain added circa 40 units in 2008, and as of the beginning of 2009 they have 345 retail units across the country. Plans include 90 new stores in 2009 in Brazil, with an investment of R$1.6 billion. The plan was programmed before the crisis and has been maintained through it. (Associação Brasileira de Shopping Centers [ABRASCE], June 9, 2009, "ignoram crise e investem").
- **Lojas Americanas** and **Sonda Supermercados** are other key national players. Regional players seem to keep expansion plans as well, although at much smaller scales: for example, Condor (the first supermarket chain in "Parana"), will keep its investment plan to open at least four more units and invest R$80 million (ABRASCE, June 9, 1009, "ignoram crise e investem").

The strong growth of retail sales and robust consumer confidence has been partly fuelled by good growth in real incomes and the rapid expansion of credit. The number of credit cards in circulation in Brazil has been increasing each year since 2000, but the growth rate has shown a slowed trend since 2007. As of August 2009, there were approximately 132 million credit cards circulating (7% more than as of the end of 2008 and 13% more than in August 2008). The total value of transactions experienced a deceleration in 2008 (although it remained growing at almost 20%), and in the first quarters of 2009 it seems to have recovered slightly, with 18% annual growth registered in August 2009 (Exhibit 5.26). The debit market is also experiencing fast growth, especially in the value of the transactions, which grew by 21% in August 2009 over August 2008.

São Paulo has the largest shopping center supply, with 130 centers as of June 2009, and around 40% of the total stock in Brazil (Exhibit 5.27). Given this large stock, shopping center density in São Paulo is higher than

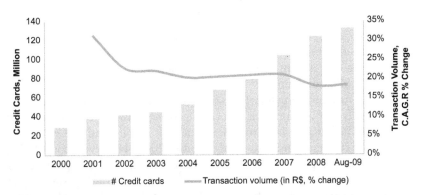

EXHIBIT 5.26 Credit Cards in Circulation and Growth Rate of Transaction Volume
Source: ABECS, ING Real Estate Research & Strategy as of October 15, 2009.
Note: "CAGR" refers to compound annual growth rate.

the national average (roughly 47 square meters per 1,000 inhabitants), but still well below levels of the more developed countries.[30] For example, the density in Portugal at 244 square meters per 1,000 inhabitants, UK with 267 square meters per 1,000 inhabitants, or Spain with 249 square meters per 1,000 inhabitants are well above Brazil's figures and the density in the

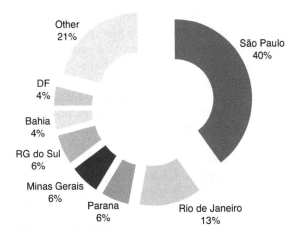

EXHIBIT 5.27 Shopping Center Gross Leasable Area ("GLA") within Brazil
Source: ABRASCE, ING Real Estate Research & Strategy, as of September 2009.
Note: "DF" represents Distrito Federal and "R.G. do Sul" represents Rio Grande do Sul.

main cities in all these countries is often even higher.[31] In 2008, the national average shopping center density in the United States was 606 square meters per 1,000 inhabitants, including only community and neighborhood centers, and shopping center density in Mexico is estimated at roughly 93 square meters per 1,000 inhabitants.[32]

The construction pipeline for new shopping centers over the coming years is relatively large in Brazil. Several projects have been delayed from 2009 to 2010, but the total for the remaining of this and the following year is 845,510 square meters, as of October 2009. However, considering the current low supply and the population growth, the shopping center density in Brazil by the end of 2010 will not have grown notably, standing at 50 square meters per 1,000 inhabitants. In São Paulo it will rise to 91 square meters per 1,000 inhabitants, still a low figure by international comparisons mentioned above.

The fast growth of the retail sector should act to lower vacancy rates and allow rents and property values to rise, particularly in modern shopping centers. According to one study, 6 out of the top 10 locations with the strongest rental growth to June 2009 were found in Brazil (most specifically, São Paulo). The retail market is still highly fragmented with the top five players holding approximately 30% of the market, and moreover they are working with foreign groups as strategic partners.

As seen in Exhibit 5.28, São Paulo and Rio de Janeiro rise to the top in a state ranking by shopping center attractiveness—they are larger and wealthier although they already have a relatively high shopping center GLA. Logically, shopping centers have generally penetrated those areas that have larger and relatively wealthier population bases from which to draw a customer base. In contrast, smaller, poorer states have nonexistent or very little shopping center penetration. It is essential to stress the sizable socioeconomic variation between municipalities, which must be considered at the asset-level trade area. Nonetheless, the framework below is an important one for assessing the relative investment attractiveness at a higher, preliminary geographic level.

The analysis in Exhibit 5.29 highlights the potential "mismatch" between shopping center density (GLA per capita) and potential spending (using GDP/capita as a proxy). It suggests that smaller, wealthier, southern and southeastern states including Santa Catarina, Rio Grande do Sul, Espirito Santo, as well as Mato Grosso have potential for greater shopping center penetration given their GDP/Capita. Espirito Santo appears especially attractive given its average GDP/capita of R$15,236 (estimated) and only 22.2 square meters of shopping center GLA per 1,000 inhabitants.

Moving down a geographic level to the municipalities, the ranking in Exhibit 5.30 outlines some of the key retail drivers and characteristics

EXHIBIT 5.28 State Rankings of Shopping Center Attractiveness (as of year-end 2008)

Federal State	Overall Ranking	GDP pc	Population	Th. R/ sq. m.	SC Density (sq. m./ 1,000 inh)	SC GLA (sq. m.)	GDP (Th. R$)
São Paulo	1	2	1	18	26	1	1
Rio de Janeiro	2	3	3	19	25	2	2
Rio Grande do Sul	3	6	5	11	22	5	4
Minas Gerais	4	10	2	7	12	4	3
Santa Catarina	5	4	11	10	23	8	7
Espírito Santo	6	5	14	2	10	16	11
Paraná	7	7	6	17	24	3	5
Distrito Federal	8	1	20	16	27	6	8
Amazonas	9	9	15	6	15	15	14
Goiás	10	12	12	15	19	11	9
Mato Grosso	11	8	19	13	20	13	15
Bahia	12	19	4	14	11	7	6
Mato Grosso do sul	13	11	21	9	17	18	17
Pará	14	22	9	3	5	17	13
Pernambuco	15	21	7	20	16	9	10
Rondônia	16	14	23	5	8	23	22
Ceará	17	23	8	22	13	10	12
Maranhão	18	26	10	1	4	21	16
Tocantins	19	17	24	8	9	24	24
Roraima	20	13	27	27	3	27	27
Sergipe	21	16	22	21	18	19	21
Amapá	22	15	26	26	2	26	25
Alagoas	23	25	16	4	6	22	20
Rio Grande do Norte	24	20	18	24	21	12	18
Paraíba	25	24	13	23	14	14	19
Acre	26	18	25	25	1	25	26
Piauí	27	27	17	12	7	20	23

Sources: IBGE, ABRASCE, ING Real Estate Research & Strategy, as of February 2009.

Notes: Indicators are weighted as follows: GDP/capita 50%, Population 25%, GDP/sq. m. 7.5%, Shopping Center Density (sq. m./1,000 inhabitants), 7.5%, Shopping Center GLA 5%, GDP 5%. States ranked 1 being the highest value and 27 the lowest, except for SC density, where the ranking is inverse (1 being the lowest value, 27 the highest).

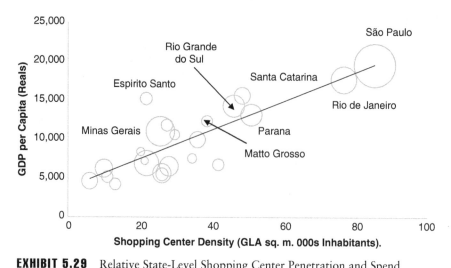

EXHIBIT 5.29   Relative State-Level Shopping Center Penetration and Spend Profiles
Source: IBGE, EIU, ABRASCE, ING Real Estate Research & Strategy as of January 30, 2009. Size of the bubble denotes population size as of 2008. GDP per capita as of 2008 estimated with 2006 data and national growth rates. Population by state as of 2008 calculated with 2007 population and 2008 population growth rate.

of the capital cities of the main states, and a broad analysis of the mismatch between current provision and demographic drivers can be found in Exhibit 5.31. Brasilia, as one of the wealthiest cities in Brazil and with its size firmly in the second tier of cities, somewhat surprisingly is revealed as only the eighth-densest municipality in the country in terms of shopping center GLA. However, these figures must be considered carefully. For example, the state of Brasilia shows a high density, which suggests that there may be a concentration of shopping centers located outside the city limits.

Industrial

The logistics industry has assumed a much greater strategic importance in Brazil in recent years. This has occurred as manufacturing developed into an important component of the Brazilian economy and as domestic consumption in the emerging, modern retail sector took hold. The industrial sector made up around 29% of Brazil's GDP in 2008 (EIU, 21 January 2009) and the long-term trend is for this sector to continue in its economic importance, particularly in light of government policy to encourage more value-added processing of agricultural and mineral commodities. Since October 2008,

EXHIBIT 5.30 City Rankings of Shopping Center Drivers (capital cities only, end 2008)

Capital City	Ranking by Main City	GDP pc	Population	Th. R/ sq. m.	SC Density (sq. m./ 000s Inh)	SC GLA	GDP (Th. R$)
São Paulo	1	2	1	6	16	1	1
Brasilia	2	1	6	2	8	7	3
Rio de Janeiro	3	4	2	8	15	2	2
Manaus	4	5	8	1	5	13	6
Porto Alegre	5	3	10	14	20	4	7
Belo Horizonte	6	8	5	9	10	6	4
Curitiba	7	6	7	13	17	5	5
Recife	8	11	9	10	7	9	10
Goiania	9	10	12	12	9	10	11
Fortaleza	10	16	4	11	6	8	9
São Luis	11	12	13	3	1	19	13
Florianopolis	12	7	20	15	18	16	17
Campo Grande	13	13	16	4	2	20	14
Salvador	14	18	3	20	12	3	8
Cuiaba	15	9	18	17	19	12	16
Belem	16	19	11	5	3	15	12
Natal	17	15	15	19	14	11	15
Aracaju	18	14	19	16	13	17	20
Teresina	19	20	14	7	4	18	18
João Pessoa	20	17	17	18	11	14	19

Sources: IBGE, ABRASCE, ING Real Estate Research & Strategy, as of April 2008.
Notes: Indicators are weighted as follows; GDP/capita (in USD) 50%, Population 25%, GDP/Capita/sq. m. 7.5%, Shopping Center Density (sq. m./1,000 inhabitants), 7.5%, Shopping Center gross lettable area (GLA) 5%, GDP (*reals*) 5%. Numbers in the table refer to rankings where "1" is the most attractive ranking.

Brazil has not escaped the effects of the global economic downturn and it initially affected industrial confidence and production. However, the sector recovered quickly and the depreciating Real at the beginning of the crisis provided exporters with some support (see Exhibit 5.32).

After the quick recovery that started in the second quarter of 2009, forecasts for Brazilian exports and imports were marginally reviewed upwards (Exhibit 5.33). Although both imports and exports were expected to fall by roughly 10% in 2009, forecast figures turn positive for 2010. Thus, we believe that entering the industrial market could position the investor well, given the forecast growth of trade in 2010 and 2011 and beyond.

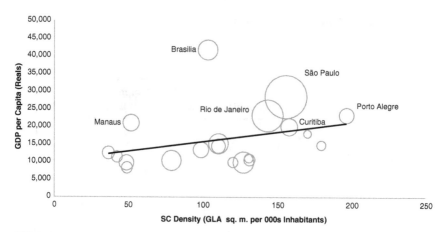

EXHIBIT 5.31 Relative Capital-City–Level Shopping Center Penetration and Spend Profiles
Source: IBGE, EIU, ABRASCE, ING Real Estate Research & Strategy, as of January 30, 2009. Size of the bubble denotes population size as of 2008. Population and GDP per capita as of 2008 estimated with 2006 data and national growth rates by EIU.

Much of the industrial production in Brazil is destined for the domestic market, and although exports are important, Brazil has one of the lowest ratios of exports to GDP of any major country in the world. In 2008, exports represented just 14.4% of GDP (compared to 30.3% for Mexico, 38.8% for China, and 77.5% for the Netherlands).[33] Thus, there is plenty of potential in Brazil for international trade to assume an even greater economic role in the medium to longer term, while for the short term its lesser reliance on exports has shielded it from the worst of the current slide in global export markets.

The industrial property market in Brazil—and throughout much of South America—is still relatively underdeveloped, with most facilities in the sector being owner-occupied. For the most part, logistical facilities are smaller and use lower technology inputs compared to facilities in Europe or North America. Although somewhat variable figures are available on modern Class A buildings, only about one-fourth of the industrial built area in São Paulo industrial parks surpasses 10 meters of height, which can be used as a proxy for investment-grade stock. It must be highlighted, as well, that in spite of Brazil's large size (it is the world's fifth-biggest country in area) land for logistics development is scarce in proximity to the most populated regions, due to topographic constraints, and so the logistics pipeline may not be as affected by the lower barriers to entry evident in other markets such as Mexico.

EXHIBIT 5.32 Industrial Market Overview

Market Factor	Market Characteristics	Drivers	Future Trends	Business Opportunity
Demand for New Development	Demand is high as the country continues its expansion in commodities, agricultural, and industrial manufacturing.	Globalization, growth of industrial manufacturing and exports.	Demand for new, institutional-grade warehouse and logistics facilities is strong, particularly in key port locations and around major population centers.	Limited supply of suitable land surrounding primary markets limits development opportunities; second- and third-tier cities may have more favorable options for industrial development.
Supply of New Development	Supplies largely concentrated in primary markets; secondary markets are gaining attention.	Increasing demand, limited suitable land is pushing prices up.	More domestic industries and logistics are creating increasing demand for industrial property.	Market in primary cities are well developed and tight, while the second-tier markets offering new opportunities.
Investment Market Support	Demand is mainly for primary market properties, but development in secondary markets may gain traction as global economy expands.	Brazil is a leader in agricultural and commodity production; growing export industry; strong domestic demand.	This should be an important investment sector given Brazil's ongoing economic development.	There could be significant financial interest in the sector if there were more investable assets and companies.
Debt Market	Plenty of commercial lending from domestic banks for now.	Opportunities exist for the foreign lender if Brazilian government and domestic banks discourage lending.	Still a nascent sector, underwriting is becoming easier with higher-quality developers interested in borrowing.	Better lending opportunities may exist in secondary markets.

EXHIBIT 5.33 Brazil's Goods and Services Export and Import Real Growth Rates

	2008	2009F	2010F	2011F	2012F	2013F
Exports	−0.7	−9.9	4.4	6.2	6.5	5.6
Imports	17.8	−9.8	8.3	10.4	8.4	8.4

Sources: EIU, ING Real Estate Research & Strategy, as of July 26, 2010.

Industrial production had been growing steadily and robustly in Brazil up to 2008, but the global volatility and economic weakness in world demand have finally affected it, and negative figures were recorded in the first half of 2009. The trend was a worldwide phenomenon at this point, and much deeper industrial production declines were found in other global manufacturing hubs throughout Europe and Asia. São Paulo and the northeast region have outperformed the national average recently, with higher monthly growth rates, while Rio de Janeiro and Minas Gerais registered lower growth rates (Exhibit 5.34).

Confidence among Brazil's industrialists revealed record high levels at the end of 2007 (Exhibit 5.35). This confidence moderated through 2008 and finally fell steeply in February 2009, but, together with other markets, it started to rebound in the second quarter of 2009. Brazilian industrial confidence has remained at higher levels through the downturn, and although it suffered a steep slump in the first quarter, the fall has been less prolonged and deep than in markets like the United States, Mexico, or the OECD.

Industrial yields in Brazil stood at a relatively high level (12.75%) at the end of 2008, which represents a premium over the other sectors in Brazil and over many developed and emerging markets around the world (Exhibit 5.36).

Industrial yields have compressed since 2005, and we expect them to compress further over the medium to long terms, given the increasing investment interest observed in the region and the current high level of industrial

EXHIBIT 5.34 Brazil's Industrial Production (% growth)

Aug 2009	São Paulo	Rio de Janeiro	Minas Gerais	Regiao Nordeste
Monthly Change (%)	3.4	0.6	1.2	6.7
Year-over-Year Change (%)	−6.9	−2.8	−13.7	−4.8

Source: Central Bank of Brazil, IBGE, ING Real Estate Research & Strategy, as of October 15, 2009.

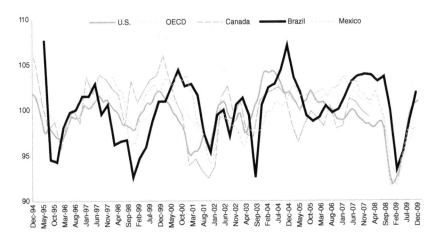

EXHIBIT 5.35 Industrial Confidence Index
Sources: Thomson Financial Datastream; Organization for Economic Cooperation and Development (OECD); ING Real Estate Research & Strategy, as of October 15, 2009.

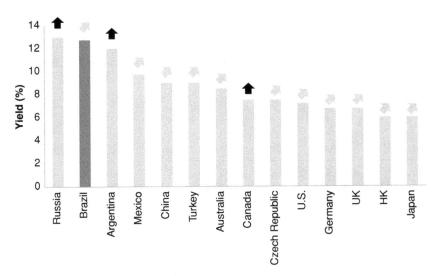

EXHIBIT 5.36 Industrial Yields (Percent) in Selected Markets and Observed Trend
Source: CW International Investment Atlas summary 2009; ING Real Estate Research & Strategy, as of June 23, 2009.
Note: Gross yields for Russia, Mexico, China, Turkey, and Czech Republic.

yields. As with the other property types, yields flattened towards the end of 2008 and the beginning of 2009, and in some cases market indications suggest they have moved out during the first half of 2009.

Brazil is currently embarking on a "growth acceleration program," whereby a sizable amount of public and private investment is targeting new projects around the country. Logistics infrastructure benefited from R$13 billion in new investments in 2007, and further investments up to R$58 billion are planned up to 2010 (Banco Nacional de Desenvolvimento Econômico e Social, 2008). Highways and roads take up 57% of the program's budget, but rail, port, and airport projects are also sizable.

The location of any logistics asset must be assessed in reference to its proximity to this sizable roll-out of new infrastructure. This new system will act to render certain old sites obsolete at worst or less efficient at best. Most important, it will open up new areas of strategic importance and reveal places where we believe that modern logistics facilities should perform well.

Almost 42% of all port tonnage handled in the Western Hemisphere south of the U.S.-Mexican border is handled by Brazilian ports (ECLAC). Tonnage handled by Brazilian ports has exhibited impressive growth rates given its very large base. Double-digit growth of cargo handled at these ports has been observed in the five largest Brazilian ports this decade (Exhibit 5.37).[34]

Brazil's airports have been especially stretched in terms of both passenger and cargo growth in recent years. Although air cargo handled has

EXHIBIT 5.37   Brazil's Major Ports (by TEU movement)

Port/Year	2000	2005	2006	2007	2008	CAGR 2000–2008
Santos	800,898	2,336,292	2,488,031	2,577,187	2,574,920	16%
Rio Grande	217,332	591,207	595,802	607,275	613,700	14%
Paranagua	252,879	378,834	253,202	598,479	595,729	11%
Salvador	95,307	191,834	214,513	191,015	248,345	13%
Vitoria	91,738	218,267	251,987	267,494	191,316	10%
São Francisco do Sul	168,355	238,962	218,970	226,806	187,548	1%
Suape	62,822	179,229	196,709	237,077	122,268	9%

Sources: ECLAC (Economic Commission for Latin America and the Caribbean): 2000 data, 2005 data for Paranagua and Salvador; ANTAQ (National Agency for Marine Transport); ING Real Estate Research & Strategy, as of January 2009. No update available for Itajai, and Sepetiba, which are the other three ports among the 10 largest.

grown at more modest rates compared to that through seaports in Brazil, planned improvements and expansions to several of the country's airport hubs should relieve the current bottlenecks in coming years. Such capacity constraints have therefore hampered the growth potential of Brazil's major airports. Nonetheless, this problem has been recognized by the public sector, and upgrades and expansions of key airports around the country are underway. This offers considerable potential for improving logistical efficiencies, for example, for airfreight between Europe and South America using São Paulo or Rio as hubs for further transshipment to other cities in the region.

São Paulo and Rio clearly emerge as attractive areas for industrial real estate given their underlying drivers (Exhibit 5.38). São Paulo has the largest base of workers, both in industrial production and in transport and affiliated sectors, while its industrial GDP is also far larger than the rest of the country. Guarulhos, the municipality to the north of São Paulo and the location of its international airport, is also high on this ranking as are São Bernardo do Campo and at least five other neighboring or nearby municipalities. Some of them are located on the new ring road circling São Paulo and are on the route to Santos, which serves as the key port for the São Paulo metro region and therefore is a key industrial location as well.

Greater São Paulo is the largest industrial market in South America. The total built area of industrial and logistics property in São Paulo is estimated at around 16 million square meters "Usable" stock in the industrial parks of São Paulo and the Campinas area is estimated at around 2.9 million square meters. As São Paulo is an hour inland, the corridor between this metro and its main port city of Santos is a relevant and sizable submarket within the country, and São Paulo's southern region accounts for roughly 35% of the industrial stock in the state. Campinas is the second-largest industrial hub and the main market for high-technology companies. Rio, as the country's second-largest metropolitan area is another important hub for domestic and international logistics. Second-tier Brazilian coastal cities also have strong potential, particularly in light of several significant new infrastructure projects that will boost their efficiencies and competitiveness for trade. A common feature across these submarkets is the lack of quality supply of Class A buildings.

Throughout Brazil, current demand continues to be for better stock with higher ceiling heights. Currently there is an emerging trend for industries to relocate from urban centers to recently built industrial parks in the interior regions, partly underpinned by the desire of reduce costs and find more efficient spaces.

Tax incentives are helping the decentralization of some industrial activity to second-tier cities including Campinas, Curitiba, Bahia, and

EXHIBIT 5.38　Ranking of Municipalities for Industrial Real Estate

Overall Ranking	Municipality	Industrial GDP Ranking	GDP Ranking	Industrial Employment Ranking	Transport Employment Ranking
1	São Paulo	1	1	1	1
2	Rio de Janeiro	3	2	2	2
3	Manaus	4	4	4	5
4	Guarulhos	8	5	3	4
5	Curitiba	10	3	6	3
6	São Bernardo do Campo	7	9	5	7
7	Campinas	14	6	10	6
8	Duque de Caxias	6	8	18	9
9	Betim	5	10	17	14
10	São José dos Campos	9	12	13	20
11	Joinville	15	17	8	19
12	Santo André	17	13	15	12
13	Contagem	23	1	5	11
14	Campos dos Goytacazes	2	7	28	27
15	Jundiá	22	14	14	16
16	Camaçari	11	20	19	24
17	Caxias do Sul	27	23	7	13
18	Serra	16	22	20	17
19	Macaé	19	29	25	18
20	São José dos Pinhais	25	26	16	21

Sources: IBGE; ING Real Estate Research & Strategy, as of February 2009.
Notes: Indicators are weighted as follows; Industrial share of GDP 35%, Number of Employees in the Industrial Sector 25%, Number of Employees in the Transport (and related) Sector 25%, and GDP 15%. Industrial employment ranking is by number of employed people in transformation industries. Transportation employment ranking is by number of employed people in transport activities.

Pernambuco. In such places, land is cheaper and more plentiful while labor is still qualified yet generally lower cost and there is less union pressure.

Residential

Three broad patterns characterize the residential sector in Brazil. First, there is a deficit of more than 6 million units of housing. Second, the highly unequal nature of Brazil's society has meant that the shortage is most acute in the lower-middle-class, working-class, and affordable housing strata. Third, monetary policy has induced interest rates to come down significantly in recent years (the SELIC rate was 26.5% in 2003, and it has come down to

8.75% as of October 2009, an all-time low), which we believe has made home ownership much more affordable (see Exhibit 5.39).

Brazil's housing deficit is one of the largest in the world, and the current regime has taken notable steps to redress this problem. It has been successful in creating an enabling environment for homebuilders to construct residential units and for the population to access mortgages by which to purchase the stock. The relative financing conditions have improved significantly and especially so for lower-income buyers.

The pent-up demand for owner-occupier housing was brought about due to a sustained period of high (over 20%) interest rates. Housing, together with transport infrastructure has been a prime focus of Brazil's Growth Acceleration Plan (PAC). Home ownership is quite high even among the poorer strata of Brazilians, and this is achieved because their housing is of poor quality and is often self-built.

Additionally, strong household formation supports increasing residential demand (Exhibit 5.40). According to EIU estimates, 960,000 new households were formed in 2008, summing a total of 55.5 million households at the end of the year. The trend will remain strong, with more than 900,000 households expected to be created each year up to 2013.[35] A stable fall in the number of members per household has been observed in recent decades, following the trend toward smaller households that took place in North America, Europe, and elsewhere for several decades. The average size of households in Brazil is estimated at 3.5 members for 2008 (it is 2.7 in North America and 2.4 in Western Europe) and is forecast (EIU, June 2009) to decrease slightly in 2009 to 3.4 and remain stable at that level.[36] This will support strong household formation for the next few years as well.

Nevertheless, uncertainty about the job market at the local level, deterioration of confidence and inflationary or other threats to the purchasing power of buyers would affect this growth rate of household formation. The lower-income segments are still very much dependent on government incentive programs and mortgage policy. The high costs and high volatility of raw material prices and supply-demand issues at the local level, in addition to increasing land prices in some areas, may emerge as concerns.

At the end of 2008, mortgage loans represented less than 3% of Brazil's GDP (Exhibit 5.41), and the trend remains for 2009. The latter figure is a far lower proportion than in Mexico (9%) or Chile (13%). This comparatively low mortgage penetration compared to other Latin American countries is also vastly lower than economies in Asia (China 10%, Malaysia 30%, Singapore 32%) and certainly compared to developed economies such as the UK (84%) or the United States (85%).[37] In addition to the decrease in interest rates, other mortgage terms have recently made home ownership more favorable. Brazilian mortgage specialist BM Sua Casa extended a

EXHIBIT 5.39 Residential Market Overview

Market Factor	Market Characteristics	Drivers	Future Trends	Business Opportunity
Demand for New Housing Stock	Extreme shortage of housing, especially for lower-income population; nonetheless, relatively high proportion of ownership.	Increasing urban population; insufficient quantity of housing; expanding mortgage market.	Demand for higher quality of housing will increase as the middle class in the country increases; small-to-medium-size housing is in short of supply.	Development of full range of housing options, from low-income to luxury, expected to meet with strong demand.
Supply of New Housing Stock	Highly concentrated in primary and secondary cities, expanding to surrounding markets.	Increased home ownership, accessibility to financing, government investment.	Local builders are ramping up production and increasing expertise.	Lower- to middle-income housing in urban areas is undersupplied.
Investment/ Developer Market	Short project cycle and abundant capital support first mover advantage to existing players.	Increasing urban population; increasing living standards.	Should be increased domestic and international competition in residential development. Competition for the best deals and development partners to heighten. Additional regulation likely because of unscrupulous developers.	Entity-level investments in national and regional development partners. Provide capital (preferred equity) to local developers; leverage local expertise.
Debt Market	For homeowners: 30-year mortgages are now available.	Opportunities exist if government and domestic banks reduce lending.	Interest rates are dropping, making debt and home ownership more affordable.	Mortgage lending is possible, but investment returns may be inferior to preferred equity.

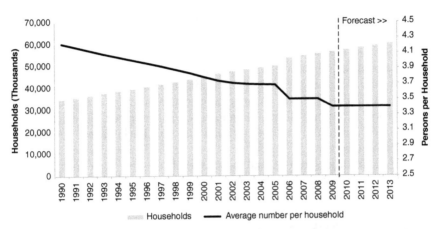

EXHIBIT 5.40 Number of Households and Members per Household in Brazil
Sources: EIU; ING Real Estate Research & Strategy, as of June 2009.

30-year maturity to its "special rate" mortgage product in 2007, thereby becoming the first lender in Brazil to offer a mortgage product with a 30-year term.

Most mortgage loans for housing purchase in Brazil are not directly related to the SELIC—the reference interest rate. In 2007, 90% of the financing to build or acquire a residential property was structured under the

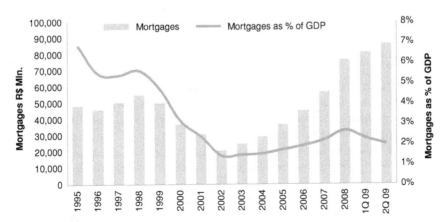

EXHIBIT 5.41 Number of Households and Members per Household in Brazil
Sources: Economist Intelligence Unit, Brazil Central Bank, IBGE, ING Real Estate Research & Strategy, as of October 2009.

SFH (Residential Financing System), which is supervised and subsidized by the government. Private market operations are growing, and they represented 35% of the total mortgages initiated in 2008 (including commercial buildings and with data available only up to October 2008, BCB). Interventions to offset the rising SELIC by continuing to make finance affordable to both homebuilders and homebuyers were enacted and demonstrate the administration's commitment to the importance of this sector. We believe that the new downward trend of interest rates will thus likely benefit demand in the residential sector.

Federal reform by the Lula administration has been a key element of this growth. There is a requirement that 65% of each private sector bank's total amount of savings deposits be used to finance the construction or purchase of residential real estate. Yet by the end of 2007, outstanding mortgage balances for all banks represented less than a quarter of eligible savings deposits—far below the mandatory level of 65% (according to Goldman Sachs, 2008). Hence, additional finance will have to flow to the sector.

Additionally, one of the programs recently adopted by the administration, as a response to the crisis, is "Minha Casa, Minha Vida," in which the federal government will invest R$34 billion (US$17 billion, with the exchange rate as of June 23, 2009). The program aims to finance the building of 1 million housing units for low-income households in joint projects among the states, the local authorities, and private investment. The program aims both to support housing demand and support households' efforts to acquire a property and to facilitate financing to homebuilders.

Many homebuilders listed in the Bovespa stock market in recent years as their work continues to address the huge housing shortage in the country. Building construction in São Paulo eased in 2005 and 2006 but recovered in 2007. In 2008, residential projects represented 56% of the total permits (according to the "Prefeitura" of São Paulo, the local administration), just slightly down from 61% in 2003.

A dramatic decline in interest rates and new government regulations that favor the development of the residential sector have been part of the government's flagship growth acceleration program, and these have been coupled with tax breaks for the construction sector. The recovery has been of benefit to companies targeting the upper-middle class, and the outlook for lower income residential sector construction now looks more promising.

Over 20 real estate companies have launched IPOs since 2005 when interest rates began falling in Brazil. Five of the most important players are Cyrela Brazil Realty, MRV Engenharia, PDG Realty, Rossi Residencial, and Gafisa. Through 2008, the returns of most of these homebuilders moved into negative territory suggesting that their IPO pricing had been too high. Some consolidation and potentially some distressed positions in this sector are likely to occur, and this may present opportunities. Given the economic and investment uncertainty, the trend has to be carefully monitored especially as such trends in the public markets usually lead the unlisted markets.

The credit crunch of 2009 presented a new set of challenges and opportunities not experienced in the country over the past few years. Homebuilders face much stricter standards for obtaining working capital funding as lenders have adopted a more cautious assessment of builders' financial strength. This has been occurring despite the continuation of strong sales.

In Exhibit 5.42, those municipalities with the highest velocity of home sales in the last twelve months to 1Q 09—São Paulo, Belo Horizonte, and Porto Alegre appear the most attractive, keeping the same pattern as in our last update. We assume that the sales velocity is a reasonable indicator of how well these markets have recently been clearing. In general terms, sales velocity is slowing down, with Belo Horizonte and São Paulo showing much more resilience. Most major cities have clustered around sales velocities of roughly 6% (the total range being 4.6% to 7.6%), while the two outper-forming cities continue to experience much higher rates. The size of each

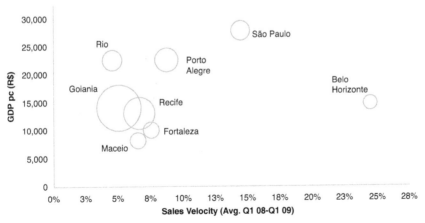

EXHIBIT 5.42 Residential Sales Velocity in Brazil's Major Municipalities
Source: IBGE, CBIC, ING Real Estate Research & Strategy, as of June 23, 2009.
Note: Size of the bubbles denotes the available stock offered per capita in the last 12 months Q1 08–Q1 09 (avg. p.a.). Sales velocity = Sold units/(Stock for sale at the end of t − 1 + launched units in t—sold units in t).

bubble in that figure indicates the amount of stock offered during the last 12 months, in per capita terms, suggesting that the smaller bubbles represent those places with further potential to build or where prices might be higher comparatively. That indicator is more stable than the sales velocity, and sizes (and relative sizes) have not changed as much as sales velocity. On that indicator, the two largest municipalities in the country remain attractive. If we consider GDP per capita (with ING estimates for 2008) Belo Horizonte appears as a good opportunity for medium or low-medium income segments, and Porto Alegre, together with São Paulo and Rio, offer a good opportunity for more expensive products.

Another way of considering investment potential is simply the estimated shortfall of housing unit stock, and estimates of this deficit classified by income category and by geographic region are provided in Exhibit 5.43. It can be observed that the southeast (as the most populated region) is the one with a higher housing deficit, which is much deeper for lower income categories.

PRIMARY MARKETS

As mentioned previously, Brazil's investment-grade real estate markets are dominated by the two largest cities: Rio de Janeiro and São Paolo. In addition

EXHIBIT 5.43   Estimated Housing Deficit by Income Group and Region

	Total Units	% Housing Units	Urban Units
North	652,684	16.7	487,357
Northeast	2,144,384	15.0	1,461,669
Southeast	2,335,415	9.3	2,222,957
São Paulo	1,234,306	9.6	1,195,800
RM São Paulo	628,624	10.3	611,936
Rio de Janeiro	478,901	9.1	471,872
RM Rio de Janeiro	378,797	9.5	376,139
RM Belo Horizonte	129,404	8.5	129,171
South	703,167	7.9	617,333
Center-West	436,995	10.5	390,447
Brazil	6,272,645	11.1	5,179,763

Source: Ministerio das Cidades, Fundaçao João Pinheiro (Déficit Habitacional no Brasil 2007, Table 3.1), ING Real Estate Research & Strategy, as of October 2009.
Note: RM: Metropolitan Region.

to these primary markets, a number of smaller, secondary markets may present increasing investment opportunities, Belo Horizonte, Curitiba, Porto Alegre, and Brasilia.

São Paulo

São Paulo is the largest office market in Latin America, with 8 million rentable square meters of office inventory, of which around 2.2 million square meters, or just around one-third, is defined as Class A/AA. Around 40% of the market is considered Class B and the remainder is Class C. Class A office buildings are spread throughout the city, but most of them are located in four submarkets: Paulista, Faria Lima, Marginal, and Berrini (Exhibit 5.44). New stock continues to be developed at sustainable levels.

The greatest amount of office space in São Paulo is in the geographic and historic center of the city. The overwhelming majority of that stock, however, is B or C grade, much of it having been built in Brazil's previous periods of expansion in the 1960s or 1970s. Much of it is not of investment grade for international institutions. Several smaller, newer office precincts have emerged, of which Berrini has the greatest stock of AA grade office space.

The economic downturn and the depreciation of the currency have pushed São Paulo to rank as the world's 33rd most expensive as of May 2009 according to CBRE's "Global MarketView." São Paulo remains

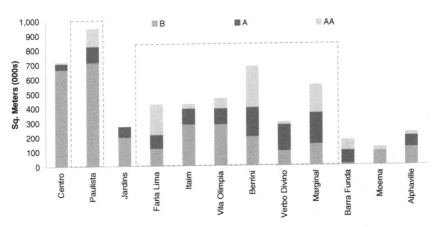

EXHIBIT 5.44 São Paulo Stock Distribution
Source: Jones Lang LaSalle, ING Real Estate Research & Strategy, estimates as of December 2008.

affordable by global standards, with rents at one-third of the most expensive rents in the world (found in Tokyo). However, the good performance of previous years keeps São Paulo with higher rents than those found in other emerging countries (like the Czech Republic, Poland, or South Korea) and some developed markets like Toronto or Washington.

Rio de Janeiro

There are more than 5 million rentable sqm of office space in Rio de Janeiro. Approximately 25% is classified as Class A space (Exhibit 5.45). With the central business district ("CBD") of Rio constricted given its location between the ocean and the mountains and the downtown lacking a large supply of Class A and AA office space, firms unable to find quality space in the center have moved to the second largest submarket of Orla or to the area of Barra de Tijuca, a new seaside business district. Cidade Nova and Zona Sul are other small submarkets with Class A stock. Repositioning the lower-grade offices in the downtown area of Rio is one potentially compelling investment strategy.

The overall vacancy rate for Rio is very low—at only 2.8% and currently represents one of the lowest office vacancy rates of any major market in the world. The development pipeline is expected to be lower in the short term, partly due to scarce financing for developments. As a consequence of the low pipeline delivered and a relatively robust net absorption, the vacancy rate for the general market fell to a record low in early 2009. Despite the

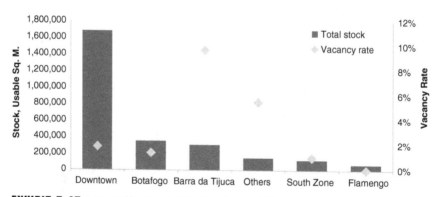

EXHIBIT 5.45 Rio Office Stock Distribution and Vacancy Rate by Submarket
Source: CBRE MarketView Rio de Janeiro Office 2Q 09, ING Real Estate Research & Strategy, as of September 15, 2009.

tight markets, the weakened economic activity might defer the absorption of the new space delivered in the coming months. A large development pipeline may put pressure on vacancy rates going forward.

INVESTMENT STRATEGIES

Buying/Developing Office Properties

The office sector is expected to experience favorable conditions in several key submarkets of São Paulo and Rio de Janeiro in the medium and long terms. Prime office towers with credit worthy tenants will continue to be sought after, but demand will likely weaken in the short term. The leasing law in Brazil allows tenants to end the lease at will in certain cases, regardless of the tenant lease length, so these leases will never be totally solid, especially in the current economic environment. Some exceptions that allow the relationship to be excluded from regulation by the leasing legislation are the build-to-suit projects and other agreements like forcible arbitration.

Value-added opportunities will likely arise as well for the retrofit of lesser-grade assets in low vacancy submarkets. Most developments are taking place in specific markets, usually at new business locations away from the city center. As a consequence, some of the strong, city-center districts remain with out of date buildings. However, these locations, with better connections and comparatively lower rents are still the most attractive for many companies. Therefore, we believe that refurbished, upgraded existing buildings in such areas may likely enjoy strong demand. An opportunity would be the codevelopment of office buildings in prime locations with favorable demand prospects. Tenant base diversification and close attention to market differentiation are advisable. Value-adding to higher environmental standards may appeal especially to certain multinational firms operating in Brazil, which are increasingly demanding greener standards for their properties in their home countries (see Exhibit 5.46).

Buying/Developing Residential Properties

In Brazil, foreign investment has entered the residential sector in joint venture with local developers/construction companies. There is the potential to finance homebuilders active in larger cities.

The primary focus is on housing for the middle class, since this segment possesses sufficient disposable income, it is an expanding class, and its income level is rising. However, projects for slightly higher socioeconomic

EXHIBIT 5.46   Buying/Developing Office Properties

Factor	Comments
Risk Factors	Most Class A properties are held in strata title, making negotiations difficult and complicating exit strategies. Tenants have significantly more rights than in many more developed countries, including the ability to unilaterally terminate lease agreements. This presents additional risks as cash flows are not as certain as in some other countries. Long due diligence and negotiations periods translate into closing times that extend many months causing deals to fall through. Title and due diligence is spotty.
Execution and Implementation	The single-ownership leasing model is still a relatively new concept in Brazil. Until the market adjusts to this practice there will continue to be impediments to the attractiveness of the market. Many large corporate tenants are making due with relatively low quality space and do not see the need to move up to institutional-quality real estate. Investment requires a significant amount of searching, negotiating, due diligence, and then much work to bring the asset up to international standard. All of this is management-intensive work.
Returns	Current yields range from 9 to 11%. Capital appreciation has been robust in recent years attracting increasing international investment to the market.
Reg./Legal	Leasing law allows tenants to end leases at will in some circumstances, limiting visibility of cash flows.
Market Size	There are a limited number of institutional-quality assets, primarily located in São Paolo and Rio de Janeiro. The number of investable core office assets is further limited because of strata title and substandard features of design and construction. Significant new development is anticipated, which will be the primary entry point to the market for much international capital.
Competition	There are numerous local developers active in the major and secondary markets, but none command a significant market share. There has been an increase in fundraising and active investment by international real estate funds.
Barriers to Entry and Exit	The lack of existing institutional-quality office product is the key impediment at the time, along with the restrictions imposed by strata title ownership. The opportunities are expected to improve for both ease of entry and exit over time. Long prospecting, due diligence, and closing periods are the norm.

segments (with higher disposable income) and slightly lower socioeconomic segments (for which the housing deficit is estimated to be larger) may also be attractive. Those regions with high velocity and low stock-to-population ratios will be prioritized. Much of the housing deficit is in the lower income segment, so how well the listed companies or other unlisted homebuilders perform in that sizable market gives an indication of opportunities ahead for offering equity or equity-like instruments as a strategy. Homebuilders in Brazil have been expanding rapidly and deploying equity at high speed. The provision of further equity would complement their continued expansionary plans. Despite the recent slowdown, income levels are growing in Brazil, and the housing deficit is large, so the downturn is not expected to change prospects for the housing sector in the medium and longer terms.

Housing projects in areas with a good level of infrastructure—access to downtown and employment areas in those cities—should also be an emphasis in seeking value. As with the retail sector, much more detailed attention at the submunicipal level is needed to support a development in a given area. Units must be priced at levels appropriate to demographic fundamentals driving demand at that more localized level (see Exhibit 5.47).

Buying/Developing Retail Properties

Higher disposable income and private consumption is expected to support the retail sector in the medium and longer terms. The short-term outlook is comparatively weaker, but we believe that the sector seems to be holding up better than expected and better than other major markets. Additionally, the expansion of the middle class amid its rising income level will likely create a broader public for shopping centers in the long run, but in the short term consumers are likely to exercise more caution. Prime shopping centers in good locations in the main population centers are expected to benefit from strong demographic and economic drivers. However, the primary locations seem to have comparatively more supply, and the current customer base of shopping centers in Brazil is limited. Therefore, selected medium-size cities with smaller projects but relatively high income may gain support.

Although returns might be lower in retail than in other sectors, it is still a property type with room for attractive returns. However, given the structure of the market, the existence of strong local players and the relatively strong competition from international investors—who appear to be part of a consolidation phase in the Brazilian shopping center sector—the entry to the market may be best done through a joint venture agreement with prominent retailers or with local developers, or through buyout of minority partners and small investors.

EXHIBIT 5.47   Buying/Developing Residential Properties

Factor	Comments
Risk Factors	The economic downturn has limited potential in the short-term, but strong demographics and income growth plus enhanced availability of credit should result in growing demand in the mid- to long-term.
Execution and Implementation	Partnering with experienced local partners is essential to success in order to tap expertise in land sourcing, entitlements, construction, and financing.
Returns	Returns can be extremely high, but risks are also high and timeline for investments are generally longer than other development strategies. Some risks may be mitigated through presales, which have been highly successful in well-located and priced developments.
Reg./Legal	Because strategy likely involves partnering with local firms, the legal issues are primarily around deal structuring, rather than property ownership.
Market Size	Tremendous undersupply of housing in relation to both current and forecast population. Growing middle class is particularly in need of housing options, but there are also shortages at the top and bottom end of the market.
Competition	Domestic firms have been successfully adding to the market, especially in the middle-income sector.
Barriers to Entry and Exit	Long prospecting, due diligence, and development timeline. Significant on-the-ground presence required. Easiest exit, especially when presales are successful.

Opportunities for investment should be prioritized in those regions where a mismatch of current GLA to purchasing power is present, mainly in second-tier cities throughout the wealthier regions. Close consideration must be given to the format appropriate in each market/submarket. With homebuilding booming in many areas of the country, retailers of household durables should make for a growing tenant base. Increasing numbers of Brazilians purchase groceries from supermarkets and hypermarkets—which can be competitively priced compared to the smaller corner stores where urban Brazilians have long bought such goods. Joint venture with a local developer seems to be a good option, especially where demand appears warranted for a specific product (see Exhibit 5.48).

EXHIBIT 5.48 Buying/Developing Retail Properties

Factor	Comments
Risk Factors	Short lease terms and tenant ability to terminate leases limit reliability of cash flows. Relatively large amount of new development planned, though still well below the level of retail in some similar developing countries. Strong local players and international competition are already established in the market.
Execution and Implementation	Lack of institutional-quality properties for purchase. Focus on markets where there is a mismatch of current retail space to purchasing power, which is particularly evident in some of the secondary markets.
Returns	Relatively lower yields are anticipated in the retail space compared to other sectors due to enhanced competition for these properties. Nonetheless, strong capital appreciation has been evident in recent years helping to improve total returns.
Reg./Legal	Leasing law allows tenants to end leases at will in some circumstances, limiting visibility of cash flows.
Market Size	São Paulo has the largest shopping center supply with around 40% of the total stock in Brazil. Retail space on a per capita basis is lower than in many comparable developing countries, though the development pipeline is large.
Competition	Increasing international presence in terms of both retailers and investors.
Barriers to Entry and Exit	Long prospecting, due diligence, and closing periods. Barriers to exit are minimal and expected to improve.

Buying/Developing Warehouse Distribution Properties

A general global trend is for owner-occupiers to sell and leaseback their facilities; this has been strong in North America and is gaining favor in Europe. Such a trend, however, has yet to emerge strongly in Brazil. There had been a notable absence of large institutional investors holding prime-grade logistical facilities in Brazil until very recently. Most local or multinational logistics operators have tended to build their own facilities. Build-to-suit and sale-and-leaseback strategies to deliver high-quality properties to large distribution companies are suggested. Venturing with a major international logistics operator with Brazilian expansion plans would also be desirable.

The global economic downturn has affected the industrial sector in Brazil. However, given the improved confidence indicators and the forecasts by major agencies, we believe that it will be a short-term crisis, which has likely passed its bottom. Thus, we believe that Brazil remains an attractive location for certain industrial investments. São Paulo state is the country's premier industrial hub and of prime importance for productive activities. Given its large population, it also comprises a large proportion of Brazil's consumption. Thus, continued potential for wholesalers and retailers to

EXHIBIT 5.49 Buying/Developing Warehouse Distribution Properties

Factor	Comments
Risk Factors	The industrial property market in Brazil is still relatively underdeveloped, with most facilities in the sector being owner-occupied. Distribution facilities are smaller and use lower technology inputs compared to facilities in Europe or North America, limiting the attractiveness of existing facilities to institutional owners.
Execution and Implementation	Introduce build-to-suit and sale-leaseback strategies to the market. Work with international firms to establish distribution systems in the country.
Returns	Industrial yields in Brazil stood at a relatively high level (12.75%) at the end of 2008, which represents a premium over the other sectors in Brazil and over many developed and emerging markets around the world.
Reg./Legal	Leasing law allows tenants to end leases at will in some circumstances, limiting visibility of cash flows.
Market Size	Assets are concentrated in São Paolo state, including the area between the city and the coast. Less than one-quarter of warehouse space is considered institutional quality. Opportunities in secondary markets may be more compelling and constraints on new development are lower.
Competition	There has been an increase in fundraising and active investment by international real estate funds and industrial REITs.
Barriers to Entry and Exit	Long prospecting, due diligence and closing period. Land for industrial development is scarce in proximity to the most populated regions, due to topographic constraints.

focus their distributive activities there is highly likely. Expansion of seaports and airports throughout the country indicates strong potential as does the ongoing development of multimodal hubs, highways and ring-roads as essential for locational priorities. Rio de Janeiro is another relevant market, given the size of its population and its subsequent importance as a nucleus of consumption (see Exhibit 5.49).

NOTES

1. Estimates for the end of 2009, EIU, as of September 2009.
2. Goldman Sachs, "BRICs and Beyond" (2007), measured in terms of purchasing power parity.
3. This is according to a World Bank framework whereby economies are classified according to their income per capita. The groups are low income, US$905 or less; lower-middle-income, US$906–US$3,595; upper-middle-income, US$3,596–US$11,115; and high income, US$11,116 or more. Brazil is included under the "upper-middle income" category. Indeed, Brazil's economy did grow at the rates experienced today by India and China when it was a low-income country in the 1960s and 1970s (IMF, 2009).
4. Banco Central do Brazil, September 2009.
5. Ibid.
6. Ibid., January 2009.
7. ING Real Estate Research & Strategy based on the U.S. Energy Information Administration, Short-Term Energy Outlook, May 2009.
8. "Petrobras's Tupi Viable at Third of Current Oil Price," Bloomberg.com, July 3, 2008.
9. Europe 15 is the aggregate of Austria, Belgium, Germany, Denmark, Ireland, Finland, France, Greece, Italy, Luxembourg, Netherlands, Portugal, Spain, Sweden, and the United Kingdom.
10. Instituto Brasileiro de Geografia e Estatística estimate, as of September 2009.
11. Indonesia—the world's fourth-largest country in overall population has a much larger proportion living in rural areas compared to Brazil.
12. EIU, as of September 2009.
13. U.S. Census Bureau International Database, as of June 2009.
14. Defined as people out of the labor force ages (0–14 years + 65 years and over) divided by the total population within the labor force ages (15–64 years old). Source: U.S. Census Bureau.
15. Australia 48%, Germany 51%, Japan 54%, UK 49%, U.S. 49%. Source: U.S. Census Bureau, ING Real Estate Research & Strategy, as of February 2009.
16. IBGE, 2008 population projections revision, as of June 2009.
17. IBGE, as of September 2009.
18. IBGE, population estimations for mid-2008, as of June 2009.
19. Getulio Vargas Foundation, 2008.

20. The minimum salary was raised to R$415 (approximately US$200) as of October 14, 2008 and to R$465 in January 2009. The 2009 increase is not factored in the statistics.
21. IBGE, Pesquisa Mensal de Emprego. This figure refers simply to the change in the number of people occupied in the labor force from December 2003 to December 2007.
22. IBGE, as of September 2009.
23. Especially given the very favorable political and financial environments, which are highly supportive of home ownership.
24. The only exchanges that expanded at a greater pace in that period were Shanghai and Shenzen in China, the Bombay Stock Exchange and NSE India, and the Luxembourg Stock Exchange (rates of expansion in USD terms).
25. IBGE data, as of June 2009, enterprise survey of 2006.
26. Ibid.
27. According to latest IBGE data, the share is 6% for São Paulo, 7% for Curitiba, 9% for Porto Alegre, 11% for Belo Horizonte, and 13% for Rio de Janeiro, according to the 2006 database for municipios.
28. Known as ABRASCE (the Brazilian Association of Shopping Centers).
29. Reuters, "Wal-Mart is to invest US$649 million in Brazil next year," November 27, 2007.
30. Property Market Analysis (PMA) Winter 2008, City Markets.
31. PMA Autumn 2008 Comparative Shopping Center Market Indicators.
32. Considering a total GLA of 120,500,000 sqm (CREA 2006) and EIU 2008 population data. No hard figures for the total GLA in Mexico are available, and the figure is an estimation.
33. Economist Intelligence Unit, January 2009.
34. For which updated cargo movement was available.
35. Economist Intelligence Unit, as of July 2009.
36. Ibid.
37. According to EIU and BCB data. Brazil figures as of the end of 2008. Levels for the rest of the countries are as of 2007.

A
Country Risk

EXHIBIT A.1 Country Risk by Income Level

Country	IMF 2007 GDP per capita (US$)	World Bank 2007 GDP (US$ billion)	IMF 2008 (estm.) Inflation (%)	Fraser Institute 2005 EFW Rating
HIGH INCOME				
Luxembourg	104,673	47.9	2.89	7.8
Norway	83,922	382.0	3.12	7.5
Iceland	63,830	19.5	5.50	7.8
Ireland	59,924	255.0	3.21	7.9
Switzerland	58,084	415.5	2.00	8.3
Denmark	57,261	308.1	2.30	7.7
Sweden	49,655	444.4	2.80	7.5
Finland	46,602	246.0	2.80	7.8
Netherlands	46,261	754.2	2.35	7.7
United States	45,845	13,811.2	3.02	8.1
United Kingdom	45,575	2,727.8	2.50	8.1
Austria	45,181	377.0	2.80	7.6
Canada	43,485	1,326.4	1.60	8.1
Australia	43,312	821.7	3.55	7.9
United Arab Emirates	42,934	129.7	9.04	7.7
Belgium	42,557	448.6	3.06	7.2
France	41,511	2,562.3	2.50	7.0
Germany	40,415	3,297.2	2.50	7.6
Italy	35,872	2,107.5	2.47	7.0
Singapore	35,163	161.3	4.70	8.8
Japan	34,312	4,376.7	0.62	7.5

(Continued)

EXHIBIT A.1 (*Continued*)

Country	IMF 2007 GDP per capita (US$)	World Bank 2007 GDP (US$ billion)	IMF 2008 (estm.) Inflation (%)	Fraser Institute 2005 EFW Rating
Kuwait	33,634	102.1	6.48	7.3
Spain	32,067	1,429.2	3.99	7.1
New Zealand	30,256	129.4	3.39	8.5
Hong Kong SAR	29,650	206.7	3.60	8.9
UPPER-MIDDLE INCOME				
Latvia	11,985	27.2	15.30	7.5
Croatia	11,576	51.3	5.54	6.4
Lithuania	11,354	38.3	8.27	7.5
Poland	11,041	420.3	4.11	6.9
Chile	9,879	163.9	6.58	7.8
Turkey	9,629	657.1	7.54	6.2
Russia	9,075	1,291.0	11.41	5.8
Mexico	8,479	893.4	3.77	7.1
Romania	7,697	166.0	7.00	6.4
Uruguay	7,172	23.1	7.40	6.9
Malaysia	6,948	180.7	2.43	6.8
Brazil	6,938	1,314.2	4.77	6.0
Argentina	6,606	262.3	9.18	5.4
South Africa	5,906	277.6	8.66	6.8
LOWER-MIDDLE INCOME				
Peru	3,886	109.1	4.20	7.2
Thailand	3,737	245.8	3.52	6.8
Colombia	3,611	172.0	5.50	5.8
Ukraine	3,046	140.5	21.92	5.8
China	2,461	3,280.1	5.86	6.3
Indonesia	1,925	432.8	7.12	6.3
Philippines	1,625	144.1	4.44	6.6
India	978	1,171.0	5.18	6.6
LOW INCOME				
Zambia	918	11.4	6.64	6.7
Vietnam	818	71.2	16.00	6.1
Ghana	676	15.2	8.90	6.2
Bangladesh	455	67.7	9.30	6.0

Sources: ING Clarion Research & Investment Strategy; IMF; World Bank; and The Fraser Institute.

Property Market Practice in China

EXHIBIT B.1 Key Terms and Practices in the Chinese Property Market

Standard Unit of Measurement	
Unit of Measurement	Square meter (sqm) is the standard.
Quotation of Floor Area	In China, most office building areas are quoted on gross area with a smaller proportion based on the usable or net area. The most common definitions use are:
	• Gross Area—All areas within the perimeter of the outside walls including the wall thickness, service cores, lift lobbies, passenger and service lift wells, staircases, lavatories, pantries, and mechanical and electric areas.
	• Net Area—The carpetable area on an office floor, plus columns but excluding all service cores. Typically, 65–75% of gross area in Shanghai, 70–75% in Beijing, and 70% in Guangzhou are usable.
Operating Costs	
Rents	Rents are generally quoted in US$ psm of gross space per day in Shanghai and in RMB psm of gross space per month in Beijing. Although sometimes quoted in US$, rents are paid in RMB. Some landlords are now also beginning to quote and include RMB rental rates in their contracts. In Guangzhou, rents are quoted in RMB psm per month.
	Paid monthly or quarterly in advance.
	For US$ leases, payments are generally made in RMB at the exchange rate as announced by the People's Bank of China.

(Continued)

EXHIBIT B.1 *(Continued)*

Standard Unit of Measurement	
Management Fees	In Grade A buildings, management fees are usually quoted in US$ psm per month on the gross area in Shanghai, and in RMB psm per month in Beijing and Guangzhou. They are additional to the rental charge and are payable monthly or quarterly in advance. Provision is usually made for management fees to be reviewed during the lease term.
Utilities	Electricity and telecommunications are separately metered and payable directly by tenant. In most commercial buildings, water rates are included in the building management charges. In domestic properties, the tenant will pay for the water charges.
Insurance	There is no rule of thumb for building insurance. However, typically tenants insure their own property with cover for third party liability. Landlords of established, well-managed buildings will insure buildings.
Car Parking	Allocated parking is in limited supply and is charged on a monthly basis, quoted in US$ or RMB, and paid in RMB. In some cases car parking may be purchased.
Government Rates	Tenants must pay stamp duty on lease contracts, but otherwise they do not have to pay any taxes on the property.
Tax	Property tax is payable by the owner and is levied on the original purchase price less 20% depreciation each year at a rate of 1.2% annually. It is only payable on property for which rental income is received. A further property tax of 12% of rental income is payable by the lessor. In Beijing and Shanghai, stamp duty of 0.1% of contract value is payable on leases in equal parts by both parties. In Guangzhou, stamp duty of 0.2% of contract value is payable on leases in equal parts by both parties.
Purchasing Property Land Title	In the PRC, all land belongs to the State. The State grants Land Use Rights for a period of time, which varies according to usage. Land Use Rights are typically granted for:

EXHIBIT B.1 *(Continued)*

Standard Unit of Measurement

	Usage	Period of Land Use Right
	Commercial, Tourism/Recreational	40 years
	Comprehensive developments (i.e., offices with Retail/residential component)	50 years
	Educational, Scientific, and Cultural	50 years
	Residential	70 years
	Industrial	50 years
Foreign Ownership	There are no restrictions on foreign investors or end-users purchasing Granted Land Rights.	
Strata Title (Partial Ownership of the Building)	"Selling" or "strata titling" part of a building is a common phenomenon in the PRC. Although owners can be required to sign a Deed of Mutual Covenant governing management, repairs, and upkeep of a building, management of such buildings can vary considerably and is usually of a lower standard than single ownership developments.	
Agency Fees	Purchase fees are generally about 1.5% to 2% of the acquisition price.	
Legal Fees	It is usual practice for each party to bear its own legal costs in a property transaction.	
Deed Tax	This tax is payable upon the purchase of property. The tax is levied at 3.0% of the total contract value.	
Property Transfer Fee	Payable by the purchaser at 0.5% of the contract value.	
Stamp Duty	Generally levied at 0.03% of the contract value payable in equal parts by both parties to the contract. In Guangzhou, it is levied at 0.05%.	

Source: Jones Lang LaSalle, Corporate Occupiers' Guide, 2006.

Bibliography

Barboza, David. "China Builds Its Dreams, and Some Fear a Bubble." *New York Times*, Oct. 18, 2005.

Bellman, Timothy, Shane Taylor, and Maria Luisa Paradinas. *The Case for Real Estate: Asset Class Performance at the Cusp of Recession.* ING Real Estate, Internal Publication. 2008.

Capital Flows to Emerging Market Economies. Rep. Institute of International Finance, 2008.

China. Ministry of Commerce. *China Commerce Yearbook 2008.* China Business, 2008.

Development—Urban Development and China. *The World Bank.* http://go.worldbank.org/LHTNOP9GU0.

Ernst & Young. *2008 Real Estate Market Outlook*, 9.

Fiorentino, Roberto V., Luis Verdeja, and Christelle Toqueboeuf. *The Changing Landscape Regional Trade Agreements: 2006 Update.* Geneva: WTO Publications, 2007.

Global Economic Prospects: Managing the Next Wave of Globalization. Washington, DC: International Bank for Reconstruction and Development / The World Bank, 2007.

Goldman Sachs Group. *BRICs and Beyond. Goldman Sachs.* The Goldman Sachs Group, Inc. http://www2.goldmansachs.com/ideas/brics/book/BRIC-Full.pdf.

Goldman Sachs Group. *Dreaming with the BRICs: The Path to 2050.* Global Economic Paper No. 99, 2003.

Goldman Sachs Group. *The N-11: More Than an Acronym.* Global Economics Paper No: 153, 2007.

Hax, A. C., & Majluf, N. *Strategy Concept and Process: Pragmatic Approach.* Prentice-Hall, (1995), 307.

Huang, Haibo, and Susan Hudson-Wilson. "Private Commercial Real Estate Equity Returns and Inflation." *The Journal of Portfolio Management* 33, no. 5 (2007): 63–73.

James, Gwartney, Robert Lawson, Russell S. Sobel, and Peter T. Leeson. "Economic Freedom of the World, 2005." *Economic Freedom of the World: 2007 Annual Report.* Fraser Institute (2007), 9.

Kalamaros, Alexander E. "Shanghai's Sustainable New Towns." *Urban Land* (Feb. 2006): 54–58.

Kobayashi-Hillary, M. *Building a future with BRICs: The next decade for off shoring.* Berlin: Springer, 2008.

Leather, Gareth, and Gerald Walsh, eds. *Country Report China*. Rep. Economist Intelligence Unit, 2010 (July 2010). http://www.eiu.com/index.asp?layout= country&geography_id=1800000180.

National Bureau of Statistics of China, Communiqué on 2004 Rural Poverty Monitoring of China (2005).

Pals, Fred. *Petrobra's Tupi Viable at Third of Current Oil Price*. Rep. Bloomberg. July 3, 2008. http://www.bloomberg.com/apps/news?pid=newsarchive&sid= ahZp9lZIwwQU&refer=energy.

Porter, Michael E. *The Competitive Advantage of Nations: With a New Introduction*. New York: Free Press, 1998.

Sivitanides, P. "Why Invest in Real Estate: An Asset Allocation Perspective." *Real Estate Issues* 22, April 1997, 30–37.

Transparency International. *Global Corruption Report 2008: Corruption in the Water Sector*, ed. by Dieter Zinnbauer and Rebecca Dobson. New York: Cambridge University Press, 2008.

Wheaton, W. C. "The Cyclic Behavior of the National Office Market." *Real Estate Economics* 15, no. 4 (1987): 281–299.

Wilson, Dominic, and Roopa Pereshothaman. *Dreaming with BRICS: The Path to 2050*. Working Paper no. 99. Goldman Sachs, Oct. 2003. http://www2 .goldmansachs.com/ideas/brics/brics-dream.html.

World Bank. "China's Rapid Urbanization: Benefits, Challenges, & Strategies." Weblog post. *News & Broadcast*, June 19, 2008. http://web.worldbank.org/ WBSITE/EXTERNAL/NEWS/0,,contentMDK:21812803~pagePK:64257043~ piPK:437376~theSitePK:4607,00.html.

World Bank. "Urban Development and China." http://go.worldbank.org/ LHTNOP9GU0.

About the Authors

DAVID J. LYNN, PH.D., MBA, MS, MA, CRE

Dr. David Lynn is an institutional real estate investor, strategist, and portfolio manager with extensive experience in national and international markets. At ING Clarion Partners, he is Managing Director, Head of the Research and Investment Strategy Group, and Generalist Portfolio Manager for the firm. In this capacity, he directs the firm's strategic and tactical investment strategy. He is a member of the Investment and Operating Committees, where he makes decisions on billions of dollars of new investments, portfolios, fund strategies, and dispositions. In his team's propriety, numbers-driven approach, he directs asset selection, portfolio analytics, market targeting, econometric forecasting, and market entry and exit. He assists the firm's fund and product development initiatives. His group provides real-time market intelligence for the U.S. and global markets. He also participates in numerous client presentations and consultations.

He has held senior investment and development positions at AIG Global Real Estate, AvalonBay Communities, The Keppel Corporation (Singapore), and the Target Corporation (Property Development Group) where he achieved well above benchmark economic returns on his portfolios and investments.

His theoretical work has yielded new approaches and analytical techniques in the areas of market forecasting, active portfolio management, financial distress, supply constrained markets, high beta sectors, and global industrial markets. He has published widely on the subjects of real estate investment, development, economics, and land use. He has translated his research and management expertise into a wide array of style-based investment strategies. Dr. Lynn has written or coauthored over 70 articles, internal investment and strategy papers, three major books (including *Active Private Equity Real Estate Strategy*, and *Emerging Market Real Estate Investment*), book chapters, and founded an academic journal called *Colloqui*. He writes a highly-regarded column, called "Capital Trends" in the *National Real Estate Investor*. He is widely quoted in major real estate periodicals and is a regular speaker and presenter at industry conferences and meetings.

Dr. Lynn earned his Ph.D. in Financial Economics at the London School of Economics, where he also earned a Master of Science specializing in Finance. His doctoral research focused on financial distress in emerging market countries. He earned a Master of Business Administration (MBA) from the Sloan School of Management, MIT, where he specialized in Finance and Real Estate. He earned a Master's in City and Regional Planning with an emphasis in Real Estate from Cornell University. His thesis research explored the application of strategic planning to the real estate industry. He earned a B.A. in Architecture from the University of California at Berkeley. He is a Counselor of Real Estate (CRE), a Certified Portfolio and Investment Manager (CPIM), a Chartered Management Analyst (CMA), a Homer Hoyt Fellow, an ISO 9000 Certified Auditor and a Certified Planner (AICP). He is a member of the American Real Estate Society (ARES), National Council of Real Estate Investment Fiduciaries (NCREIF), National Association for Business Economics (NABE), International Council of Shopping Centers (ICSC), Pension Real Estate Association (PREA), and the Urban Land Institute (ULI) (full member). He serves on the Editorial Board of the Counselors of Real Estate and the Board of PREA's Real Estate Research Institute.

TIM WANG, PH.D., HEAD OF MACROECONOMIC ANALYSIS AND STRATEGY

Tim Wang, PhD, is Senior Vice-President and Senior Investment Strategist with the Research and Investment Strategy Group at ING Clarion Partners. Dr. Wang joined ING Clarion Partners in 2006 and has authored more than 50 internal and external real estate investment strategy and market research articles and book chapters. He is a frequent speaker at industrial conferences. Tim holds an MBA from New York University and a PhD from University of Georgia.

Index

CPSIA information can be obtained
at www.ICGtesting.com
Printed in the USA
LVHW010919170920
666247LV00006B/175